TOP 500 PRESSURE COOKER RECIPES

Written by: Jamie Stewart

Warning-Disclaimer

The purpose of this book is to educate and entertain. The author or publisher does not guarantee that anyone following the techniques, suggestions, tips, ideas, or strategies will become successful. The author and publisher shall have neither liability or responsibility to anyone with respect to any loss or damage caused, or alleged to be caused, directly or indirectly by the information contained in this book.

****

Download a FREE PDF file with photos of all the recipes.

Link located at the end of the book.

*****

Table Of Contents

LUNCH RECIPES

Easy Sloppy Joes	79
Winter Beef Chili	79
Mom's Beef Casserole	80
Beef and Pasta Casserole	81
Vegetarian Tomato and Cheese Casserole	81
Classic Italian Pasta with Tomato Sauce	82
Herbed Eggplant Pasta	82
Easy Vegetarian Lentil	83
Risotto with Peas and Cheddar Cheese	83
Summer Eggplant Stew	84
Bean and Pumpkin Stew	84
Juicy Chicken in Beer Sauce	85
Country Poached Chicken Breasts	85
Saucy Chicken Breasts with Goat Cheese	86
Chicken Curry in Coconut Sauce	86
Hearty Chicken Stew	87
Lime Chicken Drumsticks with Raisins and Olives	87
Bean and Corn Salad	88
Lentil with Tomatoes and Kale	88
Yummy Lentil Curry	89
Yummy Potato with Cauliflower	89
Vegan Mushroom Stew	90
Meatball Soup with Noodles	90
Creamy Cauliflower and Cheese Soup	91
Mom's Corn Chowder	91
Chunky Butternut Bean Soup	92
Cheesy Potato and Spinach Soup	92
Creamed Sausage and Spinach Soup	93
Cheese and Onion Soup	94
Rich Garbanzo Bean Soup	94
Winter Hearty Chili	95
Chicken Soup with Farfalle	95
Creamed Tomato Soup	96
Soup with Cheese Tortellini	96
Jalapeño Chicken Soup with Corn	97
Lentil and Swiss Chard Soup	97
Delicious Pea and Ham Soup	98
Black Bean Salad	98
Easiest Adzuki Beans Ever	99
Easiest Pinto Beans Ever	99
Yellow Lentil with Kale	100
Delicious Red Lentil Curry	100
Lentil and Tomato Delight	101
Indian-Style Potato and Broccoli	101

DINNER RECIPES

Pressure Cooking: Tasty One-Pot Recipes

Pressure cooker brings a real culinary Renaissance to us, the old-fashioned cooking adapted for the modern family and the pace of modern life. Actually, the pressure cooker was a 17th century invention. It has been around for a long time. A stovetop pressure cooker has become popular twenty years ago. However, modern-day pressure cooker has become trendy because of its great improvement such as lots of digital functions and backup safety system.

If you'd like to cook the homey soups, the hearty stews, sophisticated braised meat and other five-star recipes, pressure cooker is the great choice. If you like one-pot meals, the pressure cooker is the right solution for you. The pressure cooker is one of the most versatile kitchen tools. You will enjoy different cooking methods such as browning, sautéing, deglazing, and frying without another skillet or pan.

Using a pressure cooker isn't just about quicker and easier cooking; it's about better and healthier cooking, too. If you have been wondering how to make meals like grandma used to make, give some of your favorite recipes a try in the pressure cooker.

The benefits of pressure cooking are numerous:

- Your food retains most of its valuable nutrients so your meals are healthier and better. Pressure cooker prepares your food quickly, with very little fat and water. A number of studies have shown that pressure cooking can help to preserve nutrients in food better than any other cooking technique.

- You will significantly save time and energy in preparing meals. The pressure cooker is an efficient kitchen device because it cooks meals seventy percent faster than conventional cooking methods.

- The food from the pressure cooker tastes great.

- It can be used to preserve food as well.

We have got 250 recipes ahead: a terrific oatmeal to bread puddings, awesome casseroles to easy chilies, cold appetizers to holiday desserts. Add some wow factor to your everyday cooking. Make amazing holiday dinner for your family and friends. Enjoy!

Using a Pressure Cooker: Methods & Techniques

A pressure cooker is a sealed pot that builds up the pressure using a large amount of steam. Therefore, the principle is simple. The high pressure helps the food to cook easier. It helps your food get tender while cooking. This is especially important for tough pieces of food such as meat, beans, certain vegetables, and so on. The high pressure also helps them cook faster. Vegetables and meat cooked in your pressure cooker turn out moist with lots of juices.

There is no doubt that the pressure cooker is perfect for many dishes. You can actually cook almost all meals in your pressure cooker, from breakfast and appetizers to dinners and desserts. All you need to know is the technique that you will find in this cookbook. These hand-picked recipes contain detailed explanations, including tips and tricks to make the best dishes in the easiest way ever!

Regardless of whether you are very beginner or an old hand in pressure cooking, here are some tips for successful pressure cooking:

1. **Browning and Deglazing**. It is good to know that pressure cooking promotes browning of your food. Therefore, at first, try to brown fresh meats, bacon, poultry, ground meat and some vegetables (e.g. onion, garlic, carrot, celery, mushrooms, etc.). After that, deglaze the pot with some water, wine, or broth. The flavors will be enhanced, so it will make your meals taste better.

2. **Make Meal Preparation Easier.** Chop the vegetables into uniform-sized pieces so that everything will cook evenly. Besides that, please follow the recipes instructions because some pieces of food cook faster than others.

3. **Never Overfill your Cooker.** Don't fill your pressure cooker more than two-thirds full with ingredients. If you do not follow this rule, your cooker can not operate properly and this is important for safety reasons.

4. **Always Use Some Liquid**. Therefore, make sure to prepare some water, wine, broth or some juice. You should follow the recipe instructions, and you can freely use more liquid, but never use less liquid than recommended.

5. **The Heat is Very Important**. Therefore, start cooking over high heat for the best results. Once your cooker comes up to pressure, turn the heat to a low setting so that it maintains pressure.

6. **How Long Do I Pressure-Cook?** You can find pressure-cooking time tables on the Internet. However, each and every recipe in this cookbook contains this information and you shouldn't worry about that. You can always taste your food for the doneness, but keep in mind that it's better to undercook your meal than overcook it.

Pressure cooking is an amazingly useful way to cook old-fashioned and modern dishes for a short time and with a minimum of effort. How to find the best one? Just a little searching on the Internet will bring up a lot of information, stories, and testimonials. You can choose the size according to your personal preferences. You can purchase Conventional Pressure Cooker or Electric Pressure Cooker. However, your own experience is the best teacher. So, you can immediately purchase your pressure cooker and start cooking like a pro. However, before embarking on this extraordinary culinary experience, you should read the manufacturer's instructions thoroughly. It is extremely important to make sure to follow all safety precautions. After that, roll up your sleeves and let's get down to work!

BREAKFAST RECIPES

Pearl Barley with Blueberries

(Ready in about 20 minutes | Servings 8)

Ingredients

1 ½ cups pearl barley, rinsed and drained

2 tablespoons canola oil

1 teaspoon kosher salt

4 cups water

2 tablespoons orange juice

1 ½ cups fresh blueberries

3/4 cup slivered almonds, lightly toasted

Directions

Combine barley, oil, salt, and water in your pressure cooker that has been oiled with non-stick cooking spray.

Close and lock the lid. Set the heat to HIGH. When your pressure cooker reaches a HIGH pressure, reduce the burner heat to LOW and maintain HIGH pressure.

Now cook for 18 minutes. Remove your cooker from the heat. Open it carefully using the Natural Release method; allow it to sit for 10 minutes. Drain.

Add the remaining ingredients and stir to combine. To serve, divide prepared barley salad among individual bowls. Enjoy!

Coconut Barley with Grapes

(Ready in about 30 minutes | Servings 8)

Ingredients

For the Salad:

1 ½ cups pearl barley, rinsed and drained

2 tablespoons sesame oil

1 teaspoon kosher salt

4 cups water

1½ cups grapes, halved

3 baby tangerines, peeled and broken into sections

¾ cup sweetened shredded coconut

For the Dressing:

5 tablespoons plain Greek yogurt

1 tablespoon olive oil

1 tablespoon lemon juice

1 teaspoon lemon zest

Directions

Combine barley, sesame oil, kosher salt, and water in your pressure cooker that has been oiled with non-stick cooking spray.

Close and lock the lid. Set the heat to HIGH. When your pressure cooker reaches a HIGH pressure, reduce the burner heat to LOW and maintain HIGH pressure.

Now cook for 18 minutes. Remove your cooker from the heat. Open it carefully using the Natural Release method; allow it to sit for 10 minutes. Drain and let cool to room temperature.

Add grapes, tangerines, and shredded coconut. Stir to combine.

In a mixing bowl, whisk together the dressing ingredients. Toss the salad with the dressing. Serve chilled and enjoy!

Spring Veggies with Seeds

(Ready in about 15 minutes | Servings 4)

Ingredients

2 cups water

1 teaspoon sea salt

8 cups kale leaves, chopped

2 tablespoons olive oil

2 tablespoons green onion, chopped

1 tablespoon green garlic, minced

1/2 teaspoon dried dill weed

2 tablespoons flax seeds

1 teaspoon dried red pepper flakes

1/2 cup vegetable stock

Ground black pepper, to your liking

Directions

First, pour the water into your pressure cooker. Add salt; bring water to a boil. Add the kale leaves and blanch it approximately 1 minute; drain and reserve.

Warm the olive oil in the pressure cooker over MEDIUM heat. Stir in green onion, garlic, dill weed, flax seeds and red pepper flakes; cook for about 1 minute.

Pour in the vegetable stock; sprinkle with black pepper and salt to taste. Afterwards, add reserved kale. Give it a gentle stir.

Cover the pressure cooker and bring it to HIGH pressure; maintain pressure for about 6 minutes.

Remove from the heat; carefully and slowly remove the lid by following the manufacturer's instructions; serve and enjoy!

Cold Breakfast Barley Salad

(Ready in about 25 minutes | Servings 8)

Ingredients

For the Salad:

1 ½ cups pearl barley, rinsed and drained

2 tablespoons butter, melted

1 teaspoon kosher salt

4 cups water

1½ cups fresh blackberries, halved

1/2 cup slivered almonds

For the Dressing:

5 tablespoons plain yogurt

1 tablespoon orange oil

1 tablespoon lemon juice

1 teaspoon orange zest

Directions

Treat your pressure cooker with nonstick cooking spray. Then, add barley, butter, kosher salt, and water to your cooker.

Close and lock the lid. Set the heat to HIGH. When your pressure cooker reaches a HIGH pressure, reduce the burner heat to LOW in order to maintain high pressure.

Next, cook for about 18 minutes. Remove your cooker from the heat.

Then, use the Natural Release method to open your cooker safely; allow it to sit for 10 to 20 minutes. Drain; allow to cool completely.

Add blackberries and almonds. Stir to combine.

In a mixing bowl, whisk together the dressing ingredients. Toss the salad with the dressing. Serve chilled and enjoy!

Cheese Mexican-Style Barley

(Ready in about 20 minutes | Servings 6)

Ingredients

2 tablespoons olive oil

1 onion, peeled and chopped

1 chili pepper, finely minced

2 cloves garlic, finely chopped

1 cup pearl barley, rinsed and drained

2 ¼ cups water

1 cups vegetable stock

3/4 cup Cheddar cheese, shredded

Salt and ground black pepper, to taste

Directions

In a pressure cooker, warm the oil over medium-high heat. Add the onion; sauté until it is translucent and soft.

Add the chili peppers and garlic; cook, stirring frequently, for 1 to 2 minutes. Add the barley; continue stirring until it is lightly toasted, about 2 minutes.

Pour in the water and stock. Now lock the lid. Set the burner heat to HIGH.

When it reaches high pressure, reduce the burner; maintain HIGH pressure. Cook for 18 minutes. To open your cooker, use the Quick Release method. Let stand for 5 to 10 minutes.

Stir in the cheese, salt, and black pepper. Serve in individual bowls and enjoy.

Barley with Mushrooms and Cheese

(Ready in about 25 minutes | Servings 6)

Ingredients

2 tablespoons vegetable oil

3 spring onions, chopped

1 ½ cups mushrooms, chopped

1 cup hulled barley, rinsed in a colander

3 cups broth

1 cup water

Sea salt and freshly cracked black pepper, to taste

1/2 cup Parmesan cheese, grated

1 tablespoon fresh basil, chopped

1 tablespoon butter, melted

Directions

In a pressure cooker, heat vegetable oil over medium-high heat. Then, sauté spring onions until they are softened, or 2 to 3 minutes.

Add chopped mushrooms and cook 3 to 5 more minutes. Stir in the barley; continue to cook until lightly toasted, approximately 2 minutes.

Stir in the broth, water, salt, and black pepper. Bring to a boil. Next, close and lock the lid. Cook for 20 minutes at HIGH pressure.

Open the cooker with the Natural Release method; allow to stand for 10 to 15 minutes. Open your cooker according to manufacturer's directions.

Divide the mixture among individual bowls. Sprinkle with cheese and fresh basil. Dot with melted butter and serve.

Elegant Scotch Eggs

(Ready in about 20 minutes | Servings 6)

Ingredients

6 whole eggs

1 ½ pounds ground sausage

2 tablespoons olive oil

Fresh chives, for garnish

Directions

Place a steamer basket in your pressure cooker. Stir in the water and the eggs.

Lock the lid and cook on HIGH pressure for 6 minutes.

Next, let the pressure release naturally. Now remove the steamer basket from the pressure cooker. Transfer prepared eggs to cold water; remove the shells.

Divide the sausage into six equal pieces. Flatten each piece into a flat round; put the eggs into the center; wrap the sausage around the eggs.

When your cooker is hot, add oil; cook the Scotch eggs on all sides.

Barley with Shallots and Mushrooms

(Ready in about 25 minutes | Servings 6)

Ingredients

2 tablespoons butter

1/2 cup shallots, chopped

1 ½ cups mushrooms, chopped

1/2 cups carrots, thinly sliced

1 cup hulled barley, rinsed in a colander

2 cups water

2 cups vegetable stock

1 teaspoon cayenne pepper

Sea salt and freshly cracked black pepper, to taste

1/2 cup cheddar cheese, grated

2 tablespoons fresh chives, chopped

Directions

In your pressure cooker, melt butter over medium-high heat. Then, sauté the shallots until they are softened, approximately 3 minutes.

Stir in the mushrooms and carrots; cook for 5 minutes longer. Stir in the barley; continue cooking until lightly toasted, for about 2 minutes.

Stir in the water, vegetable stock, cayenne pepper, sea salt, and black pepper. Bring to a boil. Next, close and lock the lid. Cook for 20 minutes at HIGH pressure.

Afterward, allow to stand for about 15 minutes. Open your cooker according to manufacturer's directions.

Divide the mixture among individual bowls. Sprinkle with cheddar cheese and fresh chives. Serve.

Garden Breakfast Salad

(Ready in about 20 minutes | Servings 6)

Ingredients

2 cups bulgur, cracked wheat, rinsed and drained

2 teaspoons salt

2 tablespoons vegetable oil

4 cups water

1 large-sized yellow summer squash, cubed

2 medium-sized bell peppers, chopped

3 ribs celery, chopped

For the Dressing:

Grated zest of 1 small-sized lemon

Juice of 2 small-sized lemons

1/3 cup extra-virgin olive oil

Sea salt and freshly ground black pepper, to your liking

Directions

Combine the bulgur, salt, vegetable oil, and water in a pressure cooker pot.

Close and lock the lid. Cook at HIGH pressure for 6 minutes.

Open your cooker with the Natural Release method; let stand for 10 minutes. Drain the bulgur; fluff it using a fork. Let it cool completely.

Now, add yellow summer squash, bell pepper, and celery. Stir to combine.

In a mixing bowl, combine all the dressing ingredients; whisk until everything is well mixed. Drizzle the dressing over your salad. Serve chilled and enjoy!

Pressure Cooker Hard-Boiled Eggs

(Ready in about 10 minutes | Servings 8)

Ingredients

8 eggs

1 cup water

Directions

Put a steamer basket into your pressure cooker. Add the water and the eggs.

Lock the lid in place; now cook the eggs under HIGH pressure for 6 minutes.

Lastly, allow the pressure to release naturally for 10 minutes. When the pressure is released, remove the lid.

Transfer the eggs to cold water to cool completely. Sprinkle the eggs with your favorite spices and herbs; serve.

Bulgur with Peppers and Summer Squash

(Ready in about 20 minutes | Servings 6)

Ingredients

2 cups bulgur, rinsed and drained

2 teaspoons sea salt

2 tablespoons sesame oil

4 cups water

1 large-sized yellow summer squash, cubed

1 green bell pepper, chopped

1 red bell pepper, chopped

1 jalapeño pepper, chopped

2 carrots, chopped

For the Dressing:

2 tablespoons orange juice

1/3 cup extra-virgin olive oil

1 teaspoon cayenne pepper

Sea salt and freshly ground black pepper, to your liking

Directions

Combine the bulgur, sea salt, sesame oil, and water in your pressure cooker pot.

Close and lock the lid. Cook at HIGH pressure for 6 minutes.

Open your cooker with the Natural Release method; let stand for 10 minutes. Drain the bulgur; then, fluff it with a fork. Allow it to cool completely.

Now, add yellow summer squash, peppers, and carrots. Give it a good stir.

In a mixing bowl, combine all the dressing ingredients; whisk until everything is well incorporated. Drizzle the dressing over your salad. Serve chilled.

Mediterranean Deviled Eggs

(Ready in about 20 minutes | Servings 8)

Ingredients

1 cup water

8 eggs

2 tablespoons mayonnaise

2 tablespoons plain yogurt

1/2 teaspoon onion powder

1/2 teaspoon garlic powder

Sea salt and freshly ground black pepper, to taste

Directions

Put a steamer basket into your pressure cooker. Add the water and the eggs.

Lock lid in place; now cook the eggs on HIGH pressure for 6 minutes.

Lastly, allow the pressure to release naturally for 10 minutes. When the pressure is released, remove the lid.

Transfer the eggs to ice cold water to cool completely.

Slice each egg in half; discard the yolks. Mash the yolks using a fork.

Add the rest of the above ingredients.

Divide the yolk mixture among egg whites. Arrange on a serving platter, add some chopped olives if desired, and serve.

Pomegranate Deviled Eggs

(Ready in about 20 minutes | Servings 8)

Ingredients

1 cup water

8 eggs

1/4 cup mayonnaise

2 teaspoons mustard

1 teaspoon balsamic vinegar

1/2 teaspoon dried oregano

1/4 cup pomegranate seeds

Seas salt to taste

Directions

Place a steamer basket in the pressure cooker pot. Add the water and the eggs.

Lock the lid and cook the eggs on HIGH pressure for 6 minutes.

Next, remove the lid according to manufacturer's instructions.

Replace the eggs to ice cold water to cool completely. Sprinkle the eggs with your favorite spices and herbs; serve.

Slice the eggs into halves; transfer the yolks to a mixing bowl. Mash the yolks using a fork. Stir in the remaining ingredients; stir until everything is well combined.

Divide the yolk mixture among egg whites. Serve and enjoy!

French-Style Salad

(Ready in about 20 minutes | Servings 6)

Ingredients

1 ¼ cups bulgur, rinsed and drained

1 teaspoon salt

1/2 teaspoon cayenne pepper

2 ½ cups water

2 tablespoons olive oil

1 shallot, minced

1 cucumber, diced

1 red bell pepper, seeded and chopped

1/2 cup fresh basil, minced

1/3 cup fresh lemon juice

1/3 cup extra-virgin olive oil

Sea salt and freshly cracked black pepper

Directions

Place the bulgur, salt, and cayenne in a pressure cooker. Add the water and olive oil.

Close the lid. Select HIGH pressure and 6 minutes cook time.

Open the cooker with the Natural Release method; allow it to stand for 10 to 12 minutes.

Fluff the bulgur with a fork and add the remaining ingredients. Give it a good stir and serve.

Collard Greens with Bacon

(Ready in about 10 minutes | Servings 6)

Ingredients

4 slices bacon, diced

2 cloves garlic, crushed

1 small-sized shallot, diced

3 bunches collard greens, rinsed, stems trimmed off and chopped

3 cups vegetable stock

Sea salt and freshly ground black pepper, to your liking

Fresh juice of 1 lemon

Directions

First, brown the bacon, garlic and shallot in your pressure cooker over medium-high flame.

Then, add the greens and vegetable stock, pushing down on the greens until they are wilted.

Close and lock the lid. Set the burner heat to HIGH. Set a timer for 8 minutes. Remove the pot from the heat. Use the Quick Release method to open your cooker.

Add salt, black pepper, and lemon juice. Serve warm.

Spiced Basmati Rice with Tomatoes

(Ready in about 15 minutes | Servings 6)

Ingredients

2 ½ cups chicken broth

1 ¾ cups canned tomatoes, chopped

1 ½ cups basmati rice

1/2 stick unsalted butter, cut into small pieces

1/4 teaspoon salt

1/2 teaspoon dried oregano

1/2 teaspoon dried basil

Directions

Combine the chicken broth, tomatoes, basmati rice, butter, and salt in a pressure cooker. Add dried oregano and basil.

Lock the lid onto the cooker. Set the pot over HIGH heat; bring to high pressure. Cook for 10 minutes.

Lastly, use the quick-release method to reduce the pot's pressure. Now set aside for 10 minutes.

Unlock the cooker. Serve warm.

Mushroom-Tomato Jasmine Rice

(Ready in about 15 minutes | Servings 6)

Ingredients

2 ½ cups vegetable stock

1/2 cup mushrooms, chopped

1 ¾ cups canned tomatoes, chopped

1 ½ cups jasmine rice

1/2 stick butter, cut into small pieces

1/4 teaspoon salt

1/4 teaspoon turmeric powder

1/2 teaspoon dried basil

1 tablespoon parsley

Directions

Combine all of your ingredients in a pressure cooker.

Lock the lid onto the cooker. Set the pot over HIGH heat; bring to high pressure. Cook for 10 minutes.

Lastly, use the quick-release method to reduce the pot's pressure.

Now set aside for 10 minutes. Unlock the cooker. Taste and adjust the seasonings. Serve right now.

Spiced Kale with Bacon

(Ready in about 10 minutes | Servings 6)

Ingredients

4 slices bacon, diced

1 cup onion, diced

3 bunch kale, rinsed, stems trimmed off and chopped

3 cups beef stock

1 teaspoon granulated garlic

1 teaspoon red pepper flakes, crushed

1/2 teaspoon cloves, ground

Sea salt and freshly ground black pepper, to your liking

Directions

First, brown the bacon and onion in your pressure cooker over medium-high heat.

Then, add the kale and beef stock; cook until your greens have wilted. Add granulated garlic, red pepper, cloves, salt, and black pepper.

Close and lock the lid. Set the burner heat to HIGH. Set a timer to 8 minutes. Remove the pot from the heat. Use the Quick Release method to open your cooker. Serve immediately.

Breakfast Rice with Veggies

(Ready in about 15 minutes | Servings 6)

Ingredients

2 tablespoons olive oil

1/2 cup white onion, chopped

1/2 cup carrots, grated

2 cloves garlic, finely minced

2 ½ cups vegetable stock

1 ¾ cups canned tomatoes, chopped

1 ½ cups long-grain white rice

1/2 teaspoon kosher salt

1/4 teaspoon ground black pepper

1/2 teaspoon dried basil

Chopped fresh chives, for garnish

Directions

In a pressure cooker, heat olive oil over medium heat, sauté the onions until translucent. Then, add the carrots and garlic; continue sautéing for a few minutes more.

Add the rest of the above ingredients, except for fresh chives. Lock the lid onto the cooker.

Set the pot over HIGH heat; bring to high pressure. Cook for 10 minutes. Lastly, use the quick-release method to reduce the pot's pressure.

Now, set it aside for 10 minutes. Unlock the cooker. Taste and adjust the seasonings. Sprinkle with fresh chives and serve.

Yummy Sausage Gravy with Biscuits

(Ready in about 15 minutes | Servings 8)

Ingredients

1 ¼ pounds sausage, chopped

1 teaspoon dried oregano

1 teaspoon rosemary

1 teaspoon dried thyme

1/2 teaspoon onion powder

1/2 cup vegetable stock

1/4 cup wheat flour

1 ½ cups milk

1/2 teaspoon salt

Cracked black pepper, to your liking

Prepared biscuits

Directions

To make the sauce, set your pressure cooker to HIGH pressure. Then, place the sausage in the bottom of your cooker; sauté until they begin to turn brown, about 7 minutes.

Sprinkle with oregano, rosemary, thyme, and onion powder. Pour in stock. Now securely lock the lid and set on HIGH for about 5 minutes. Now release the cooker's pressure, according to manufacturer's instructions.

In a measuring cup, whisk the flour with milk. Add this mixture to your cooker; let simmer for about 3 minutes, or until the juice has thickened.

Season with salt and black pepper. To serve, spoon prepared gravy over the biscuits.

Mustard Greens with Bacon and Shallots

(Ready in about 10 minutes | Servings 6)

Ingredients

1 cup shallots, diced

2 cloves garlic, peeled and minced

4 slices bacon, diced

3 bunches mustard greens, rinsed, stems trimmed off and chopped

3 cups beef stock

1/4 teaspoon granulated sugar

Sea salt and freshly ground black pepper, to your liking

Directions

In the pressure cooker over medium-high heat, cook shallots, garlic, and bacon for about 4 minutes.

Then, add the mustard greens and beef stock; cook until your greens have wilted. Add granulated sugar, sea salt and black pepper.

Close and lock the lid. Set the burner heat to HIGH. Set a timer to cook for 8 minutes.

Remove the pot from the heat. Use the Quick Release method to open your cooker. Divide among individual bowls and serve right now.

Biscuits with Bacon Gravy

(Ready in about 15 minutes | Servings 8)

Ingredients

6 slices bacon

2 tablespoons bacon grease

1/2 teaspoon granulated garlic

1 teaspoon rosemary

1 teaspoon dried thyme

1/2 cup vegetable stock

1 ½ cups milk

1/4 cup all-purpose flour

Sea salt and black pepper, to taste

6 biscuits

Directions

To make the gravy, set the pressure cooker to HIGH. Then, add the bacon and bacon grease; sauté until bacon has browned, about 7 minutes.

Sprinkle with garlic, rosemary, and thyme. Pour in vegetable stock. Now securely lock the lid and set on HIGH for about 5 minutes.

Next, release the pressure according to manufacturer's instructions.

In a mixing bowl, combine the milk and flour; whisk until everything is well combined. Add the milk mixture to your cooker; let it simmer 3 minutes longer, or until it has thickened.

Season with salt and black pepper. To serve, spoon prepared gravy over the biscuits.

23. Zesty Orange Marmalade

(Ready in about 30 minutes | Servings 18)

Ingredients

1 ½ pounds Seville oranges, halved

Juice of 2 small-sized limes

3 pounds granulated sugar

Spices to your liking

Directions

Squeeze the juice from the oranges. Chop the orange peel; place the pith and pips in a muslin bag. Soak the peel together with muslin bag in 1-pint water overnight.

Transfer to the pressure cooker; add the lime juice.

Close the lid and bring to HIGH pressure; cook for about 15 minutes. Reduce the pressure at room temperature.

Next, squeeze the juice from the muslin bag; discard the bag. Add the sugar and spices; heat gently, stirring often, until the sugar is dissolved. Open the cooker and bring to a boil.

Cool your marmalade slightly. Divide among sterilized jars.

Breakfast Spoon Bread

(Ready in about 20 minutes | Servings 6)

Ingredients

Nonstick cooking spray

2/3 cup cornmeal

1 cup baking mix

1 cup milk

2 cups vegetable broth

1 cup cheddar cheese, shredded

2 whole eggs, beaten

1/4 stick butter, melted

A pinch of sugar

1/2 teaspoon black pepper

1 teaspoon salt

1/2 teaspoon onion powder

1/2 teaspoon garlic powder

Directions

Treat the inside of your pressure cooker with nonstick cooking spray.

In a large-sized bowl, combine all the above components. Then, add this mixture to your pressure cooker. Securely lock the lid and set for 10 minutes on LOW pressure.

Turn off the heat and let stand for about 10 minutes before serving. Serve in individual bowls. Enjoy!

Honey Creamy Apricots

(Ready in about 20 minutes | Servings 4)

Ingredients

8 apricots, pitted and halved

1/4 cup apple juice

1/4 cup water

2 tablespoons brown sugar

1/4 teaspoon vanilla extract

1/4 teaspoon ground cinnamon

2 tablespoons honey

1 cup cream cheese

Directions

Add all the above ingredients, except for honey and cream cheese, to a pressure cooker. Securely lock the lid and cook on LOW approximately 5 minutes.

Release pressure, according to manufacturer's instructions. Remove apricots from the cooker; set aside.

Combine honey and cream cheese; whisk to combine well.

To serve, place four apricot halves on each serving plate. Serve topped with a dollop of cream cheese mixture.

Oatmeal with Almonds

(Ready in about 10 minutes | Servings 4)

Ingredients

3 tablespoons butter

1 cup steel-cut oats

3 ½ cups water

1/4 teaspoon grated nutmeg

1/2 teaspoon ground cinnamon

A pinch of salt

1/4 cup milk

1/4 cup sugar

1/2 cup slivered almonds

Directions

Warm butter on HIGH until melted.

Then, add the steel-cut oats, water, nutmeg, cinnamon, and salt. Seal the cooker's lid; cook under HIGH pressure for 5 minutes.

Next, release pressure according to manufacturer's directions. Stir in the milk and sugar; give it a good stir. Divide among individual bowls and sprinkle with slivered almonds. Serve right away.

Apple and Pear Oatmeal

(Ready in about 25 minutes | Servings 6)

Ingredients

6 cups water

1 cup almond milk

1 ½ cups steel-cut oats

1/2 cup dried figs, chopped

1/2 cup dried currants

2 pears, cored and diced

1 apple, cored and diced

1 teaspoon cinnamon powder

1/2 teaspoon ground nutmeg

Directions

Add the ingredients to a pressure cooker.

Now set your cooker to HIGH; cook for 18 minutes.

Sweeten with maple syrup or honey if desired. Serve.

Eggnog Rice Pudding

(Ready in about 15 minutes | Servings 6)

Ingredients

1/4 stick butter

1 cup jasmine rice

2 cups water

1/2 teaspoon vanilla extract

1/2 teaspoon rum extract

1/2 teaspoon ground nutmeg

1/4 teaspoon ground cinnamon

1 ½ cups eggnog

1/4 cup maple syrup

Directions

In a pressure cooker, warm butter on HIGH.

Stir in jasmine rice, water, vanilla extract, rum extract, nutmeg, and cinnamon.

Then, lock the pressure cooker's lid; set to 7 minutes on HIGH. Now release the cooker's pressure according to manufacturer's directions.

Stir in eggnog and maple syrup; divide among individual bowls and enjoy.

Pepper Risotto with Peas

(Ready in about 15 minutes | Servings 6)

Ingredients

2 tablespoons vegetable oil

1 medium onion, chopped

1 yellow bell pepper, stemmed, cored, and chopped

1 red bell pepper, stemmed, cored, and chopped

1/2 teaspoon saffron

1 ½ cups long-grain white rice

3 cups vegetable broth

1/4 cup black olives, sliced and pitted

1 cup frozen peas, thawed

Directions

Warm the oil in a pressure cooker; set over medium heat. Then, sauté the onion and bell peppers, stirring frequently, until they have softened, for 3 to 4 minutes.

Add the saffron, white rice, broth and olives.

Lock the lid onto the pressure cooker. Raise the heat to HIGH; bring the pot to high pressure. Once the pressure has been reached, reduce the heat as much as possible while maintaining the pressure. Cook for 10 minutes.

Lastly, use the quick-release method and set aside for 5 minutes.

Then, open the lid; stir in the peas. Serve warm.

Basmati Rice with Corn

(Ready in about 15 minutes | Servings 6)

Ingredients

2 tablespoons olive oil

1 small-sized leek, chopped

2 cloves garlic, finely minced

1 carrot, chopped

1 green bell pepper, stemmed, cored, and chopped

1 ½ cups basmati rice

Salt and ground black pepper, to your liking

3 cups chicken stock

1/4 cup black olives, sliced and pitted

1 cup frozen corn, thawed

Directions

In a pressure cooker, warm olive oil over medium heat. Then, sauté the leek and garlic until they are browned and softened. Now add carrot and bell peppers; cook, stirring continuously, for 3 to 4 minutes.

Add the white rice, salt, black pepper, stock, and black olives.

Lock the lid onto your pressure cooker. Raise the heat to HIGH; bring the pot to high pressure. Once the pressure has been reached, reduce the heat as much as possible while maintaining the pressure. Cook for 10 to 12 minutes.

Lastly, use the quick-release method; open the cooker according to manufacturer's directions. Then, open the lid; stir in the thawed corn. Serve warm.

Peach and Hazelnut Bread Pudding

(Ready in about 45 minutes | Servings 8)

Ingredients

Nonstick cooking spray

6 cups stale bread chunks

1 cup peach, pitted and chopped

1/3 cup hazelnuts, chopped

5 whole eggs

1 ½ cups almond milk

1/2 cup heavy cream

1/2 cup brown sugar

3 tablespoons butter, melted

1 tablespoon flour

1/2 teaspoon rum extract

1/2 teaspoon cinnamon powder

Directions

Brush your cake pan with nonstick cooking spray. Then, add the bread, peach, and hazelnuts to the pan; toss to combine.

In a bowl, whisk together the remaining ingredients; pour this mixture over the top of the bread mixture in the pan; press the bread mixture down to saturate. Allow it to sit for 10 to 15 minutes.

Place a metal rack at the bottom of the pressure cooker. Pour in 2 cups of water. Cover cake pans with an aluminum foil; then, place them on the metal rack.

Now set the cooker to HIGH; cook for 25 minutes. Let the pressure release according to manufacturer's instructions.

Allow the pudding to stand for about 15 minutes before serving.

Date and Cranberry Croissant Pudding

(Ready in about 45 minutes | Servings 8)

Ingredients

Nonstick cooking spray

6 cups croissants, torn into pieces

1/2 cup dried cranberries

1/2 cup dried dates, chopped

5 large eggs, beaten

1/2 cup heavy cream

1 ½ cups whole milk

1/2 cup sugar

2 tablespoons margarine, room temperature

1/2 teaspoon ground cinnamon

1/2 teaspoon pure vanilla essence

Directions

Coat a soufflé dish with nonstick cooking spray.

In a mixing bowl, combine croissants, cranberries, and dates; toss to combine well. Then, transfer the mixture to the soufflé dish.

In a separate bowl, combine the remaining ingredients; stir to combine well. Let it soak for 10 minutes.

Lay a trivet at the bottom of a pressure cooker. To make a water bath, pour 2 cups of water.

Cover the dish with foil. Bring to HIGH pressure; cook for 25 minutes.

Release pressure according to manufacturer's directions; let it stand for 10 minutes before serving.

Morning Cilantro Rice

(Ready in about 35 minutes | Servings 6)

Ingredients

2 tablespoons butter

2 green onions, minced

2 cloves garlic, minced

1 ½ cups brown basmati rice

3 ½ cups chicken broth

1/4 cup packed fresh cilantro leaves, minced

1/2 teaspoon salt

1/4 teaspoon ground black pepper

Directions

Melt the butter in your pressure cooker pot over medium heat. Then, sauté green onions and garlic, stirring frequently, until they have softened, about 2 minutes.

Add the rice and cook for 1 to 2 minutes more. Stir in the remaining ingredients. Lock the lid onto the pressure cooker pot.

Raise the heat to HIGH; bring the pot to high pressure. Make sure to maintain this pressure. Cook for about 20 minutes.

Use the quick-release function; unlock and open the cooker. Give it a good stir before serving.

Mediterranean Rice Breakfast

(Ready in about 35 minutes | Servings 6)

Ingredients

3 tablespoons vegetable oil

2 Roma tomatoes, chopped

1 tablespoon packed fresh oregano leaves, chopped

1 teaspoon kosher salt

1/2 teaspoon cayenne pepper

1/4 teaspoon ground black pepper

1 ½ cups long-grain brown rice, such as brown basmati

2 ½ cups vegetable stock

1/3 cup olives, pitted and chopped

1/4 cup packed fresh parsley leaves, chopped

2 ½ ounces feta cheese, crumbled

Directions

Heat the vegetable oil in a pressure cooker; set over medium heat.

Add the tomatoes, oregano leaves, salt, cayenne pepper, and black pepper; cook, stirring continuously for about 3 minutes.

Next, add the rice and cook for one more minute. Add the stock, olives, and parsley leaves. Lock the lid onto the cooker.

Raise the heat to HIGH; bring the pot to high pressure. Make sure to maintain this pressure. Cook for about 20 minutes.

Afterward, use the quick-release method, and allow it to stand for about 10 minutes. Unlock and open the cooker. Add crumbled cheese and serve.

Mixed-Berry Jam

(Ready in about 1 hour 20 minutes | Servings 16)

Ingredients

1 pound strawberries, hulled and halved

1/2 pound blackberries

1/2 pound blueberries

1 vanilla bean, halved lengthwise

1 ½ pounds honey

Directions

Put all of the above ingredients into your pressure cooker. Then, place the cooker over medium-high heat, bringing it to a boil; make sure to stir the mixture often.

Now lock the cooker's lid into place; bring it to HIGH pressure. After that, lower the heat to MEDIUM-LOW for 10 minutes. Now allow pressure to release naturally.

Uncover the pressure cooker pot; place it back over medium-high heat; bring to a boil for about 5 minutes, stirring frequently.

Spoon the jam into sterilized jars. Serve with your favorite biscuits.

Chocolate Oatmeal with Almonds

(Ready in about 15 minutes | Servings 2)

Ingredients

1 cup water

3/4 cup almond milk

1 cup quick-cooking oats

2 peaches, pitted and diced

1/2 teaspoon pure almond extract

1/2 teaspoon vanilla essence

1 teaspoon ground cinnamon

1/2 cup dark chocolate, broken into chunks

2 tablespoons slivered almonds

Directions

Throw all the ingredients, except for chocolate and almonds, in your pressure cooker. Now lock the lid. Bring to HIGH pressure; maintain the pressure for about 6 minutes.

Remove the pressure cooker pot from the heat; allow pressure to release gradually.

Add chocolate and gently stir to combine. Divide the chocolate oatmeal among serving bowls and scatter slivered almonds over the top. Serve right now.

Biscuits with Bacon Gravy

(Ready in about 15 minutes | Servings 8)

Ingredients

2 bacon strips, finely diced

1 pound sausage

1 teaspoon rosemary, chopped

1 teaspoon dried thyme, chopped

1/2 cup vegetable broth

1/4 cup wheat flour

1 ½ cups whole milk

1/2 teaspoon salt

1 teaspoon cracked black pepper

Prepared biscuits

Directions

First of all, make the sauce. Set your pressure cooker to HIGH. Then, place bacon strips and sausage in the bottom of your cooker; sauté until they are browned, approximately 7 minutes.

Sprinkle with rosemary and thyme. Pour in vegetable broth. Now securely lock the lid and set on HIGH for about 5 minutes. Now release the cooker's pressure.

In a bowl or a measuring cup, whisk the flour and milk. Add this mixture to the cooker; let simmer for 3 minutes, or until the juice has thickened.

Season with salt and black pepper. To serve, spoon the bacon gravy over prepared biscuits and enjoy.

Cheese Spoon Bread

(Ready in about 20 minutes | Servings 6)

Ingredients

1 cup whole milk

2 cups vegetable stock

2/3 cup cornmeal

1 cup baking mix

1 cup sharp cheese, shredded

2 eggs

2 tablespoons butter, melted

2 teaspoons sugar

1/2 teaspoon black pepper

1 teaspoon salt

1/2 teaspoon onion powder

1 teaspoon granulated garlic

Directions

Brush the inside of the cooker with nonstick cooking spray.

In a bowl, combine all the above components. Now add this mixture to the pressure cooker. Securely lock the lid and set for 8 minutes on LOW.

Then, leave steam valve open. Set the cooker to "Brown" and let it cook approximately 5 minutes. Turn off the heat and let stand for 5 minutes before serving.

Super Creamy Potato Salad

(Ready in about 20 minutes + chilling time | Servings 6)

Ingredients

8 small-sized red potatoes, scrubbed

1 cup water

1 medium-sized onion, chopped

1 carrot, chopped

1 stalk celery, chopped

1 teaspoon cayenne pepper

1/2 teaspoon dried rosemary

3/4 teaspoon sea salt

1/4 teaspoon black pepper, freshly cracked

3 whole hard-boiled eggs, chopped

1/2 cup mayonnaise

1 teaspoon apple cider vinegar

Directions

Place potatoes together with water in your pressure cooker. Then, you should cook them on high pressure for about 3 minutes. Now let steam release for 2 to 3 minutes.

Now, quickly release the pressure in order to open pressure cooker. Allow the potatoes to cool enough to handle. Peel and slice them. Place a single layer of potatoes in a bowl.

Alternate potato layers with onions, carrot, and celery layers. Sprinkle each layer with cayenne pepper, rosemary, salt, and freshly cracked black pepper. Top your salad with the eggs.

In a mixing bowl, mix together the mayonnaise and apple cider vinegar. Now fold this mayonnaise mixture into the vegetables. Allow the salad to chill in a refrigerator before serving. Serve chilled.

Protein Lentil Salad

(Ready in about 20 minutes | Servings 6)

Ingredients

1 cup dried lentils, rinsed

2 cups chicken broth

1 bay leaf

1 medium-sized carrot, diced

1 medium-sized onion, finely diced

2 tablespoons olive oil

2 tablespoons white wine

1 clove garlic, minced

2 tablespoons fresh cilantro, chopped

1/2 teaspoon dried basil

3/4 teaspoon salt

1/4 teaspoon pepper

Directions

Add lentils, chicken broth, and bay leaf to the pressure cooker.

Securely lock the lid and then, set on HIGH for 8 minutes. Remove the lid; then, drain lentils and discard the bay leaf.

Combine prepared lentils with the remaining ingredients. Serve warm or at room temperature.

Apples and Pears in Strawberry Sauce

(Ready in about 25 minutes | Servings 4)

Ingredients

2 medium-sized pears, peeled, cored, and halved

2 medium-sized apples, peeled, cored, and halved

1 cup water

1 pint strawberries

1 vanilla bean, sliced lengthwise

1/2 teaspoon grated nutmeg

1/4 teaspoon ground cardamom

1/2 cup light brown sugar

1 tablespoon cornstarch

Directions

Put all ingredients, except for brown sugar and cornstarch, into the pressure cooker. Now securely lock the pressure cooker's lid.

Set the cooker on LOW for 7 minutes. Then, remove pears and set aside.

Next, mash the strawberries with a heavy spoon. Combine the sugar and cornstarch with 1 tablespoon of water.

Now, set cooker to "Brown,"; stir in dissolved sugar-cornstarch mixture. Allow it to simmer for 3 to 5 minutes, or until strawberry sauce has thickened.

Divide the pears and apples among serving plates. Top with strawberry sauce, serve and enjoy.

Peach and Cottage Breakfast

(Ready in about 20 minutes | Servings 4)

Ingredients

4 peaches, pitted and halved

1/4 cup water

1/4 cup apple juice

1/4 teaspoon vanilla extract

2 tablespoons brown sugar

1/8 teaspoon grated nutmeg

1/4 teaspoon ground cinnamon

1 cup cottage cheese

2 tablespoons maple syrup

Directions

Add all the above ingredients, except for cottage cheese, to your pressure cooker. Securely lock the lid and cook on LOW for 4 to 5 minutes.

Release pressure, and adjust the seasonings. Remove peaches from the cooker and reserve.

Combine cottage cheese with maple syrup.

To serve: place one peach on each serving plate. Serve topped with a dollop of cheese mixture. Enjoy!

Quick and Easy Aromatic Oatmeal

(Ready in about 10 minutes | Servings 4)

Ingredients

3 tablespoons butter

1 cup steel-cut oats

3 ½ cups water

1/4 teaspoon grated nutmeg

1/2 teaspoon ground cinnamon

A pinch of salt

1/4 cup low-fat milk

1/4 cup light brown sugar

Directions

Warm butter on HIGH until melted.

Then, add the steel-cut oats, water, grated nutmeg, cinnamon, and salt. Seal the cooker's lid and cook under HIGH pressure for 5 minutes.

Next, release pressure and uncover. Add the milk and brown sugar; stir to combine and serve right away.

Fruit Steel-Cut Oats

(Ready in about 25 minutes | Servings 6)

Ingredients

1 ½ cups steel-cut oats

1/2 cup dates, chopped

1/2 cup dried currants

3 apples, cored and diced

1 teaspoon pumpkin pie spice

6 cups water

1 cup soy milk

Directions

Prepare the ingredients according to the manufacturer's directions. Then, transfer them to a pressure cooker.

Now set your cooker to HIGH and cook for 18 minutes.

Sweeten with some honey if desired. Enjoy!

Holiday Eggnog Rice Pudding

(Ready in about 15 minutes | Servings 6)

Ingredients

2 tablespoons butter

2 cups water

1 cup rice

1/2 teaspoon rum extract

1/4 teaspoon ground cinnamon

1 ½ cups eggnog

1/4 cup honey

Directions

First of all, warm butter on HIGH or "Brown,".

Add the water, rice, rum extract, and cinnamon. Then, lock the pressure cooker's lid and set to 7 minutes on HIGH. Now release the cooker's pressure.

Stir in eggnog and honey; divide among serving plates and serve.

Apricot and Almond Bread Pudding

(Ready in about 45 minutes | Servings 8)

Ingredients

Non-stick cooking spray

6 cups stale bread chunks

1 cup apricots, pitted and chopped

1/3 cup almonds, chopped

5 whole eggs

1 ½ cups whole milk

1/2 cup heavy cream

1/2 cup sugar

3 tablespoons butter, melted

1 tablespoon flour

1 teaspoon vanilla extract

1/8 teaspoon cardamom

1/4 teaspoon ground cinnamon

Directions

Coat cake pans with cooking spray. Then, add the bread, apricots, and almonds to the pans and toss to combine.

In a mixing bowl, whisk together the rest of the above ingredients; pour this mixture over top of the bread mixture in the pans; press the bread mixture down to saturate. Allow it to sit for about 10 minutes.

Place a metal rack at the bottom of a pressure cooker. Pour in 2 cups of water. Cover cake pans with an aluminum foil; then, place them on the metal rack.

Now set the cooker to HIGH for 25 minutes. Let the pressure release for 10 minutes. Allow bread pudding to rest 10 to 15 minutes before serving.

Date and Walnut Bread Pudding

(Ready in about 45 minutes | Servings 8)

Ingredients

5 cups stale bread chunks

1 cup dates, pitted and chopped

1/3 cup walnuts, chopped

5 whole eggs

2 cups whole milk

1/4 cup honey

3 tablespoons butter, melted

1 tablespoon flour

1/42 teaspoon ground cinnamon

1/2 teaspoon almond extract

Directions

Brush your cake pans with non-stick cooking spray. Toss together bread chunks, dates and walnuts, and drop them into the pans.

In a bowl, combine together the remaining ingredients; add the mixture to the pans. Let it soak for about 10 minutes.

Place a trivet at the bottom of your pressure cooker. Then, pour in 2 cups of water. Cover the pans with a foil and place them on the trivet.

Set the cooker to HIGH for 25 minutes. Serve warm or at room temperature.

Banana and Cranberry Croissant Pudding

(Ready in about 45 minutes | Servings 8)

Ingredients

6 cups croissants, torn into pieces

1/2 cup dried bananas, chopped

1/2 cup dried cranberries

5 large eggs

1 ½ cups milk

1/2 cup heavy cream

1/2 cup sugar

2 tablespoons butter, melted

1/4 teaspoon grated nutmeg

1/2 teaspoon ground cinnamon

Directions

Brush a soufflé dish with non-stick cooking spray.

In a bowl, combine together torn croissants, dried bananas, and cranberries; toss to combine. Then, add this croissants mixture to the soufflé dish.

In a bowl, combine together the remaining ingredients; stir to combine. Let it soak for 10 minutes.

Lay a trivet at the bottom of a cooker. Pour 2 cups of water to create a water bath. Cover the dish with a foil, and place on trivet in the cooker. Bring to HIGH pressure and cook for 25 minutes.

Release pressure and allow your pudding to rest for 10 minutes before serving.

Healthy Strawberry Jam

(Ready in about 1 hour 20 minutes | Servings 16)

Ingredients

2 pounds strawberries, hulled and halved

1 vanilla bean, halved lengthwise

1 ½ pounds honey

Directions

Put all the above ingredients into the pressure cooker. Then, place the uncovered cooker over medium-high heat, bringing it to a boil; make sure to stir frequently.

Now lock the cooker's lid into place and bring it to pressure. After that, lower the heat to medium-low for 10 minutes. Take your pressure cooker off the heat; allow pressure to release naturally.

Uncover the cooker and place it back on medium-high heat; bring to a boil for about 4 minutes, stirring constantly.

Spoon the jam into hot sterilized jars. Seal the jars properly. Serve with your favorite biscuits. Enjoy!

Breakfast Dessert Oatmeal

(Ready in about 15 minutes | Servings 2)

Ingredients

3⁄4 cup water

1 cup coconut milk

1 cup quick-cooking oats

2 pears, peeled, cored, and diced

1/2 teaspoon vanilla essence

1/2 teaspoon cardamom

1 teaspoon ground cinnamon

2 tablespoons almonds, chopped

Directions

Put all of the above ingredients into your pressure cooker. Now lock the lid. Bring to HIGH pressure and maintain for 5 to 6 minutes.

Remove the cooker from the heat; allow pressure to release gradually.

Serve with some extra milk if desired.

Banana Pecan Oatmeal

(Ready in about 10 minutes | Servings 2)

Ingredients

3⁄4 cup water

1 cup soymilk

1 cup toasted quick-cooking oats

2 bananas, sliced

1/4 cup golden raisins

2 tablespoons honey

2 teaspoons cinnamon

2 tablespoons pecans, chopped

Directions

Drop all of the ingredients into the cooker.

Lock the lid. Bring it to HIGH pressure and maintain for about 5 minutes. Remove from the heat and bring pressure down

Uncover and stir the mixture. Serve with some extra dried fruits or milk if desired.

Vegan Cranberry Oatmeal

(Ready in about 15 minutes | Servings 2)

Ingredients

3 cups water

1 cup steel-cut oats

2 teaspoons vegan margarine

1 cup apple juice

4 tablespoons dried cranberries

1-2 tablespoons brown sugar

1/4 teaspoon cardamom

1/4 teaspoon ground cinnamon

Directions

Place a metal rack in the pressure cooker; pour in 1/2 cup of water.

Add all the above ingredients to a metal bowl that fits inside the pressure cooker. Stir to combine.

Cover and bring to LOW pressure. Then, maintain pressure for 8 minutes.

Next, allow pressure to release naturally. Serve right away!

Maple Apple Oatmeal

(Ready in about 15 minutes | Servings 2)

Ingredients

3/4 cup water

1 cup milk

2 tablespoons dried apricots

1 apple, cored and diced

1 cup toasted quick-cooking oats

2 tablespoons maple syrup

2 tablespoons walnuts, chopped

Directions

Simply throw all the above ingredients into your pressure cooker.

Now lock the lid into place. Then, maintain HIGH pressure for 5 minutes.

Next, remove the cooker from the heat; allow pressure to release. Serve right now and enjoy!

Sausage Breakfast Casserole

(Ready in about 15 minutes | Servings 4)

Ingredients

2 tablespoons canola oil

1 yellow onion, diced

1 small-sized red bell pepper, seeded and chopped

1/2 pound sausage

3 cups potatoes, shredded

6 eggs, beaten

1 cup Ricotta cheese

2 cups Cheddar cheese

3/4 teaspoon salt

1/4 teaspoon ground black pepper

Directions

Warm canola oil in the pressure cooker; now sauté the onion and bell pepper until they are tender. Add the sausage and cook for about 3 more minutes.

Add the remaining ingredients to the pressure cooker. Lock the lid into place; then, maintain HIGH pressure for about 5 minutes.

Remove from the heat. Serve warm and enjoy!

Mom's Berry Jam

(Ready in about 1 hour 20 minutes | Servings 16)

Ingredients

1 pound raspberries

1 pound blackberries

1 vanilla bean, halved lengthwise

1 ½ pounds honey

Directions

Throw all the above ingredients into your pressure cooker. Now place the cooker over medium-high heat, bring it to a boil; stir often.

Cover and bring it to pressure. Next, lower the heat to medium-low for 10 minutes. Allow pressure to release naturally.

Uncover the pressure cooker and place it back on medium-high heat; bring to a boil for 4 to 5 minutes, stirring frequently.

Lastly, ladle your jam into hot sterilized jars. Seal the jars. Serve with English muffins if desired. Enjoy!

Old-Fashioned Grits

(Ready in about 15 minutes | Servings 4)

Ingredients

4 cups water

A pinch of salt

1/4 teaspoon grated nutmeg

1 cup stone-ground grits

1 tablespoon ghee

Directions

Bring the water, salt, and nutmeg to a boil in your pressure cooker over HIGH heat.

Gradually stir in the grits and lock the lid into place. Bring to high pressure over high heat; maintain pressure for 10 minutes.

Allow steam to release naturally. Lastly, stir in ghee just before serving. Serve and enjoy!

Winter Spiced Grits

(Ready in about 15 minutes | Servings 4)

Ingredients

2 cups water

2 cups vegetable broth

A pinch of salt

1/4 teaspoon dried thyme

1 cup grits

1/2 tablespoon cayenne pepper

Directions

Bring the water, vegetable broth, salt, and thyme to a boil in your pressure cooker over HIGH heat.

Slowly add the grits to the cooker. Put the lid on and bring to pressure over high heat; maintain pressure for about 10 minutes.

Cool down and remove the lid. Divide the grits among four serving plates; sprinkle with cayenne pepper and serve.

Breakfast Hash Browns

(Ready in about 15 minutes | Servings 4)

Ingredients

2 tablespoons vegetable oil

2 tablespoons margarine

6 russet potatoes, peeled and grated

1/2 teaspoon paprika

3/4 teaspoon sea salt

1/4 teaspoon freshly ground black pepper

Directions

Warm vegetable oil and margarine in the pressure cooker over medium heat.

Add the russet potatoes to the pressure cooker. Then, cook for 5 minutes, stirring periodically, until the potatoes are just browned. Season with paprika, salt, and black pepper.

Next, press the potatoes down firmly with a wide metal spatula.

Cover the cooker and bring it to LOW pressure; maintain pressure for about 6 minutes. Afterwards, quick-release the pressure. Serve warm.

Hash Browns with Sausage and Apples

(Ready in about 20 minutes | Servings 4)

Ingredients

3 tablespoons butter

1 (12-ounce) bag frozen hash brown potatoes

3/4 teaspoon sea salt

1/4 teaspoon freshly ground black pepper

6 ounces cooked sausage, chopped

2 apples, sliced

1 tablespoon maple syrup

1 teaspoon granulated garlic

Directions

Add the butter to the pressure cooker and warm it over medium heat.

Add the hash brown potatoes and cook for about 5 minutes, stirring occasionally. Season with the salt and black pepper.

Use a wide spatula to press the potatoes down. Add the chopped sausage and apples. Then, drizzle with the maple syrup and sprinkle with granulated garlic.

Now lock the lid in place and bring to low pressure for 6 minutes. Afterwards, quick-release the pressure. Divide among four serving plates and serve.

Bacon Hash Browns

(Ready in about 20 minutes | Servings 4)

Ingredients

2 tablespoons canola oil

1 pound russet potatoes, peeled

2 tablespoons fresh chopped parsley

2 cups crumbled bacon

3/4 teaspoon kosher salt

1/2 teaspoon freshly ground black pepper

Toast, for serving

Directions

Warm canola oil over medium heat in the pressure cooker. Add the potatoes to the pressure cooker.

Sauté for 5 to 6 minutes, stirring occasionally, until they are browned.

Add the parsley, bacon, salt, and black pepper. Mix well to combine. Then, press the potatoes down with a wide spatula.

Cover the pressure cooker and bring it to low pressure; cook for 6 to 7 minutes. Now remove from the heat; quick-release the pressure, and serve with toast.

Saucy Morning Ham

(Ready in about 20 minutes | Servings 4)

Ingredients

1 tablespoon lard

4 slices ham

3/4 cup coffee

1 tablespoon sugar

Directions

Heat the lard in a pressure cooker. Stir in the ham slices and fry them for 2 minutes on both sides. Pour in the coffee.

Lock the lid into place. Then, bring to low pressure; maintain for 7 to 8 minutes. Now quick-release the pressure. Remove prepared ham to the plates.

Add the sugar to the pan; stir until it dissolves. Pour dissolved sugar over the ham. Serve with fresh fruit juice if desired and enjoy!

French-Style Vegetarian Sandwiches

(Ready in about 30 minutes | Servings 6)

Ingredients

1 (13-ounce) package tempeh, cut into strips

3 cups vegetables broth

3 cups water

2-3 green garlics, minced

1 cup soy sauce

2 tablespoons canola oil

1 red onion, sliced

1 small-sized bell pepper, sliced

Salt and pepper, to taste

6 French rolls

6 slices Mozzarella cheese

Directions

Add the tempeh, vegetable broth, water, green garlic, and soy sauce to your pressure cooker. After that, lock the lid into place; bring to HIGH pressure approximately 20 minutes. Then, quick-release the pressure. Reserve the tempeh.

Warm canola oil in a saucepan; sauté the onion and bell pepper until they are softened and caramelized. Add the tempeh, salt, and black pepper.

Preheat your oven to 450 degrees F. Now divide prepared mixture among 6 French rolls. Add Mozzarella cheese. Bake your sandwiches in the preheated oven for about 5 minutes, or until Mozzarella slices have melted. Serve right away and enjoy!

Pumpkin Steel Cut Oats

(Ready in about 20 minutes | Servings 6)

Ingredients

1 tablespoon butter

1 cup steel-cut oats

3 cups water

1 cup pumpkin puree

1/4 cup honey

1/2 teaspoon cardamom

1 teaspoon cinnamon

1/4 teaspoon grated nutmeg

A pinch of salt

Directions

Select 'Sauté' and warm the butter in your pressure cooking pot until it's melted. Now add the oats; toast the oats, stirring often, about 3 minutes.

Add the rest of the above ingredients. Select HIGH pressure and maintain it for 10 minutes.

After that, release the pressure for 10 minutes. Then, carefully remove the cooker's lid.

Serve warm with some extra milk if desired. Enjoy!

Smoky Tofu Sandwiches

(Ready in about 20 minutes | Servings 6)

Ingredients

1 (16-ounce) package firm tofu, crumbled

1/4 cup mustard

3/4 cup brown sugar

1/4 cup water

3/4 cup apple cider vinegar

1 tablespoon chili powder

1 tablespoon soy sauce

1 teaspoon smoked paprika

2 tablespoons butter

A few drops of liquid smoke

1/2 teaspoon salt

1/4 teaspoon black pepper

6 burger buns

Directions

Press the tofu for 5 minutes. Then, crumble the tofu and transfer to the pressure cooker.

In a bowl, whisk the rest of the ingredients, except for buns. Now pour the mustard mixture into the pressure cooker.

Lock the lid into place, and bring to HIGH pressure; maintain for 5 minutes. Use a natural pressure release. Serve with your burger buns.

Quick and Easy Hard-Boiled Eggs

(Ready in about 40 minutes | Servings 6)

Ingredients

2 cups water

8 eggs

4 cups cold water

Directions

Fill a pressure cooker with the water according to the manufacturer's directions. Put the eggs into the steamer basket above the water. Now seal the lid. Bring the pressure cooker to LOW pressure.

Cook for about 6 minutes. Then, allow the pressure to drop for 5 minutes.

Replace the hot eggs to the cold water. Allow the eggs to cool completely. Serve.

Chia and Raspberry Oatmeal

(Ready in about 25 minutes | Servings 4)

Ingredients

1 tablespoon ghee

1 cup steel-cut oats

3 cups water

1/2 cup heavy cream

2 tablespoons maple syrup

1/4 teaspoon kosher salt

1 cup raspberries

1/4 cup chia seeds

Directions

Add ghee to pressure cooking pot, and select "Sauté"; warm ghee and add steel-cut oats. Toast the steel-cut oats until they smell nutty, or 3 to 4 minutes.

Add water, cream, maple syrup, and kosher salt. Select HIGH pressure and cook for 10 minutes. After that, turn off pressure cooker; gradually release the pressure.

Stir in raspberries and chia seeds. Then, let sit until your oatmeal reaches desired thickness. Serve with a splash of milk if desired.

Coconut and Chili Tofu

(Ready in about 25 minutes | Servings 6)

Ingredients

1 (16-ounce) package firm tofu

2 green chilies, seeded and minced

2 green garlics, finely chopped

4 green onions, chopped

1 tablespoon soy sauce

1/2 cup fresh cilantro, chopped

2 tablespoons water

2 tablespoons olive oil

1 (13-ounce) can coconut milk

Salt and pepper, to taste

4 cups hot cooked rice

Directions

Wrap the tofu in the paper towels and press for 10 minutes. Then, cut the tofu into pieces.

In your food processor, puree green chilies, green garlic, green onions, soy sauce, cilantro, and water. Puree until you get a smooth paste; add extra water as needed.

Warm the oil in the pressure cooker; sauté the tofu pieces until they are lightly browned. Now add the coconut milk and the prepared chili paste.

Select HIGH pressure and maintain it for 5 minutes. Turn off pressure cooker and allow pressure to release gradually and naturally. Sprinkle with salt and black pepper, as needed. Serve over hot cooked rice.

Sweet and Spicy Tofu

(Ready in about 15 minutes | Servings 4)

Ingredients

1 (16-ounce) package extra-firm tofu

2 cups water

2 tablespoons cornstarch

2 scallions, minced

1 teaspoon ginger, minced

1/4 cup soy sauce

2 tablespoons maple syrup

1/4 cup sherry wine

2 teaspoons paprika

2 tablespoons canola oil

2 cups broccoli, blanched and chopped

Directions

First of all, press the tofu for about 5 minutes by adding weight on top. Cut into chunks.

To make the sauce: In a bowl, whisk together 1 cup water, cornstarch, scallions, ginger, soy sauce, maple syrup, sherry wine, and paprika. Set aside.

Heat canola oil in your pressure cooker; now sauté the tofu until it is browned on all sides. Add the blanched broccoli and continue sautéing for 1 minute more. Add the reserved sauce. Season to taste.

Cover and bring to HIGH pressure; maintain for 5 minutes. Afterwards, turn off pressure cooker and allow pressure to release naturally. Serve with quinoa if desired.

Coconut and Pumpkin Oatmeal

(Ready in about 20 minutes | Servings 4)

Ingredients

1 tablespoon vegan margarine

1 cup steel-cut oats

2 cups water

1 cup coconut water

1 cup pumpkin puree

1/4 cup maple syrup

1 teaspoon cinnamon

1/4 teaspoon grated nutmeg

A pinch of salt

Coconut shreds, as garnish

Directions

First, melt the vegan margarine in a pressure cooker. Next, add steel-cut oats and toast them, stirring constantly, for about 3 minutes.

Add the remaining ingredients, except for coconut. Select HIGH pressure and cook for 10 minutes.

Next, release the pressure for 10 minutes. Afterwards, remove the cooker's lid.

Serve warm sprinkled with coconut shreds. Enjoy!

Family Grape Jelly

(Ready in about 15 minutes | Servings 12)

Ingredients

5 cups grape juice

2 (1 3⁄4-ounce) packages dry pectin

1⁄2 cup sugar

Directions

Add grape juice and pectin to your pressure cooking pot; bring to medium-high heat.

Lock the cooker's lid and maintain HIGH pressure for 1 minute. Remove from the heat and remove the lid. Add the sugar and stir to combine.

Now discard any foam. Replace your jelly to hot sterilized glass containers. Seal the containers and allow them to cool at room temperature.

Serve with peanut butter if desired.

Everyday Tomato Chutney

(Ready in about 15 minutes | Servings 12)

Ingredients

4 pounds tomatoes, peeled

2 red onions, peeled and diced

3 cloves garlic, peeled and minced

1 ¾ cups white sugar

1 cup wine vinegar

1⁄4 cup raisins

1⁄2 teaspoon ground coriander

1⁄4 teaspoon ground cloves

1 teaspoon ground ginger

1 teaspoon chili powder

1 tablespoon curry paste

Directions

In a food processor or blender, purée the tomatoes.

Add the puréed tomatoes to the pressure cooker. Stir in the rest of the above ingredients. Stir to combine, lock the lid, and cook at LOW pressure for 10 minutes.

Afterwards, turn off pressure cooker. Let pressure release naturally. Serve chilled over flat bread and enjoy.

Green Tomato Chutney

(Ready in about 15 minutes | Servings 12)

Ingredients

2 pounds green tomatoes, diced

2 garlic cloves, peeled and minced

1 leek, thinly sliced

1 jalapeño pepper, minced

2 bell peppers, diced

1/4 cup dried cherries

1 tablespoon fresh ginger, grated

3/4 cup brown sugar

3/4 cup white wine

3/4 teaspoon sea salt

Directions

Put all ingredients into the pressure cooking pot; stir to combine well. Cook on LOW pressure for 10 minutes. Remove from the heat and allow pressure to release gradually.

Place in a refrigerator before serving. You can spread your chutney over pizza crust if desired. Keep in your refrigerator for 2 months. Enjoy!

Homemade Peach Jam

(Ready in about 10 minutes | Servings 20)

Ingredients

4 cups peaches, pitted, peeled and chopped

4 cups sugar

1 teaspoon orange juice

1 teaspoon lemon juice

1 (1 3/4-ounce) package dry pectin

Directions

Add the peaches, sugar, orange juice, and lemon juice to the pressure cooking pot. Stir until the ingredients are well combined.

Bring to low pressure and maintain pressure for 3 minutes. Remove from the heat and allow pressure to release.

Uncover and place over medium-high heat. Then, stir in the pectin; bring mixture to a boil, stirring often, for 1 minute.

Spoon into the sterilized glass containers. Keep in the freezer for up to 8 months.

Fruit Breakfast Risotto

(Ready in about 15 minutes | Servings 4)

Ingredients

2 tablespoons margarine

1 ½ cups rice

1 large apple, cored and diced

1 large pear, cored and diced

1/2 teaspoon cinnamon

1/8 teaspoon grated nutmeg

1/8 teaspoon salt

1/3 cup brown sugar

1 cup apple juice

3 cups milk

1/2 cup dried cranberries

Directions

Melt the margarine in the pressure cooking pot for about 3 minutes. Add rice to the cooker; cook, stirring frequently, approximately 4 minutes.

Add the apple, pear, cinnamon, nutmeg, salt, and brown sugar. Add the apple juice and milk. Select HIGH pressure and cook 6 minutes. Then, turn off your cooker and use a quick pressure release.

Afterwards, stir in dried cranberries. Serve topped with a splash of milk if desired.

Sunday Bread Pudding with Cherries

(Ready in about 25 minutes | Servings 4)

Ingredients

5 cups bread chunks

1 cup dried cherries

2 cups evaporated milk

2 whole eggs

1 egg yolk

1/4 cup sugar

1/4 teaspoon allspice

1/4 teaspoon ground cinnamon

1/2 tablespoon butter

2 ½ cups water

Directions

Fill a metal baking dish with bread chunks. Then, add dried cherries and toss to combine.

In a mixing bowl, combine the milk, eggs, sugar, allspice, and cinnamon. Combine until it becomes frothy. Pour this custard mixture over bread-cherry mixture. Push the bread down.

Spread butter on an aluminum foil. Cover dish with the foil, butter side down; make sure to wrap tightly.

Add water to pressure cooker. Lay baking dish on a cooking rack in your pressure cooker. Allow it to cook about 15 minutes at 15 pounds pressure. Remove foil and serve warm.

Fig and Walnut Bread Pudding

(Ready in about 25 minutes | Servings 6)

Ingredients

2 tablespoons butter

4 slices day-old bread, crusts trimmed and cubed

1/2 cup dried figs, chopped

1/2 cup walnuts, chopped

1/2 cup packed light brown sugar

1/2 teaspoon ground cinnamon

1/4 teaspoon grated nutmeg

A pinch of salt

2 cups warm milk

2 eggs, beaten

3 cups water

Directions

Butter a soufflé dish that fits into your pressure cooker.

In a mixing bowl, combine the bread cubes, chopped dried figs and walnuts. In a separate mixing bowl, combine together the sugar, cinnamon, nutmeg, salt, milk, and eggs.

Pour the wet mixture into the bread mixture; stir to combine well; transfer the mixture to the prepared soufflé dish. Cover your soufflé dish with an aluminum foil.

Now pour the water into your cooker. Put the soufflé dish into the cooker steamer basket. Lock the lid in place; bring to pressure and cook for 20 minutes under HIGH pressure. Remove the lid and serve warm.

Grandma's Sweet Cornbread

(Ready in about 30 minutes | Servings 8)

Ingredients

2/3 cup flour

1 1/3 cups cornmeal

1/4 cup brown sugar

1 teaspoon baking soda

2 teaspoons baking powder

1 teaspoon kosher salt

1/2 stick butter, room temperature

1 cup buttermilk

2 whole eggs

Directions

In a mixing bowl, sift the flours; add sugar, baking soda, baking powder, and salt. Mix to combine well.

In a separate bowl, whisk together the remaining ingredients.

Add dry mixture to the wet mixture, mixing well.

Pour your batter into a greased pan. Cover with a glass lid. Place the pan inside the pressure cooker, in a steamer basket.

Pour about 2/3 cup of water into the bottom of your cooker. Lock the lid, and bring to HIGH pressure. When the pressure is reached, reduce temperature to lowest setting, and cook for about 22 minutes.

Lastly, carefully open the lid; transfer your cornbread to a wire rack to cool for 5 minutes before serving.

Morning Sausage with Gravy

(Ready in about 20 minutes | Servings 8)

Ingredients

2 pounds sausage

2 tablespoons lard

1/4 cup flour

2 cups half-and-half

3/4 teaspoon sea salt

1/4 teaspoon freshly ground black pepper

Directions

Stir the sausage into your pressure cooker. Now fry over medium-high heat for 5 minutes.

Lock the lid into place; bring to LOW pressure and maintain for 8 minutes. Then, quick-release the pressure.

Return the pressure cooker to medium-high heat. Add the lard and cook until it is melted.

Sprinkle the flour and cook, stirring continuously. Whisk in the half-and-half, stirring continuously. Bring to a boil.

Now reduce the heat and simmer for about 3 minutes or until the gravy has thickened. Season with salt and pepper. Serve warm with buttermilk biscuits if desired.

Sausage and Corn Delight

(Ready in about 20 minutes | Servings 4)

Ingredients

1 pound sausage links

1 medium onion, peeled and diced

2 green garlic, sliced

4 potatoes, peeled and sliced

1 (16-ounce) can corn

3/4 cup tomato paste

Salt and black pepper, to taste

Directions

Add the sausage to your cooker; brown the sausage over medium flame. Reserve.

Lay the onion, green garlic, potatoes, and corn in the bottom of the cooker. Place reserved browned sausage on top of the corn in the cooker.

Pour the tomato paste over the layers in the pressure cooker. Lock the lid; then, bring to HIGH pressure, and maintain for about 7 minutes.

Season with salt and pepper to taste. Lastly, allow to sit for about 10 minutes.

Delicious Sausage with Veggies

(Ready in about 20 minutes | Servings 6)

Ingredients

1 ½ pounds pork sausage

1 cup shallots, sliced

4 potatoes, peeled and sliced

1 red bell pepper, seeded and sliced

1 yellow bell pepper, seeded and sliced

3/4 cup tomato paste

1/2 teaspoon granulated garlic

Salt and black pepper, to taste

Directions

Throw pork sausage into your cooker; then, sauté the sausage for 4 to 5 minutes. Set sautéed sausage aside.

Place the shallots, potatoes, and bell peppers in the bottom of the pressure cooker. Top with the prepared sausage.

Pour the tomato paste into the pressure cooker. Sprinkle with granulated garlic, salt, and black pepper. Lock the lid; then, bring to HIGH pressure, and cook for about 7 minutes.

Let it rest for about 10 minutes before serving. Serve and enjoy!

Country Cornmeal Mush

(Ready in about 20 minutes | Servings 6)

Ingredients

4 cups water

1 cup cornmeal

3/4 teaspoon kosher salt

2 tablespoons butter

Directions

In a mixing bowl, whisk together 1 cup water, cornmeal, and kosher salt.

Pour the remaining 3 cups of water into your pressure cooker. Bring to a boil. Then, stir cornmeal mixture into the boiling water.

Add butter to the cooker and stir frequently. Lock the lid into place. Bring to LOW pressure and cook for 10 minutes.

Then, quick-release the pressure. Serve warm with your favorite milk.

Yummy Sesame Congee

(Ready in about 40 minutes | Servings 8)

Ingredients

12 cups water

2 cups brown rice

3-4 cloves garlic, peeled and minced

1 large-sized shallot, finely chopped

2 tablespoons mirin

2 tablespoons toasted sesame seeds

3/4 teaspoon salt

1/4 teaspoon freshly cracked black pepper

Directions

Throw 10 cups of water together with brown rice into your pressure cooker. Then, cook for 25 minutes on HIGH; allow pressure to release naturally.

Next, stir in the rest of the above ingredients; continue cooking until the flavors have married, or approximately 15 minutes.

Serve with sliced cucumber and avocado if desired. Enjoy!

Scallion Rice Porridge

(Ready in about 40 minutes | Servings 8)

Ingredients

2 cups long-grain rice

10 cups water

3-4 scallions, finely chopped

3 slices fresh ginger

2 tablespoons sesame oil

1/2 teaspoon ground black pepper

3/4 teaspoon sea salt

Directions

Add long-grain rice to your pressure cooker. Pour in the water and cook for about 25 minutes on HIGH; then, allow pressure to release.

Add the remaining ingredients; continue cooking for 10 to 15 minutes or until the scallions have softened.

Serve sprinkled with fresh chopped chives and enjoy!

Bean and Cherry Salad

(Ready in about 35 minutes + chilling time | Servings 12)

Ingredients

Water

2 cups dried cannellini beans

1 teaspoon lemon zest

3 tablespoons sherry vinegar

2 tablespoons tamari sauce

2 teaspoons honey

1 teaspoon chili paste

2 cloves garlic, peeled and minced

2 teaspoons sesame oil

1 cup frozen corn kernels, thawed

1 cup frozen peas, thawed

3 carrots, thinly sliced

1 medium zucchini, peeled, grated, and drained

3/4 cup dried cranberries

3 green onions, peeled and diced

Salt and freshly cracked black pepper, to taste

Directions

Place water and beans in a bowl. Let it soak overnight.

Now prepare the dressing by whisking lemon zest, sherry vinegar, tamari sauce, honey, chili paste, garlic, and sesame oil. Refrigerate the dressing overnight.

Drain the beans and cook them in your pressure cooker along with 3 cups of water for 25 minutes. Remove the cooker from the heat and allow pressure to release.

Next, drain cooked beans and transfer them to a bowl. Toss the beans with the rest of the above ingredients. Drizzle with chilled dressing. Taste and adjust the seasonings. Serve.

Vegan Banana Almond Oatmeal

(Ready in about 10 minutes | Servings 2)

Ingredients

1 cup coconut milk

3⁄4 cup water

1 cup quick-cooking oats

2 bananas, sliced

1/4 cup dried figs, chopped

2 tablespoons maple syrup

2 teaspoons cinnamon

2 tablespoons almonds, chopped

Directions

Simply drop all of the ingredients in your pressure cooker pot.

Lock the lid. Bring it to HIGH pressure; maintain the pressure for about 5 minutes. Remove from the heat and bring pressure down.

Uncover and divide prepared oatmeal among serving bowls. Serve warm.

Family Breakfast Casserole

(Ready in about 15 minutes | Servings 4)

Ingredients

2 tablespoons olive oil

1 medium-sized onion, diced

1 bell pepper, seeded and chopped

1/3 pound sausage

3 cups potatoes, shredded

6 eggs, beaten

1 cup mozzarella cheese

2 cups Colby cheese

Sea salt and ground black pepper, to taste

Directions

Warm olive oil in the pressure cooker; then, sauté the onion together with bell pepper until they are softened. Add the sausage and cook for an additional 3 minutes.

Add the remaining ingredients to the pressure cooker. Lock the lid into place; then, maintain HIGH pressure for about 5 minutes.

Remove from the heat and serve immediately.

Pumpkin Pie Breakfast Pudding

(Ready in about 20 minutes | Servings 4)

Ingredients

1 ½ cups canned pumpkin

1/2 cup brown sugar

1/2 cup heavy cream

2 eggs

2 tablespoons maple syrup

1 teaspoon vanilla extract

2 tablespoons all-purpose flour

1/2 teaspoon ground cardamom

1 teaspoon ground cinnamon

1/2 teaspoon vanilla extract

A pinch of salt

Directions

Brush a soufflé dish with nonstick cooking spray; set it aside. Whisk the ingredients in a large-sized mixing bowl.

Pour the mixture into the prepared soufflé dish. Cover it with an aluminum foil and seal well.

Set the pressure cooker rack in your cooker; pour in 2 cups water. Make an aluminum foil sling for the soufflé dish.

Set the cooker over high heat; bring it to HIGH pressure. Once this pressure has been reached, reduce the heat and maintain this pressure. Cook for 15 minutes.

Release the pressure and open the cooker. Lastly, transfer your dish to a wire cooling rack using a foil sling. Serve at room temperature.

Sunday Breakfast Potatoes

(Ready in about 10 minutes | Servings 6)

Ingredients

2 ¼ pounds russet potatoes, peeled and cut into chunks

1 teaspoon sea salt

1/4 teaspoon ground black pepper

1/2 teaspoon red pepper flakes, crushed

3 tablespoons butter, cut into pieces

3/4 cup buttermilk

Directions

Place the potatoes in a pressure cooker pot; then, fill the pot with water to cover the potatoes. Sprinkle with the salt. Close and lock the lid.

Set the burner heat to HIGH. After that, reduce the burner heat to maintain HIGH pressure. Then, cook for 6 minutes.

Open your pressure cooker with the Quick Release method. Drain prepared potatoes in a colander.

Using a potato masher, mash the potatoes. Stir in black pepper, red pepper, butter and the buttermilk. Beat the mixture to the desired consistency. Serve immediately with your favorite cheese.

Spiced Grandma's Grits

(Ready in about 15 minutes | Servings 4)

Ingredients

4 cups water

A pinch of salt

1/8 teaspoon ground cinnamon

1/4 teaspoon grated nutmeg

1 cup stone-ground grits

2 tablespoons butter

4 ounces Cheddar cheese, shredded

Directions

Bring the water, salt, cinnamon and nutmeg to a boil in your pressure cooker over HIGH heat.

Gradually and slowly stir in the grits; lock the cooker's lid into place. Bring to HIGH pressure and maintain it for 10 minutes.

Afterward, allow steam to release naturally. To serve, stir in butter and cheese: give it a good stir. Enjoy!

Easy Breakfast Hash Browns

(Ready in about 15 minutes | Servings 4)

Ingredients

3 tablespoons olive oil

6 russet potatoes, peeled and grated

1 teaspoon cayenne pepper

3/4 teaspoon sea salt

1/2 teaspoon freshly cracked black pepper

Directions

Warm olive oil in a pressure cooker pot over medium heat.

Add the potatoes to the pressure cooker. Then, cook for 5 minutes, stirring periodically, until the potatoes are just browned. Season with cayenne pepper, salt, and cracked black pepper.

Next, press the potatoes down firmly using a wide spatula.

Cover the cooker with the lid; bring to LOW pressure; maintain pressure for about 6 minutes. Lastly, quick-release the pressure. Serve right now.

Sausage Hash Browns

(Ready in about 20 minutes | Servings 4)

Ingredients

2 tablespoons olive oil

1 pound potatoes, peeled

2 tablespoons fresh cilantro, chopped

2 cups sausage crumbled

3/4 teaspoon salt

1/2 teaspoon freshly ground black pepper

Toast, for serving

Directions

Warm olive oil over medium heat. Add the potatoes. Sauté for about 6 minutes, stirring occasionally, until the potatoes are browned.

Stir in the cilantro, sausage, salt, and black pepper. Mix until everything is well combined. Then, press the potatoes down with a wide spatula.

Cover the pressure cooker and bring it to LOW pressure; cook for 7 minutes.

Lastly, remove the cooker from the heat; quick-release the pressure. To serve, divide among serving plates and arrange with toast.

Melt in your Mouth Tofu Sandwiches

(Ready in about 20 minutes | Servings 6)

Ingredients

1 (16-ounce) package firm tofu, crumbled

1/4 cup mustard

1 tablespoon sugar

1/4 cup water

3/4 cup apple cider vinegar

1 tablespoon soy sauce

1 teaspoon cayenne pepper

2 tablespoons butter

1/2 teaspoon salt

1/4 teaspoon black pepper

6 burger buns

Directions

Press the tofu and crumble it. Then, transfer the tofu to the pressure cooker.

In a bowl, whisk the remaining ingredients, except for buns. After that, pour the mixture into the pressure cooker.

Lock the lid into place; bring to HIGH pressure and maintain the pressure for 5 minutes. Use a natural pressure release. Serve with prepared burger buns.

Rich Morning Potatoes

(Ready in about 15 minutes | Servings 8)

Ingredients

3 pounds russet potatoes, peeled and diced

1 teaspoon sea salt

3/4 stick butter, softened

1 cup heavy cream, warm

1 cup whole milk, warm

Red pepper flakes, to your liking

Directions

Place the potatoes in a pressure cooker; fill with water to cover. Add the salt and lock the lid.

When the cooker reaches HIGH pressure, reduce the burner heat and maintain HIGH pressure. Then, cook for 8 minutes.

Then, remove your pot from the heat. Use the Quick Release method. Drain the potatoes.

Next, mash the potatoes; gradually add the butter pieces, heavy cream, and warm milk. Mix to combine well.

Transfer mashed potatoes to a serving bowl. Sprinkle with red pepper flakes and serve.

Creamy Berry Oatmeal

(Ready in about 25 minutes | Servings 4)

Ingredients

1 tablespoon ghee

1 cup steel-cut oats

3 cups water

1/2 cup heavy cream

2 tablespoons honey

A pinch of salt

1 cup blueberries

1/2 cup blackberries

1/4 cup chia seeds

Directions

Melt the ghee in your pressure cooking pot over medium flame. Then, toast the steel-cut oats until they smell nutty, or 3 to 4 minutes.

Add water, heavy cream, honey, and a pinch of salt. Use HIGH pressure and cook for 10 minutes. After that, turn off the pressure cooker. Gradually release the pressure according to manufacturer's instructions.

Stir in blueberries, blackberries, and chia seeds. Then, allow the oatmeal to rest until it reaches desired thickness. Serve with a splash of milk and enjoy.

Spicy Tofu with Cauliflower

(Ready in about 15 minutes | Servings 4)

Ingredients

1 (16-ounce) package extra-firm tofu

2 cups water

2 tablespoons corn flour

1 small-sized leek, finely chopped

1/4 cup tamari sauce

2 tablespoons maple syrup

1/4 cup dry wine

1 teaspoon red pepper flakes, crushed

2 tablespoons olive oil

2 cups cauliflower florets, blanched

Directions

Press the tofu for about 5 minutes. Cut into small pieces.

To make the sauce: In a bowl, whisk together 1 cup water, corn flour, leek, ginger, tamari sauce, maple syrup, wine, and red pepper. Reserve.

Warm olive oil in the pressure cooker; sauté the tofu until it is browned on all sides.

Add the cauliflower florets and continue sautéing for 1 to 2 minutes longer. Stir in the prepared sauce. Taste and adjust the seasonings.

Bring to HIGH pressure; maintain for 5 minutes. Afterward, allow pressure to release naturally. Serve warm.

Rich Bread Pudding with Dried Fruits

(Ready in about 25 minutes | Servings 4)

Ingredients

5 cups stale bread chunks

1/2 cup dried cranberries

1/2 cup raisins

2 cups milk

2 whole eggs

1 egg yolk

1/4 cup brown sugar

1/2 teaspoon ground cinnamon

1/2 tablespoon butter, softened

2 ½ cups water

Directions

Fill a baking dish with bread chunks. Then, add dried cranberries and raisins; toss to combine well.

To make the custard: In a medium-sized mixing bowl, combine the milk, eggs, egg yolk, brown sugar, and cinnamon. Combine until the mixture becomes frothy.

Pour the custard mixture over bread-fruit mixture. Push the bread down using a spatula.

Coat an aluminum foil with softened butter. Cover the baking dish with the aluminum foil, butter side down; wrap tightly.

Pour the water into the pressure cooker. Lay baking dish on a rack in your pressure cooker.

Next, cook for about 15 minutes. Serve warm and enjoy.

Old-Fashioned Sweet Cornbread

(Ready in about 30 minutes | Servings 8)

Ingredients

1 1/3 cups cornmeal

2/3 cup flour

1/4 cup sugar

1 teaspoon baking soda

2 teaspoons baking powder

1/2 teaspoon salt

1/2 stick butter, room temperature

1 cup buttermilk

2 large-sized eggs

Directions

In a bowl, sift the flours; add sugar, baking soda, baking powder, and salt. Mix until everything is well combined.

In another mixing bowl, whisk together the butter, buttermilk, and the eggs.

Combine the dry mixture and the wet mixture, mixing well.

Pour your batter into a lightly greased pan. Place the pan in a steamer basket in the pressure cooker.

Pour about 2/3 cup of water into the bottom of the pressure cooker. Lock the lid, and bring to HIGH pressure.

When the pressure is reached, reduce temperature to lowest setting; cook for 22 minutes.

Old-Fashioned Cornmeal Mush

(Ready in about 20 minutes | Servings 6)

Ingredients

1 cup cornmeal

4 cups water

3/4 teaspoon salt

2 tablespoons butter

Maple syrup, for serving

Golden raisins, for serving

Directions

In a bowl, whisk together cornmeal, 1 cup of water, and salt.

Pour the remaining 3 cups of water into the bottom of your pressure cooker; bring it to a boil. Then, stir cornmeal mixture into the boiling water.

Add butter and stir frequently. Lock the lid into place. Bring to LOW pressure; now cook for 10 minutes.

Then, quick-release the pressure. Serve warm with maple syrup and golden raisins.

LUNCH RECIPES

Family Green Soup

(Ready in about 15 minutes | Servings 4)

Ingredients

2 tablespoons vegetable oil

1 onion, peeled and chopped

2 cloves garlic, minced or pressed

1 bunch mustard greens, sliced into thin strips

3 russet potatoes, peeled and cut into chunks

2 turnips, peeled and cut into chunks

6 cups chicken stock

1/2 teaspoon kosher salt

1/2 teaspoon ground black pepper, to taste

1/2 teaspoon dried thyme

1 teaspoon cayenne pepper

1 (15-ounce) can kidney beans, drained and rinsed

1/2 cup roasted red bell peppers, diced

Directions

In a pressure cooker, heat the oil over medium heat. Then, sauté the onion and garlic, until softened, about 3 minutes.

Add the mustard greens, potatoes, turnips, and stock. Add spices and herbs.

Close and lock the lid. When the cooker reaches HIGH pressure, reduce the heat and still maintain HIGH pressure. Set a timer to cook for 6 minutes.

Remove the pot from the heat. Use the Quick Release method.

Stir in the beans and red bell peppers. Continue to cook, uncovered, for 10 to 12 minutes till it is thoroughly warmed. Serve warm and enjoy!

Vegetable Beef Soup

(Ready in about 15 minutes | Servings 6)

Ingredients

1-quart vegetable broth

1 (28-ounce) can diced tomatoes

1 pound boneless beef bottom round, diced

1 leek, chopped

1 celery stick, chopped

2 medium carrots, diced

1 teaspoon paprika

1 teaspoon sea salt

1/2 teaspoon ground black pepper

12 ounces green beans, trimmed and cut into pieces

1 cup frozen peas, thawed

Directions

Combine the vegetable broth along with tomatoes, beef, leek, celery, carrots, paprika, salt, and black pepper in a pressure cooker.

Lock the lid; bring to HIGH pressure. Cook for 10 minutes. Use the quick-release method.

Stir in the green beans and peas. Cover and lock the lid. Open the lid and stir before serving.

Hearty Beef and Mushroom Soup

(Ready in about 40 minutes | Servings 6)

Ingredients

1 tablespoon canola, corn, or vegetable oil

1 ½ pounds beef shank rounds, trimmed

1 onion, chopped

1 carrot, chopped

2 medium celery stalks, chopped

6 cups beef broth

1 cup pearl barley

1 teaspoon garlic powder

1-ounce mushrooms

1/2 teaspoon ground allspice

Sea salt and ground black pepper

Directions

Warm the oil in a pressure cooker over medium heat. Brown the beef on all sides, turning occasionally. Transfer to a large-sized bowl.

Stir in the onion, carrot, and celery; cook, stirring frequently, until the onion is translucent.

Add the remaining ingredients. Now add reserved beef back to the cooker.

Lock the lid and bring the pot to HIGH pressure. Cook for 25 minutes.

Slice the meat off the bones. Chop the meat and stir it into the soup. Serve.

Country Potato and Beef Soup

(Ready in about 15 minutes | Servings 6)

Ingredients

3 cups beef broth

1 (14-ounce) can tomatoes, diced

1 large-sized onion, diced

2 medium celery stalks, thinly sliced

2 medium carrots, thinly sliced

2 large-sized potatoes, diced

1/4 cup loosely packed fresh parsley leaves, finely chopped

Sea salt and ground black pepper

1 ½ pounds lean ground beef

Directions

First, whisk the beef broth and tomatoes in a pressure cooker.

Stir in the remaining ingredients. Lock the lid onto the cooker. Set the pot over HIGH heat. Cook for 5 minutes.

Use the quick-release method.

Beef and Sweet Potato Soup

(Ready in about 1 hour | Servings 8)

Ingredients

1 pound beef brisket, cut into pieces

1 quart vegetable broth

1 (28-ounce) can tomatoes, diced

1 (12-ounce) bottle beer

1 large carrot, chopped

2 large sweet potatoes, peeled and chopped

1/4 cup apple cider vinegar

2 tablespoons Worcestershire sauce

1 teaspoon dry mustard

1 teaspoon sea salt

1/2 teaspoon cayenne pepper

1/2 teaspoon ground black pepper

2 bay leaves

Directions

Combine everything in your pressure cooker. Lock the lid onto the pressure cooker.

Set the pot over HIGH heat. Cook for 45 minutes.

Afterward, let the pressure fall back to normal naturally, about 30 minutes. Give it a good stir. Serve.

Ground Beef Vegetable Soup

(Ready in about 15 minutes | Servings 6)

Ingredients

3 cups vegetable stock

1 (14-ounce) can tomatoes, diced

1 leek, diced

2 cloves garlic, finely minced

2 medium celery stalks, thinly sliced

2 medium carrots, thinly sliced

3 potatoes, diced

1/4 cup loosely packed fresh parsley leaves, finely chopped

Sea salt and ground black pepper

1 ½ pounds lean ground beef

Directions

First, combine the stock and tomatoes in your pressure cooking pot.

Stir in the remaining ingredients. Lock the lid onto the cooker. Set the pot over HIGH heat. Cook for 6 minutes.

Use the quick-release method. Serve warm and enjoy!

Old-Fashioned Beef Soup

(Ready in about 20 minutes | Servings 6)

Ingredients

1 ½ pounds boneless beef sirloin, cut into pieces

1 onion, chopped

2 cloves garlic, minced

3 cups vegetable broth

2 (12-ounce) bottles light-colored beer

2 tablespoons balsamic vinegar

2 tablespoons Worcestershire sauce

Sea salt and black pepper

1 pound carrots, halved widthwise

1 celery stick, chopped

1 pound Yukon Gold potatoes, diced

Directions

Stir the beef pieces, onion, garlic, vegetable broth, beer, balsamic vinegar, Worcestershire sauce, salt, and black pepper in your cooker. Lock the lid onto the cooker.

Now bring it to HIGH pressure. Cook for 5 minutes. Use the quick-release method.

Stir in the carrots, celery, and Yukon Gold potatoes.

Set the pot back over HIGH heat; bring it back to HIGH pressure. Cook for 7 minutes. Use the quick-release method. Serve warm.

Cheesy Vegetable Broth

(Ready in about 15 minutes | Servings 16)

Ingredients

3 tablespoons vegetable oil

1 onion, chopped

2 cloves garlic, peeled and crushed

1 fennel bulb, halved, cored and sliced

3 ribs celery with leaves, chopped

1 tomato, chopped

1/2 bunch fresh parsley, chopped

1 cup Parmigiano-Reggiano, cut into pieces

2 bay leaves

1/2 teaspoon dried Italian herb blend

1 teaspoon black peppercorns

10 cups water, to cover

Directions

In a pressure cooker, heat vegetable oil over medium-high heat.

Stir in the onion, garlic, fennel, and celery; cook, stirring periodically, till veggies begin to soften.

Place the tomato and parsley on top of the vegetables; top with cheese pieces. Add bay leaves, Italian herb blend, and black peppercorns.

Pour the water into your cooker. Cook for 12 minutes on HIGH. Open the cooker with the Natural Release method; allow it to stand for 15 to 20 minutes.

Set a colander lined with a double layer of cheesecloth over a large-sized bowl; then, pour the broth through to strain; press the vegetables to extract all the liquid. Your broth is ready to use.

Tortellini Tomato Soup

(Ready in about 10 minutes | Servings 6)

Ingredients

3 tablespoons olive oil

1 onion, chopped

2 cloves garlic, minced

1 carrot, coarsely chopped

6 cups chicken stock

1 (28-ounce) can tomato puree

1 (14.5-ounce) can diced tomatoes in juice

1 (9-ounce) package fresh cheese tortellini

1 cup minced fresh basil

Salt and freshly cracked black pepper, to your liking

1 cup Parmesan cheese, shredded

Directions

In a pressure cooker, warm olive oil over medium-high heat. Then, sauté the onion for about 5 minutes.

Stir in the garlic; continue to cook, stirring periodically, until just fragrant. Now add the carrot and chicken stock. Stir in the tomato puree, canned tomatoes, and tortellini.

Close and lock the lid of your cooker. Set the burner heat to high. Maintain HIGH pressure and set a timer to cook for 5 minutes.

Open the cooker with the Natural Release method. Stir in fresh basil, salt, and black pepper. Serve with Parmesan cheese on the side.

Winter Meatball Soup with Noodles

(Ready in about 20 minutes | Servings 6)

Ingredients

2 tablespoons olive oil

1 medium-sized leek, thinly sliced

1/2 cup celery stalks, chopped

1 cup carrot, sliced

6 cups vegetable stock

1 (16-ounce) bag frozen Italian meatballs

1 cup dried noodles

2 cups kale, torn into pieces

1 tablespoon balsamic vinegar

2 cloves garlic, minced

Salt and ground black pepper, to taste

Directions

Warm the olive oil on HIGH until sizzling. Sauté the leeks, celery and carrots for about 5 minutes.

Add the remaining ingredients. Securely lock the lid and set for 5 minutes on HIGH.

Serve warm in individual bowls.

Creamy Cauliflower Soup with Cheese

(Ready in about 15 minutes | Servings 6)

Ingredients

2 tablespoons olive oil

1 cup spring onions, sliced

1 medium-sized head cauliflower, chopped into small florets

2 carrots, trimmed and chopped

4 cups vegetable stock

1/2 teaspoon red pepper flakes, crushed

1 teaspoon garlic powder

1/2 teaspoon cumin powder

1/4 teaspoon allspice

1 cup heavy cream

1 cup Cheddar cheese, shredded

Salt and freshly cracked black pepper, to taste

Directions

Warm the oil in your cooker until sizzling. Then, sauté the onions until translucent.

Then, stir in the cauliflower florets, carrots, vegetable stock, red pepper, garlic powder, cumin, and allspice.

Next, lock the pressure cooker's lid; set for 5 minutes on HIGH.

Lastly, release the cooker's pressure according to manufacturer's directions.

Stir in heavy cream and Cheddar cheese; season with salt and black pepper to taste. Serve warm.

Vegetable Soup with Tortillas and Cheese

(Ready in about 10 minutes | Servings 4)

Ingredients

4 corn tortillas, cut into wide strips

Non-stick cooking spray

2 tablespoons olive oil

1 onion, chopped

2 small zucchinis, cut into bite-size pieces

1 green bell pepper, seeded and diced

1 red bell pepper, seeded and diced

2 cloves garlic, minced

1/3 cup fresh lemon juice

1 (28-ounce) can diced tomatoes in juice

1 cup canned pumpkin puree

1 teaspoon ground cumin

1 teaspoon chili powder

1/2 teaspoon dried basil

1 teaspoon dried oregano

1/2 teaspoon sea salt

3/4 teaspoon ground black pepper

3 cups water

3 cups vegetable stock

1 ½ cups frozen corn kernels

Shredded Cheddar cheese, for serving

Directions

Preheat the oven to 400 degrees F. Then, line a baking sheet with parchment paper. Lightly spray both sides of each tortilla with the non-stick cooking spray. Then, cut the tortillas into strips using a knife.

Spread the tortilla strips onto the baking sheet. Bake until they are crisp, turning once halfway through baking. It will take about 10 minutes.

In a pressure cooker, heat the olive oil over medium heat. Then, stir in the onion; sauté the onion for about 2 minutes.

Add the zucchinis, bell peppers, garlic, and lemon juice; bring to a boil and let the liquid reduce by half. Add the tomatoes, pumpkin puree, herbs, spices, water, and vegetable stock.

Close and lock the lid. Set the burner heat to HIGH. Set a timer to cook for 6 minutes.

Remove it from the heat. Open the cooker with the Quick Release method. Be careful of the steam as you remove the lid.

Stir in the corn; let it simmer, uncovered, over medium heat, approximately 2 minutes.

To serve, place tortilla chips on the bottom of each serving bowl; ladle over the soup. Sprinkle with grated Cheddar cheese. Serve immediately.

Rich Corn Chowder

(Ready in about 25 minutes | Servings 6)

Ingredients

1 tablespoon canola oil

1 onion, diced

2 cloves garlic, peeled and minced

1 celery stalk, chopped

2 carrots, chopped

5 cups fresh corn kernels, cut off the cob

3 cups vegetable stock

1 teaspoon sea salt

1/4 teaspoon freshly cracked black pepper

1 (12-ounce) can evaporated milk

2 tablespoons cornstarch

3 tablespoons butter

Directions

In a pressure cooker, heat canola oil over HIGH setting. Now, sauté the onion and garlic until they are softened or about 5 minutes.

Add celery, carrot, corn kernels, vegetable stock, salt, and freshly cracked black pepper; securely lock the lid and cook the soup for 6 minutes on HIGH.

In a mixing bowl, combine the milk and cornstarch; stir the mixture into your soup. Stir in the butter.

Now simmer the soup approximately 3 minutes, or until your soup has thickened. Serve warm with plain Greek yogurt if desired.

Chunky Bean Soup

(Ready in about 1 hour | Servings 6)

Ingredients

2 tablespoons canola oil

1 cup green onions, chopped

1 carrot, chopped medium

2 celery stalks, chopped

1 ½ pounds dried beans

9 cups chicken stock

Sea salt and ground black pepper, to taste

1/2 teaspoon dried dill weed

1/2 teaspoon dried rosemary, chopped

2 cups butternut squash, diced

1/2 cup sour cream

Directions

Warm canola oil in a pressure cooker; sauté green onions, carrot, and celery until they are soft.

Add the beans, chicken stock, salt, and ground black pepper. Cook for about 35 minutes on HIGH.

Using cold water method, open your cooker; add dill weed, rosemary, and butternut squash. Cover and cook for 10 minutes longer.

Serve your soup warm with a dollop of sour cream. Enjoy!

Hearty Sausage Soup

(Ready in about 20 minutes | Servings 6)

Ingredients

2 tablespoons canola oil

1 pound ground sausage

2 cloves garlic, peeled and minced

1 medium-sized leek, peeled and diced

6 cups vegetable stock

1 (10-ounce) bag spinach leaves

3 carrots, thickly sliced

1 celery stalk, chopped

1 teaspoon dried oregano

1 teaspoon dried thyme

Salt and ground black pepper, to taste

1/2 cup heavy cream

Directions

In a pressure cooker, heat canola oil until sizzling. Then, sauté the sausage, garlic, and leek, until the sausage has browned and the garlic is fragrant.

Add the remaining ingredients, except the heavy cream.

Securely lock the lid and set on HIGH for 3 minutes. Then, release the cooker's pressure.

To serve, add heavy cream and enjoy!

Chicken and Rice Soup

(Ready in about 30 minutes | Servings 6)

Ingredients

1 pound chicken thighs, boneless, skinless and cubed

3 tablespoons all-purpose flour

Salt and ground black pepper, to taste

1 teaspoon cayenne pepper

3 tablespoons olive oil

1 leek, diced

2 large-sized celery stalks, chopped

2 carrots, chopped

2 tablespoons tomato paste

2 thyme sprigs

1 ¼ cups wild rice

6 cups chicken broth

1 cup heavy cream

Directions

Coat the chicken thighs with flour; season with salt, ground black pepper, and cayenne pepper.

Now, heat olive oil on HIGH until melted.

Lay the chicken thighs at the bottom of your pressure cooker; cook until they have just browned, about 5 minutes.

Add the remaining ingredients, except for the heavy cream; cook for 14 minutes on HIGH setting.

Allow the pressure to release naturally. Add the heavy cream; give it a good stir. Serve warm in individual bowls.

Caramelized Onion Soup with Cheese

(Ready in about 20 minutes | Servings 6)

Ingredients

3 tablespoons butter

2 onions, peeled and thinly sliced

2 tablespoons sugar

5 cups beef stock

2 tablespoons dry wine

1 bay leaf

1 sprig rosemary

Sea salt and freshly cracked black pepper

1/2 teaspoon cayenne pepper

Colby Swiss Cheddar cheese, for garnish

Directions

In your pressure cooker, warm butter on HIGH setting until sizzling.

Then, sauté the onions together with sugar, until they are golden brown and caramelized approximately 10 minutes.

Add the beef stock, dry wine, bay leaf, rosemary, sea salt, ground black pepper, and cayenne pepper; stir to combine well.

Now lock the pressure cooker's lid and cook for about 10 minutes on HIGH.

Ladle prepared soup into individual bowls; to serve, top with shredded Colby cheese.

Quick and Easy Adzuki Beans

(Ready in about 10 minutes | Servings 4)

Ingredients

1 cup adzuki beans

4 cups water

2 tablespoons olive oil

1 teaspoon salt

1 teaspoon cayenne pepper

1/2 teaspoon black pepper, ground

2 bay leaves

Directions

Add all of the above ingredients to a pressure cooker.

Then, place the lid; bring to HIGH pressure and cook for 8 minutes.

Lastly, let the pressure release naturally. Ladle into individual bowls and serve warm.

Country Red Lentils

(Ready in about 20 minutes | Servings 8)

Ingredients

8 cups water

2 cups dried red lentils

3 tablespoons olive oil

1 teaspoon salt

1 cup onions, diced

2 cloves garlic, minced

1 teaspoon ground cumin

1 (6-ounce) can tomato paste

Salt and ground black pepper, to taste

Directions

Add the water, red lentils, 1 tablespoon of olive oil and salt to your pressure cooker.

Cover and bring to HIGH pressure for 8 minutes. Turn off the heat; allow pressure to release according to manufacturer's instructions. Drain the lentils.

In a saucepan, warm the remaining 2 tablespoons of olive oil; sauté the onions until they are caramelized.

Add the remaining ingredients; cook for about 4 minutes, stirring often.

Next, add the onion mixture to the prepared lentils; mix to combine well. Serve warm.

Chunky Potato and Corn Soup

(Ready in about 10 minutes | Servings 6)

Ingredients

2 tablespoons olive oil

1 large-sized onion, chopped

6 cups vegetable stock

6 medium-sized potatoes, peeled and diced

2 bay leaves

Salt and freshly ground black pepper, to taste

1 ½ cups corn

1/2 cup heavy cream

Directions

Heat olive oil in a pressure cooker over medium heat. Then, sauté the onions for 2 minutes. Pour in the vegetable stock. Add potatoes, bay leaves, salt, and black pepper.

Cover and bring to HIGH pressure; maintain pressure for about 5 minutes. Discard the bay leaves.

Stir in the corn and the heavy cream; give it a good stir and serve.

Yummy Chicken Pea Soup

(Ready in about 10 minutes | Servings 8)

Ingredients

4 carrots, peeled and grated

2 parsnips, peeled and finely chopped

1 celery stalk, finely chopped

1 onion, peeled and diced

2 cloves garlic, peeled and minced

1 cup mushrooms, thinly sliced

3 teaspoons butter, melted

4 cups vegetables broth

Salt and freshly ground black pepper, to taste

1 teaspoon dried thyme

8 chicken thighs, skin removed

2 cups frozen baby peas, thawed

Directions

Add the carrots, parsnips, celery, onion, garlic, mushroom, and butter to a pressure cooker. Seal the lid; bring to LOW pressure; maintain the pressure approximately 2 minutes. Lastly, open the cooker's lid naturally.

Add the broth, salt, black pepper, thyme, and chicken. Cover with the lid; bring to HIGH pressure. Then, remove the lid according to manufacturer's instructions. Stir in thawed peas and cook for 5 minutes longer. Serve right away.

Sunday Fish Chowder

(Ready in about 15 minutes | Servings 6)

Ingredients

2 tablespoons olive oil

2 yellow onions, thinly sliced

2 cups water

4 cups clam juice

6 medium-sized potatoes, peeled and diced

2 bay leaves

Salt and freshly ground black pepper, to taste

1 pound white fish, cut into bite-sized pieces

1 sprig dried thyme

1 teaspoon ground cumin

1/2 cup heavy cream

Directions

Melt the olive oil in a pressure cooker over medium heat. Then, sauté the onion for about 2 minutes. Add the water, clam juice, potatoes, bay leaves, salt, and ground black pepper.

Then, bring to HIGH pressure; maintain this pressure for about 5 minutes. Remove the lid according to the manufacturer's directions.

Add the fish and let it simmer until the fish is opaque or 3 to 4 minutes. Stir in the thyme, cumin, and heavy cream. Serve right now.

Hearty Fennel Soup with Corn

(Ready in about 15 minutes | Servings 8)

Ingredients

1 tablespoon butter

2 tablespoons olive oil

1 medium leek, white parts only and thinly sliced

6 cups vegetable stock

1 (14-ounce) can diced tomatoes

1 fennel bulb, trimmed and chopped

1 tablespoon finely chopped dill fronds

1 teaspoon salt

1/4 teaspoon ground black pepper

1/2 teaspoon red pepper flakes, crushed

2 cups fresh corn kernels

1 medium zucchini, diced

Directions

Melt the butter and the oil in a pressure cooker over medium heat. Add the leek and sauté, stirring often, until softened. Stir in the stock, tomatoes, fennel, dill, salt, black pepper, and red pepper.

Lock the lid onto your cooker.

Raise the heat to HIGH; bring the pot to high pressure. Cook for 5 minutes. Use the quick-release method. Unlock and open the cooker.

Stir in the corn and zucchini. Lock the lid back onto the pot.

Set the pot back over HIGH heat; bring it back to high pressure and cook for 1 minute more. Use the quick-release method again. Stir and serve.

Kale and Mushroom Soup

(Ready in about 15 minutes | Servings 6)

Ingredients

2 tablespoons canola oil

8 ounces cremini mushrooms, sliced

1 large onion, chopped

1 tablespoon garlic, minced

2 medium celery stalks, finely chopped

2 medium carrots, diced

1 tablespoon loosely packed fresh rosemary leaves, minced

Salt and ground black pepper, to your liking

7 cups chicken stock

1 butternut squash, peeled and diced

1/4 cup soy sauce

2 cups kale, torn into pieces

Directions

Set a pressure cooker over medium heat. Heat canola oil; then, sauté the mushrooms, onion and garlic for about 5 minutes.

Stir in celery, carrots, rosemary leaves, salt, and black pepper; cook for one more minute. Pour in the chicken stock.

Add the butternut squash and soy sauce. Stir well to combine. Lock the lid onto the pot. Bring the pot to HIGH pressure. Cook for about 10 minutes.

Use the quick-release method to bring the pressure back to normal. Unlock and open the cooker. Stir in the kale.

Cover and lock the lid onto the pot; let stand for 5 minutes to wilt the kale leaves. Enjoy!

Tomato Soup with Green Beans

(Ready in about 15 minutes | Servings 8)

Ingredients

3 tablespoons olive oil

1 medium onion, white parts only and thinly sliced

2 garlic cloves, minced

6 cups chicken stock

1 fennel bulb, trimmed and chopped

1 (14-ounce) can diced tomatoes

1 teaspoon salt

1/2 teaspoon dried thyme

1/4 teaspoon freshly cracked black pepper

1/2 teaspoon cayenne pepper

1 ¾ pounds green beans, trimmed and cut into 1-inch pieces

Directions

Warm olive oil in a pressure cooker over medium heat. Add the onion and garlic; sauté, stirring often, until softened. Stir in the stock, fennel, tomatoes, salt, thyme, black pepper, and cayenne pepper.

Lock the lid onto your cooker.

Raise the heat to HIGH; bring the pot to high pressure. Cook for 5 minutes. Use the quick-release method. Unlock and open the cooker.

Stir in the green beans. Lock the lid back onto the pot.

Set the pot back over HIGH heat; bring it back to high pressure and cook for 1 minute more. Use the quick-release method again. Stir and serve.

Easy Sloppy Joes

(Ready in about 15 minutes | Servings 8)

Ingredients

1/2 cup red quinoa

2 tablespoons olive oil

1 onion, chopped

2 cloves garlic, minced

2 pounds lean ground beef, crumbled

1 (28-ounce) can tomatoes, crushed

1/2 cup rolled oats

1/4 cup packed dark brown sugar

2 tablespoons Worcestershire sauce

2 tablespoons apple cider vinegar

1 tablespoon cayenne pepper

Directions

Pour the quinoa into a pressure cooker; fill the cooker with water. Lock the lid in place.

Set the pot over HIGH heat. Cook for 2 minutes. Use the quick-release method to open your cooker. Drain the quinoa.

Heat olive oil in the cooker; set over medium heat. Add the onion and cook, stirring often, until the onion softens.

Add the remaining ingredients and lock the lid onto the cooker. Raise the heat to HIGH. Cook for 5 minutes. Use the quick-release method.

Stir in the quinoa; stir to combine. Enjoy!

Winter Beef Chili

(Ready in about 10 minutes | Servings 6)

Ingredients

1 tablespoon olive oil

1 onion, chopped

1 large bell pepper, stemmed, seeded, and chopped

2 cloves garlic, minced

2 pounds lean ground beef

1 (28-ounce) can tomatoes, diced

2 (15-ounce) cans kidney beans, drained and rinsed

6 tablespoons chili powder

1 teaspoon dried basil

1/2 teaspoon dried thyme

1 teaspoon dried oregano

3/4 cup chicken broth

Directions

Melt olive oil in a pressure cooker over medium heat. Then, sauté the onion and bell pepper, stirring frequently, until the onions are translucent, about 4 minutes. Stir in the garlic and cook until just fragrant.

Add the remaining ingredients. Lock the lid onto the cooking pot.

Raise the heat to HIGH and bring the pot to high pressure. Once the pressure has been reached, reduce the heat maintaining this pressure. Cook for 5 minutes.

Use the quick-release method to drop the pressure. Then, open the pot and serve.

Mom's Beef Casserole

(Ready in about 10 minutes | Servings 4)

Ingredients

1 tablespoon vegetable oil

1 medium-sized onion, chopped

1 red bell pepper, seeded and chopped

1 green bell pepper, seeded and chopped

1 clove garlic, minced

1 pound lean ground beef

1 (28-ounce) can tomatoes, diced

2 cups fresh corn kernels

1 (15-ounce) can cannellini beans, drained and rinsed

1 (12-ounce) bottle dark beer, preferably a brown ale

1 tablespoon cayenne pepper

1 teaspoon dried basil

1 teaspoon dried oregano

1 teaspoon ground cumin

1 teaspoon chipotle pepper, minced

1/2 teaspoon salt

1/4 teaspoon ground black pepper

8 ounces dried pasta

Fresh chives, for garnish

Directions

Heat vegetable oil in a pressure cooking pot over medium heat. Sauté the onion, bell peppers, and garlic; cook, stirring constantly, until the onions become translucent.

Stir in the ground beef. Cook, until it has lightly browned. Add the tomatoes, corn kernels, beans, beer, cayenne pepper, basil, oregano, cumin, chipotle pepper, salt, and black pepper.

Stir in the pasta. Lock the lid onto the pot.

Raise the heat to HIGH and bring the pot to high pressure. Once the pressure has been reached, reduce the heat maintaining this pressure. Cook for 5 minutes.

Use the quick-release method and open the cooker. Unlock and remove the cooker's lid. Give it a good stir, sprinkle with fresh chives, and serve.

Beef and Pasta Casserole

(Ready in about 10 minutes | Servings 4)

Ingredients

2 tablespoons olive oil

1 pound lean ground beef

1 onion, chopped

2 bell peppers, stemmed, cored, and chopped

1 teaspoon dried oregano

1 teaspoon dried marjoram

1 teaspoon dried thyme

1/2 teaspoon cayenne pepper

1/2 teaspoon fennel seeds

Sea salt and black pepper, to your liking

3/4 cup dry red wine

1 (28-ounce) can tomatoes, crushed

8 ounces dried penne

Directions

Heat olive oil in a pressure cooking pot over medium heat.

Add the ground beef and continue to cook, stirring often, until it softens, or approximately 5 minutes. Reserve.

Add the onion and bell peppers to the cooker; cook, stirring frequently, until they soften. Stir in the oregano, marjoram, thyme, cayenne pepper, fennel seeds, salt, and black pepper.

Stir in red wine, tomatoes, and penne pasta. Stir well to combine. Lock the lid onto the cooking pot. Cook for 5 minutes on HIGH.

Afterward, use the quick-release method. Stir well before serving and enjoy.

Vegetarian Tomato and Cheese Casserole

(Ready in about 10 minutes | Servings 6)

Ingredients

1 (28-ounce) can crushed tomatoes

1 (12-ounce) can evaporated milk

1 ½ cups vegetable stock

1 teaspoon dried oregano

1/2 teaspoon ground cumin

Sea salt freshly cracked black pepper

1 pound dried pasta

6 ounces Mozzarella cheese, diced

1¼ cups Parmesan cheese, grated

Directions

Add tomatoes, milk, stock, oregano, cumin, salt, and black pepper to a pressure cooking pot. Stir until everything is well combined.

Stir in the pasta until coated. Give it another gentle stir. Lock the lid onto the pressure cooker.

Set the pot over HIGH heat. Cook for 5 minutes. Afterward, use the quick-release method.

Stir in Mozzarella cheese and Parmesan cheese. Set the lid back; set aside for 2 to 4 minutes, till cheeses have completely melted. Serve warm.

Classic Italian Pasta with Tomato Sauce

(Ready in about 30 minutes | Servings 6)

Ingredients

2 tablespoons olive oil

3 cloves garlic, minced

1/2 cup dry white wine

2 ½ pounds tomatoes, diced

1/4 cup packed fresh basil leaves, finely chopped

1 teaspoon salt

1 teaspoon ground black pepper

Cooked pasta of choice, for serving

Directions

Heat the oil in a pressure cooker over medium heat. Then, sauté garlic until tender.

Pour in the wine; stir well to combine. Add the tomatoes, basil leaves, salt, and ground black pepper.

Lock the lid onto the cooker. Then, bring the cooker to HIGH pressure and cook for 15 minutes. Use the quick-release method and open the cooker.

Use an immersion blender to puree the mixture. Bring the sauce to a simmer for about 15 minutes. Serve with your favorite pasta.

Herbed Eggplant Pasta

(Ready in about 10 minutes | Servings 4)

Ingredients

2 tablespoons canola oil

1 shallot, chopped

1 tablespoon capers, minced

1 large eggplant, stemmed and diced

2 medium bell peppers, stemmed, cored, and chopped

1 (28-ounce) can diced tomatoes

1¼ cups vegetable stock

2 teaspoons dried rosemary

1 teaspoon garlic powder

Salt to your liking

1/2 teaspoon ground black pepper

1 tablespoon apple cider vinegar

8 ounces dried pasta of choice

Directions

Heat canola oil in a pressure cooker over medium heat. Add the shallot and capers; cook, stirring often, for about 2 minutes.

Add the eggplant and bell peppers; continue cooking for 1 minute longer. Stir in the tomatoes, stock, rosemary, garlic powder, salt, black pepper, and apple cider vinegar.

Stir in the pasta until coated. Lock the lid onto the cooker.

Cook for 5 minutes on HIGH heat. Use the quick-release method to drop the cooker's pressure. Unlock and open the cooker. Stir well and serve.

Easy Vegetarian Lentil

(Ready in about 30 minutes | Servings 6)

Ingredients

1 tablespoon canola oil

1 onion, chopped

1 red bell pepper, stemmed, cored, and chopped

3 cups vegetable stock

2 cups lentils

1 (14-ounce) can crushed tomatoes

2 tablespoons soy sauce

1 tablespoon packed dark brown sugar

1/2 teaspoon cumin powder

1/2 teaspoon sea salt

1 teaspoon ground black pepper

Directions

Heat canola oil in a pressure cooker over medium heat. Stir in the onion and bell pepper; cook, stirring frequently, until the onion is translucent, about 3 minutes.

Pour in the vegetable stock; add the lentils, tomatoes, soy sauce, brown sugar, cumin powder, sea salt, and black pepper.

Lock the lid onto the cooking pot. Raise the heat to HIGH. Once the pressure has been reached, reduce the heat maintaining this pressure. Cook for 18 minutes.

Unlock and open the cooker. Stir and serve.

Risotto with Peas and Cheddar Cheese

(Ready in about 15 minutes | Servings 6)

Ingredients

2 tablespoons butter

1 onion, chopped

1½ cups white rice

1/4 cup apple cider

1 quart vegetable broth

1/4 teaspoon grated nutmeg

1 cup shelled fresh peas

4 ounces Cheddar cheese, shredded

Directions

Melt the butter in a pressure cooker over medium heat. Sauté the onion for about 4 minutes.

Stir in the rice. Pour in the apple cider; constantly stir for about 2 minutes. Pour in vegetable broth; sprinkle with grated nutmeg.

Lock the lid onto the cooker. Then, bring the pot to HIGH pressure. Cook for 7 minutes. Use the quick-release method to open your cooker.

Stir in the peas and Cheddar cheese. Afterwards, set it aside for 5 minutes. Enjoy!

Summer Eggplant Stew

(Ready in about 15 minutes | Servings 4)

Ingredients

3 tablespoons olive oil

1 large-sized shallot, chopped

1 clove garlic, minced

1/4 teaspoon cayenne pepper

3 large-sized tomatoes

1/2 cup vegetable stock

2 Yukon Gold potatoes, diced

1 large eggplant, stemmed and cut into pieces

1 teaspoon fennel seeds

1/4 teaspoon ground black pepper

1/2 teaspoon salt

Directions

Heat the oil in a pressure cooking pot; then, set over medium heat. Add the shallot and sauté for about 3 minutes.

Stir in the garlic and cayenne pepper until fragrant and aromatic, or about 30 seconds.

Stir in the tomatoes; pour in the stock. Add the remaining ingredients; stir well to combine.

Lock the lid and cook for 5 minutes using HIGH pressure. Use the quick-release method and unlock the pot. Serve warm.

Bean and Pumpkin Stew

(Ready in about 15 minutes | Servings 4)

Ingredients

2 tablespoons butter

1 medium-sized leek, chopped

2 celery stalks, chopped

1 medium-sized carrot, chopped

2 garlic cloves, minced

8 cups pumpkin, peeled, seeded, and cubed

2 cups vegetable stock

1 (15-ounce) can kidney beans, drained and rinsed

1 teaspoon dried thyme

1 teaspoon dried sage

Kosher salt and ground black pepper, to taste

Directions

Melt the butter in a pressure cooker over medium heat. Add the leeks, celery, and carrot; cook, stirring often, until the vegetables have softened, approximately 4 minutes.

Stir in the garlic and continue cooking for about 30 seconds.

Add the pumpkin, stock, kidney beans, thyme, sage, salt, and ground black pepper; stir well.

Lock the lid. Raise the heat to HIGH. Cook for 8 minutes. Use the quick-release method to release pressure. Unlock and open the cooker. Serve hot.

Juicy Chicken in Beer Sauce

(Ready in about 12 minutes | Servings 4)

Ingredients

1/2 cup potato starch flour

Sea salt and freshly ground black pepper, to your liking

1 (3-pound) chicken, cut into 10 pieces

1/2 stick butter

1 onion, chopped

1 (12-ounce) bottle beer

3/4 cup heavy cream

1 teaspoon dried sage

1 teaspoon dried thyme

1 teaspoon dried rosemary

Directions

In a small-sized bowl, combine flour, salt, and black pepper. Then, dredge the chicken in the flour mixture.

In a pressure cooker, melt the butter over medium-high heat. Then, sauté the onion until softened, about 3 minutes. Now, brown the chicken on all sides, working in batches. Reserve the chicken.

Pour in the beer and bring to a boil; cook for 1 minute. Return the chicken to the cooker along with the juice. Close and lock the lid.

Set the burner heat to HIGH. Set a timer to cook for 8 minutes. Remove the pot from the heat. Open the cooker using the Quick Release method.

Add heavy cream and herbs; simmer over MEDIUM heat for 2 minutes. Serve warm.

Country Poached Chicken Breasts

(Ready in about 30 minutes | Servings 10)

Ingredients

10 boneless and skinless chicken breast halves

1 medium-sized carrot, thinly sliced

1 rib celery, with leaves, cut into small pieces

2 cups chicken broth

Directions

Place the chicken, carrot, and celery in a pressure cooker. Add the broth to cover the ingredients.

Close and lock the lid. Set a timer to cook for 6 minutes on HIGH setting.

Afterwards, open the cooker with the Natural Release method; let it stand for 15 to 20 minutes. Serve warm.

Saucy Chicken Breasts with Goat Cheese

(Ready in about 20 minutes | Servings 6)

Ingredients

2 tablespoons vegetable oil

2 pounds chicken breast halves, boneless and skinless

1 ½ cups prepared salsa of your choice

1 teaspoon fennel seeds

1 teaspoon granulated garlic

Salt and freshly ground black pepper, to your liking

1/4 cup fresh lime juice

8 ounces goat cheese, crumbled

Directions

In a pressure cooker, heat vegetable oil over medium-high heat. Then, brown chicken breasts on all sides. Transfer them to a plate.

Add the remaining ingredients, except for goat cheese to the pot. Return the breasts to the cooking pot.

Close and lock the lid. Set the burner heat to HIGH. Set a timer to cook for 7 minutes.

Afterwards, open the cooking pot with the Quick Release method. Serve topped with the goat cheese. Enjoy!

Chicken Curry in Coconut Sauce

(Ready in about 10 minutes | Servings 8)

Ingredients

4 tablespoons olive oil

3 pounds boneless and skinless chicken breasts, cut into strips

1/2 pound scallions, diced

1/4 cup curry powder

1 (14-ounce) can unsweetened coconut milk

1 cup mango chutney, pureed

Sea salt and ground black pepper, to taste

Directions

In a pressure cooker, heat 2 tablespoons of olive oil over medium-high heat.

Then, brown the chicken strips until they're no longer pink. Transfer them to a plate.

Heat the remaining 2 tablespoons olive oil in the pot. Next, sauté the scallions for about 8 minutes or until tender and translucent. Add the curry powder and stir to combine.

Add the remaining ingredients. Close and lock the lid. Set the burner heat to HIGH. Set a timer to cook for 5 minutes.

Remove the cooking pot from the heat. Open the cooker using the Quick Release method. Serve warm and enjoy!

Hearty Chicken Stew

(Ready in about 25 minutes | Servings 4)

Ingredients

2 tablespoons olive oil

2 ½ pounds chicken wings

Sea salt and freshly ground black or white pepper

1 teaspoon cayenne pepper

1 teaspoon dried rosemary

1/2 teaspoon dried thyme

1 leek, white part only, thinly sliced

2 cloves garlic, chopped

1 tablespoon rice flour

2 cups chicken broth

1 (14.5-ounce) can diced tomatoes with juice

2 medium-sized turnips, peeled and chopped

Directions

In a pressure cooker, heat the oil over medium-high heat. Season the chicken wings with salt, black pepper, cayenne pepper, rosemary, and thyme.

Then, brown the chicken wings for about 2 minutes on each side. Stir in the leeks and cook for about 4 minutes.

Add the garlic and cook 30 seconds longer. Sprinkle with the flour and add chicken broth. Return the chicken wings to the cooker along with the juice.

Next, stir in the tomatoes and turnips. Give it a gentle stir. Close and lock the lid. Set the burner heat to HIGH. Set a timer to cook for 24 minutes.

Open the cooker with the Quick Release method. Serve warm.

Lime Chicken Drumsticks with Raisins and Olives

(Ready in about 10 minutes | Servings 6)

Ingredients

1 onion, chopped

1 spring garlic, chopped

1/4 cup olive oil

2 teaspoons cumin seeds

2 teaspoons coriander seeds

6 chicken drumsticks, skin removed

1/2 cup raisins

1 (10-ounce) jar pitted Kalamata olives, drained

1 teaspoon salt

1/2 teaspoon freshly cracked black pepper

1 lime, thinly sliced

2 cups water

Directions

In a pressure cooker, combine the onion, spring garlic, olive oil, cumin, and coriander seeds. Nestle the chicken drumsticks on top of this mixture.

Distribute the raisins and olives over the chicken drumsticks. Sprinkle with salt and black pepper. Top with the lime slices. Then, pour in the water.

Close and lock the lid. Now cook for 6 minutes on HIGH. Remove the pot from the heat and open it with the Natural Release method. Serve over rice if desired.

Bean and Corn Salad

(Ready in about 15 minutes + chilling time | Servings 6)

Ingredients

2 cups kidney beans, soaked overnight

4 cups water

1 tablespoon olive oil

1 red onion, chopped

3 cloves garlic, peeled and smashed

2 tomatoes, chopped

1 cup corn kernels

3 teaspoons olive oil

1 teaspoon balsamic vinegar

3/4 teaspoon salt

1/2 teaspoon ground black pepper

1 sprig fresh rosemary

1 sprig fresh thyme

Directions

Add beans, water, olive oil, onion, and garlic to the pressure cooker. Now lock the cooker's lid.

Turn the heat to HIGH; cook for about 8 minutes. Then, wait for the pressure to come down.

Next step, strain the beans; now transfer the beans to a refrigerator. Transfer to a serving bowl and add the remaining ingredients. Serve chilled.

Lentil with Tomatoes and Kale

(Ready in about 25 minutes | Servings 4)

Ingredients

1 tablespoon olive oil

1 medium-sized red onion, diced

1/2 teaspoon thyme

1/2 teaspoon rosemary

1/4 teaspoon cumin

1 cup dried lentils

1/2 cup water

2 tomatoes, chopped

2 cups spinach, torn into pieces

Directions

Heat olive oil in your pressure cooker over medium heat. Sauté the onion together with thyme, rosemary, and cumin for about 5 minutes.

Next, add dried lentils, water, and tomatoes; stir until everything is well combined. Close and lock the pressure cooker's lid.

Cook for about 15 minutes at HIGH pressure.

Afterwards, release the pressure according to manufacturer's directions. Stir in the spinach until it is wilted; serve.

Yummy Lentil Curry

(Ready in about 20 minutes | Servings 8)

Ingredients

2 cups dried red lentils

8 cups water

3 tablespoons olive oil

1 teaspoon salt

1/4 teaspoon black pepper

2 cloves garlic, minced

1 cup scallions, diced

3 tablespoons curry powder

1 teaspoon cumin

1 teaspoon chili powder

1 (6-ounce) can tomato paste

Directions

Add the lentils, water, 1 tablespoon of olive oil, salt, and ground black pepper to your pressure cooker.

Cover and bring to HIGH pressure for 8 minutes. Turn off the heat; let the pressure release. Drain the lentils.

To prepare curry mixture: warm the remaining 2 tablespoons of olive oil in a pan; sauté the garlic and scallions until they have softened.

Add the remaining ingredients; cook for about 4 minutes, stirring continuously.

Stir the curry mixture in the prepared lentils; mix to combine well. Serve warm and enjoy!

Yummy Potato with Cauliflower

(Ready in about 15 minutes | Servings 6)

Ingredients

2 cups potatoes, peeled and cubed

2 cups cauliflower, broken into florets

2 tablespoons canola oil

1 tablespoon scallions, chopped

2 cloves garlic, minced

1 teaspoon ginger, minced

1 teaspoon garam masala

1 teaspoon salt

1/2 teaspoon ground black pepper

Directions

Add the potatoes to a pressure cooker; cover the potatoes with the water. Seal the lid.

Then, cook under HIGH pressure for about 4 minutes. Quick-release the pressure.

Add the cauliflower. Bring to HIGH pressure and cook for 2 minutes. Drain and reserve.

Warm canola oil in a pressure cooker over LOW heat. Add the remaining ingredients; cook for 2 more minutes.

Then, add the cooked potatoes and cauliflower with 2 tablespoons of water. Let simmer over LOW heat for 10 minutes, stirring occasionally. Serve.

Vegan Mushroom Stew

(Ready in about 25 minutes | Servings 4)

Ingredients

2 tablespoons vegetable oil

1 onion, chopped

2 stalks celery, sliced

1 carrot, chopped

2 bell peppers, diced

2 cups mushroom, chopped

1 (28-ounce) can crushed tomatoes

2 cups corn kernels

1 cup tomato paste

1/2 cup barbecue sauce

1 teaspoon red pepper flakes, crushed

1 teaspoon salt

1/2 teaspoon black pepper

Directions

Heat vegetable oil in the pressure cooker over medium heat; sauté the onion, celery, carrot, and bell peppers until all the vegetables have softened, approximately 5 minutes.

Add all remaining ingredients. Cover and bring to HIGH pressure; maintain the pressure for 30 minutes. Remove from the heat and open the lid naturally; serve warm.

Meatball Soup with Noodles

(Ready in about 20 minutes | Servings 6)

Ingredients

2 tablespoons canola oil

1 onion, thinly sliced

1 cup carrot, sliced

6 cups vegetable broth

1 (16-ounce) bag frozen Italian meatballs

1 cup dried noodles

2 cups spinach, torn into pieces

1 tablespoon lemon juice

2 cloves garlic, minced

Salt and ground black pepper, to taste

Directions

First, heat the oil on HIGH until sizzling. Now sauté the onion and carrot for about 5 minutes.

Add the rest of the above ingredients. Securely lock the lid and set for 5 minutes on HIGH.

Taste and adjust the seasonings. Serve warm and enjoy!

Creamy Cauliflower and Cheese Soup

(Ready in about 10 minutes | Servings 6)

Ingredients

2 tablespoons butter

1 medium-sized leek, sliced

1 small-sized head cauliflower, chopped

2-3 baby carrots, trimmed and chopped

4 cups chicken broth

1 bay leaf

1/2 teaspoon cayenne pepper

1 teaspoon granulated garlic

1 cup heavy cream

1 cup sharp cheese, shredded

Salt and cracked black pepper, to taste

Directions

Warm the butter in your cooker until sizzling. Then, sauté the leeks until translucent, or for about 5 minutes.

Add the cauliflower, carrots, chicken broth, 1 bay leaf, cayenne pepper, and granulated garlic. Now lock the pressure cooker's lid; set for 4 minutes on HIGH. Then, release the cooker's pressure.

Stir in heavy cream and shredded sharp cheese; season with salt and black pepper. Serve.

Mom's Corn Chowder

(Ready in about 25 minutes | Servings 6)

Ingredients

1 tablespoon olive oil

1 shallot, diced

2 cloves garlic, peeled and minced

1 carrot, chopped

1 celery stalk, chopped

5 cups fresh corn kernels, cut off the cob

3 cups vegetable broth

3/4 teaspoon salt

1/4 teaspoon ground black pepper

1 (12-ounce) can evaporated milk

2 tablespoons cornstarch

3 tablespoons margarine

Directions

In your pressure cooker, heat olive oil over HIGH setting. Now, sauté the shallot and garlic for 4 to 5 minutes.

Add carrot, celery, corn kernels, vegetable broth, salt, and ground black pepper; securely lock the lid, and cook the soup for 6 minutes on HIGH.

In a small bowl, whisk together the milk and cornstarch; stir the mixture into your soup. Stir in the margarine. Let simmer for 2 to 3 minutes, or until the soup has thickened. Serve warm with the croutons if desired.

Chunky Butternut Bean Soup

(Ready in about 1 hour | Servings 6)

Ingredients

2 tablespoons olive oil

1 medium-sized leek, chopped

2 carrots, chopped medium

2 celery stalks, chopped

3 sprigs fresh thyme

16 ounces dried beans

9 cups vegetables broth

Sea salt and black pepper, to taste

1/2 teaspoon dried dill weed

1/2 teaspoon dried rosemary, chopped

2 cups butternut squash, diced

1/2 cup sour cream

Directions

Warm olive oil in your pressure cooker; sauté leek, carrot, and celery until they are softened.

Add the thyme, beans, broth, salt, and black pepper. Cook for 35 minutes on HIGH.

Using cold water method, open the cooker's lid; add dill, rosemary, and butternut squash. Cover and cook for 10 more minutes.

Serve with a dollop of sour cream. Enjoy!

Cheesy Potato and Spinach Soup

(Ready in about 20 minutes | Servings 6)

Ingredients

1/4 cup vegetable oil

6 white onions, white part only, sliced

1 red bell pepper, seeded and chopped

2 celery stalks, chopped

1/2 cup rice

3 potatoes, peeled and diced

5 cups vegetable stock

3/4 teaspoon sea salt

1/4 teaspoon ground black pepper

2 tablespoons white wine

3 tablespoons tomato paste

1 ½ cups fresh spinach, torn into large pieces

1/2 cup Monterey Jack cheese, grated

Directions

In a pressure cooker, warm vegetable oil. Add onions, bell pepper, and celery; sauté for about 2 minutes.

Stir in rice and potatoes. Continue cooking an additional minute.

Add vegetable stock, salt, black pepper, wine, and tomato paste. Stir well to combine.

Seal the lid and cook on high pressure. Now reduce the heat to maintain pressure, and cook for 4 minutes. Uncover and divide among soup bowls. Garnish with grated cheese and serve warm.

Creamed Sausage and Spinach Soup

(Ready in about 20 minutes | Servings 6)

Ingredients

2 tablespoons vegetable oil

1 pound ground sausage

3 cloves garlic, peeled and minced

1 onion, peeled and diced

6 cups chicken broth

1 (10-ounce) bag spinach leaves

4 carrots, thickly sliced

1 teaspoon sugar

1 teaspoon dried basil

1 teaspoon dried oregano

1/4 teaspoon red pepper flakes, crushed

Salt and ground black pepper, to taste

1/2 cup heavy cream

Directions

First of all, heat vegetable oil until sizzling. Then, sauté the sausage, garlic and onion, until the sausage is browned, the onion is translucent, and the garlic is fragrant.

Add the rest of the ingredients, except for heavy cream.

Securely lock the lid and set on HIGH for 3 minutes. Then, release the cooker's pressure.

Add heavy cream before serving and enjoy!

Cheese and Onion Soup

(Ready in about 20 minutes | Servings 6)

Ingredients

3 tablespoons butter

2 onions, peeled and thinly sliced

2 teaspoons sugar

5 cups beef broth

2 tablespoons red wine

1 bay leaf

1 teaspoon dried thyme

Sea salt and freshly ground black pepper

6 slices Provolone cheese

Directions

In your pressure cooker, warm butter on HIGH until sizzling.

Cook the onions and sugar in the cooker, until they are caramelized, for about 10 minutes.

Add the beef broth, wine, bay leaf, dried thyme, salt, and ground black pepper; stir to combine. Now lock the pressure cooker's lid and cook for 8 to 10 minutes on HIGH.

Ladle into soup bowls and top with Provolone cheese. Serve and enjoy!

Rich Garbanzo Bean Soup

(Ready in about 1 hour | Servings 8)

Ingredients

2 ½ cups dried garbanzo beans, soaked overnight

1/2 cup dry lentils, brown (I have never tried red)

3 ripe tomatoes, diced

1 cup fresh cilantro, finely minced

3 cloves garlic, minced

1 onion, finely chopped

2 carrots, peeled and finely chopped

2 celery ribs, finely chopped

2 tablespoons vegetable oil

Sea salt and ground black pepper, to taste

1/4 teaspoon turmeric

1/2 cup flour

3 tablespoons tomato paste

1/2 cup rice noodles

Directions

Place garbanzo beans, lentils, tomatoes, and cilantro in your pressure cooker.

Add the garlic, onion, carrots, and celery. Pour in enough water to cover the vegetables.

Next, add the vegetable oil, salt, black pepper, and turmeric; cover with the lid. Cook for about 15 minutes.

In the meantime, combine the flour with 1 cup of warm water. Add this mixture to the cooker along with tomato paste. Cook an additional 10 minutes, stirring periodically.

Stir in rice noodles and cook for 10 more minutes. Ladle into eight soup bowls and serve warm.

Winter Hearty Chili

(Ready in about 1 hour | Servings 6)

Ingredients

1 ¼ cups pinto beans, soaked for 30 minutes

3 tablespoons canola oil

1 ½ pounds sirloin steaks, cubed

2 cloves garlic, minced

1 leek, chopped

1 tablespoon chili powder

1 bell pepper chopped

3 tomatoes, chopped

1 (28-ounce) can tomato sauce

5 cups beef broth

2 teaspoons sugar

Kosher salt and black pepper to taste

Directions

Drain and rinse the soaked pinto beans.

In the meantime, heat canola oil on HIGH until sizzling. Then, cook the steak, garlic, and leek for about 5 minutes.

Add remaining ingredients; seal the pressure cooker's lid, and set on HIGH for 24 minutes.

Open the lid naturally and adjust your chili for seasonings. Serve warm.

Chicken Soup with Farfalle

(Ready in about 25 minutes | Servings 6)

Ingredients

1 pound chicken breasts, boneless, skinless and cubed

2 tablespoons flour

Salt and ground black pepper, to taste

3 tablespoons butter

1 onion, diced

2 large-sized carrots, sliced

3 large-sized celery ribs, sliced

1 ½ cups uncooked farfalle pasta

6 cups chicken stock

3/4 teaspoon salt

1/2 teaspoon black pepper

1/2 teaspoon cayenne pepper

1 cup frozen corn kernels, thawed

Directions

Toss the chicken cubes with flour; generously season with salt and ground black pepper.

Then, warm the butter on HIGH until melted and sizzling.

Lay the coated chicken at the bottom of your pressure cooker; cook for about 5 minutes or until lightly browned, turning once.

Add the onion, carrots, and celery. Top with farfalle pasta and chicken stock; season with salt, black pepper, and cayenne pepper. Seal the lid and cook for 6 minutes on HIGH.

Now, release the cooker's pressure. Afterwards, stir in corn kernels and simmer for 1 to 2 minutes. Serve warm.

Creamed Tomato Soup

(Ready in about 20 minutes | Servings 6)

Ingredients

2 tablespoons butter

1 onion, diced

1 (28-ounce) can tomato sauce

4 cups chicken broth

8 tomatoes, finely chopped

2 cloves garlic, minced

1/2 teaspoon basil

1/2 teaspoon oregano

Sea salt and ground black pepper, to taste

1 cup heavy cream

Directions

Warm the butter on HIGH until melted.

Cook the onion in the pressure cooker for about 5 minutes.

Add the remaining ingredients, except for heavy cream. Seal the lid and cook for 8 minutes on HIGH.

Let the pressure release naturally for 5 to 10 minutes. Serve topped with heavy cream.

Soup with Cheese Tortellini

(Ready in about 15 minutes | Servings 6)

Ingredients

2 tablespoons canola oil

2 garlic cloves, minced

1 onion, diced

2 carrots, sliced

2 stalks celery, cut into 1/4 inch slices

1 cup dry cheese tortellini

4 cups vegetable stock

1 (24-ounce) jar spaghetti sauce

1 (14.5-ounce) can diced tomatoes

Sea salt and ground black pepper

Directions

Heat canola oil in your pressure cooker over HIGH heat.

Sauté the garlic, onion, carrots, and celery until tender.

Add the rest of the ingredients; stir to combine. Now lock the lid, set the pressure cooker to HIGH and cook for about 5 minutes.

Serve topped with grated Cheddar cheese if desired.

Jalapeño Chicken Soup with Corn

(Ready in about 30 minutes | Servings 6)

Ingredients

1 pound chicken breasts, boneless, skinless and cubed

2 tablespoons flour

Sea salt and ground black pepper

2 tablespoons canola oil

1 onion, diced

2 celery stalks, sliced

1 jalapeño pepper, seeded and diced

5 cups tomato soup

1/2 teaspoon ground cumin

Sea salt and black pepper, to taste

1 cup frozen corn kernels, thawed

4 corn tortillas, cut into strips

Directions

Dust the cubed chicken breasts with flour; season with salt and black pepper.

Then, heat oil on HIGH until sizzling. Lay the coated chicken in the cooker; sauté until they are lightly browned, or about 5 minutes.

Sauté the onion, celery, jalapeño pepper for about 1 minute. Add the tomato soup, cumin, salt, and black pepper.

Seal the pressure cooker's lid and set on HIGH for 7 minutes. Stir in corn and tortilla strips. Serve.

Lentil and Swiss Chard Soup

(Ready in about 35 minutes | Servings 4)

Ingredients

2 tablespoons olive oil

1 small-sized white onion, chopped

3 garlic cloves, minced

2 carrots, chopped

1 parsnip, chopped

1 celery rib, chopped

4 cups vegetable broth

1 cup dry lentils, rinsed and picked

1 cup Swiss chard leaves

Sea salt and freshly cracked black pepper

Directions

First, heat olive oil in your pressure cooker. Then, sweat the onion and garlic for a few minutes.

Add the carrots, parsnip, and celery; sauté for 1 to 2 minutes.

Add the vegetable broth and dry lentils, and cook for about 20 minutes.

Open the pressure cooker; add Swiss chard, and stir until it wilts. Season with salt and black pepper to taste. Serve.

Delicious Pea and Ham Soup

(Ready in about 30 minutes | Servings 8)

Ingredients

1 pound dried split peas

8 cups water

1 ham bone

1 cup scallions, chopped

2 carrots, diced

2 parsnips, diced

1 teaspoon mustard seed

1 teaspoon dried basil

2 tablespoons sherry wine

Directions

Fill the pressure cooker with all the above ingredients, except for sherry wine.

Put the lid on your pressure cooker, and bring to HIGH pressure. Cook for 20 minutes.

Add sherry and stir to combine. Serve and enjoy!

Black Bean Salad

(Ready in about 10 minutes + chilling time | Servings 6)

Ingredients

4 cups water

2 cups black beans, soaked overnight

1 tablespoon canola oil

1 red onion, chopped

2 cloves garlic, peeled and smashed

2 tomatoes, chopped

1 cup corn kernels

3 teaspoons olive oil

1 teaspoon apple cider vinegar

3/4 teaspoon salt

1/2 teaspoon white pepper

1 sprig fresh thyme

Directions

Add water, beans, canola oil, red onion, and garlic to the pressure cooker. Now lock the lid.

Turn the heat to HIGH; cook approximately 8 minutes.

Next, wait for the pressure to come down.

Strain the beans and transfer them to a refrigerator in order to cool completely. Transfer to a serving bowl and add the rest of the ingredients. Enjoy!

Easiest Adzuki Beans Ever

(Ready in about 10 minutes | Servings 4)

Ingredients

4 cups water

1 cup adzuki beans

2 tablespoons canola oil

1/2 teaspoon black pepper, ground

1 teaspoon salt

1 bay leaf

Directions

Fill the pressure cooker with all the above ingredients.

Seal the lid; bring to HIGH pressure and maintain for 8 minutes.

Then, allow pressure to release naturally. Ladle into soup bowls and serve hot.

Easiest Pinto Beans Ever

(Ready in about 1 hour 15 minutes | Servings 6)

Ingredients

8 cups water

1 cup dried pinto beans

2 tablespoons canola oil

2 bay leaves

1 teaspoon salt

3/4 teaspoon ground black pepper

Directions

Add 4 cups of water and pinto beans to your pressure cooker. Cover with the lid and bring to HIGH pressure for 1 minute. Then, quick-release the pressure.

Drain and rinse the beans; add the beans back to the pressure cooker. Let them soak for about 1 hour.

Add the rest of the ingredients; bring to HIGH pressure and maintain for about 11 minutes. Serve warm and enjoy!

Yellow Lentil with Kale

(Ready in about 25 minutes | Servings 4)

Ingredients

1 tablespoon canola oil

1 medium-sized leek, diced

1/4 teaspoon coriander

1/2 teaspoon thyme

1/4 teaspoon cumin

1 cup yellow dried lentils

2 tomatoes, chopped

1/2 cup water

2 cups kale, torn into small pieces

Directions

Heat canola oil in your pressure cooker over medium heat. Sauté the leeks together with coriander, thyme, and cumin for about 5 minutes. Then, add lentils, tomatoes, and water; stir well to combine. Close and lock the pressure cooker's lid.

Cook for about 12 minutes at HIGH pressure.

Afterwards, release the pressure according to manufacturer's instructions. Mix in the kale; stir until it is wilted; serve.

Delicious Red Lentil Curry

(Ready in about 20 minutes | Servings 8)

Ingredients

8 cups water

2 cups dried red lentils

3 tablespoons canola oil

3/4 teaspoon salt

1 cup scallions, diced

2 cloves garlic, minced

3 tablespoons curry powder

1 teaspoon cumin

1 teaspoon chili powder

1 (6-ounce) can tomato paste

Salt and ground black pepper, to taste

Directions

Add the water, lentils, 1 tablespoon of canola oil and salt to your pressure cooker.

Cover and bring to HIGH pressure for 8 minutes. Turn off the heat and allow pressure to release according to manufacturer's directions. Drain the lentils.

To prepare curry mixture: In a saucepan, warm the remaining 2 tablespoons of canola oil; sauté the scallions until they are caramelized.

Add the rest of the ingredients and cook for about 4 minutes, stirring frequently.

Add curry mixture to the prepared lentils; mix to combine. Serve warm and enjoy!

Lentil and Tomato Delight

(Ready in about 15 minutes | Servings 6)

Ingredients

1 tablespoon vegetable oil

1 parsnip, chopped

1 carrot, chopped

1 stalk celery, chopped

1 red bell pepper, chopped

1 green bell pepper, chopped

1 onion, chopped

1 cup dried lentils

1 (14.5-ounce) can tomatoes, chopped

2 cups water

1 teaspoon red pepper, flakes, crushed

Kosher salt and ground black pepper, to taste

Directions

Heat vegetable oil in a pressure cooker over medium heat. Add parsnip, carrot, celery, bell peppers, and onion. Sauté until the vegetables have softened.

Then add dried lentils, tomatoes, and water, and stir well. Seal the lid. Cook for 10 minutes at HIGH pressure.

Open the cooker according to manufacturer's directions. Season with red pepper, salt and black pepper. Enjoy!

Indian-Style Potato and Broccoli

(Ready in about 15 minutes | Servings 6)

Ingredients

2 cups potatoes, peeled and cubed

2 cups broccoli, broken into florets

2 tablespoons olive oil

2 cloves garlic, minced

1 teaspoon ginger, minced

1 teaspoon garam masala

1/2 teaspoon ground black pepper

1 teaspoon salt

Directions

Add the potatoes to your pressure cooker; cover with water. Seal the lid and cook under HIGH pressure for about 4 minutes. Then, remove the cooker from the heat; quick-release the pressure.

Add the broccoli. Bring to HIGH pressure; cook for 2 minutes. Drain and reserve. Clean the cooker.

Warm olive oil in the pressure cooker over LOW heat. Add the rest of the ingredients and cook for about 2 minutes.

Then, add the cooked potatoes and broccoli, along with 2 tablespoons of water. Let simmer over LOW heat for 10 minutes; stir periodically. Serve and enjoy!

Green Onion and Asparagus Salad

(Ready in about 10 minutes | Servings 4)

Ingredients

1 ½ pounds fresh asparagus, snap off the ends

1/2 cup water

1/2 cup green onions, minced

2 tablespoons lemon juice

3 tablespoons olive oil

1 teaspoon cayenne pepper

Salt and freshly ground white pepper, to taste

Directions

Place the asparagus flat in the pressure cooker; add the water.

Lock the lid and cook on HIGH for 3 minutes. Then, allow pressure to release naturally and gradually. Transfer the asparagus to a serving platter.

To make the dressing: In a measuring cup, whisk together the rest of the ingredients. Dress the asparagus and serve.

Easy Lemony Asparagus

(Ready in about 10 minutes | Servings 4)

Ingredients

1 cup water

Rind of 1 organic lemon

1 pound asparagus

Sea salt and ground black pepper, to taste

2 tablespoons olive oil

Directions

Place water and lemon rind in the pressure cooker; add a steamer basket.

Arrange the asparagus in the steamer basket. Close and lock the cooker's lid. Cook for 2 to 3 minutes at HIGH pressure. Next, open the cooker by releasing pressure.

Transfer to a serving platter. Sprinkle with salt and black pepper; drizzle with olive oil. Serve.

Sour Mushroom and Tofu Soup

(Ready in about 10 minutes | Servings 4)

Ingredients

2 tablespoons sesame oil

1 onion, thinly sliced

1 cup mushrooms, quartered

5 cups vegetable broth

1 (8-ounce) can sliced water chestnuts

3 tablespoons wine vinegar

3 tablespoons soy sauce

1/4 teaspoon white pepper

2 tablespoons cornstarch

1 (8-ounce) package tofu, cubed

1/2 scallions, thinly sliced

Directions

First, heat sesame oil in your cooker; next, sauté the onion until it's translucent or 3 to 4 minutes.

Add mushrooms, broth, water chestnuts, wine vinegar, soy sauce, and white pepper to the cooker.

Securely lock the lid and set for 5 minutes on HIGH. Then, release the cooker's pressure.

Next, mix the cornstarch with 2 tablespoons of water. Add the cornstarch mixture along with tofu; simmer for 2 minutes. Serve warm topped with scallions.

Basic Beef Broth

(Ready in about 1 hour 30 minutes | Servings 12)

Ingredients

1 tablespoon vegetable oil

1 ½ pounds bone-in chuck roast

1 pound beef bones, cracked

1 red onion, slice into rings

1 parsnip, peeled and chopped

1 carrot, peeled and chopped

1 celery stalk, cut and chopped

4 cups water

Directions

First of all, heat the vegetable oil over high heat. Then, add chuck roast and bones; brown on all sides for a few minutes, turning a few times.

Turn the heat to medium; add the onion, parsnip, carrot, and celery, and enough water to cover your ingredients. Close the cooker's lid.

Cook for about 1 hour 30 minutes at HIGH pressure. Open the cooker with the natural release method.

Next, remove the roast and beef bones with a slotted spoon. Discard the bones. Keep your broth 1 or 2 days in the refrigerator or 3 months in the freezer.

Easy Traditional Borscht

(Ready in about 25 minutes | Servings 6)

Ingredients

1 ½ tablespoons ghee

2 cloves garlic, peeled and minced

1/2 pound lamb, cut into bite-sized pieces

1 onion, peeled and diced

1 pound red beets, peeled, diced and rinsed

1 small-sized head cabbage, cored and chopped

1 (15-ounce) can tomatoes, diced

6 cups beef broth

1/4 cup wine vinegar

Sea salt and freshly ground black pepper, to taste

Sour cream, for garnish

Directions

Add the ghee, garlic, and lamb to your pressure cooker. Cook the lamb over medium heat, until it is browned. Add the onion and cook until translucent and fragrant.

Then, add the beets, cabbage, tomatoes, beef broth, wine vinegar to the pressure cooker.

Then, cook for 10 to 15 minutes at LOW pressure. Turn off the heat and quick-release the pressure.

Season with sea salt and black pepper according to your taste. Ladle your soup into serving dishes and garnish with sour cream. Enjoy!

Green Bean and Chicken Soup

(Ready in about 10 minutes | Servings 8)

Ingredients

6 carrots, peeled and grated

1 turnip, peeled and finely chopped

2 stalks celery, finely chopped

1 large-sized onion, peeled and diced

1 cup chicken breasts, boneless and cubed

2 tablespoons extra-virgin olive oil

2 teaspoons butter, melted

2 cloves garlic, peeled and minced

4 cups chicken stock

6 medium potatoes, peeled and diced

1 teaspoon dried rosemary

2 bay leaves

2 strips orange zest

Salt and freshly ground black pepper, to taste

8 chicken thighs, skin removed

2 (10-ounce) packages frozen green beans, thawed

Directions

Add the grated carrot, turnips, celery, onion, chicken meat, olive oil, and butter to your pressure cooker. Lock the lid into place. Bring to LOW pressure and maintain for 1 minute. Open the lid naturally.

Add the rest of the ingredients, except for green beans. Cover and bring to HIGH pressure. Then, allow pressure to release naturally and remove the lid.

Return the uncovered pressure cooker to MEDIUM heat and add the green beans. Now cook for 5 minutes. Taste for seasonings and serve warm.

Potato and Corn Chowder

(Ready in about 10 minutes | Servings 6)

Ingredients

2 tablespoons butter

2 white onions, chopped

6 cups vegetable stock

6 Idaho potatoes, peeled and diced

2 bay leaves

Salt and freshly ground black pepper, to taste

1 ½ cups corn

1/2 cup heavy cream

Directions

Melt the butter in your pressure cooker over medium heat. Then, sauté onions for 2 minutes. Pour in the vegetable stock. Add potatoes, bay leaves, salt, and black pepper.

Cover with the lid and bring to HIGH pressure; maintain pressure for 4 to 5 minutes. Discard the bay leaves.

Stir in the corn and heavy cream and serve warm.

Hearty Clam Chowder

(Ready in about 15 minutes | Servings 4)

Ingredients

4 thick strips bacon, diced

2 stalk celery, finely diced

1 carrot, finely diced

1 parsnip, finely diced

2 shallots, peeled and minced

1 pound potatoes, peeled and diced

3 (6 1/2-ounce) cans chopped clams, drained and liquid reserved

2 ½ cups vegetable broth

1 cup frozen corn

2 cups milk

1/2 teaspoon dried rosemary

1 teaspoon cayenne pepper

Sea salt and freshly ground black pepper, to taste

Directions

Fry the bacon over medium-high heat until it is just crisp. Add the celery, carrot, parsnip, and shallot; sauté for 3 to 5 minutes.

Stir in the potatoes and stir-fry for a few minutes longer. Stir in the clam liquid and vegetable broth.

Then, bring to HIGH pressure; maintain pressure for about 5 minutes. Allow pressure to drop naturally.

Stir in frozen corn, milk, rosemary, cayenne pepper, salt, black pepper, and reserved clams. Bring to a gentle simmer for 5 minutes. Serve.

Mushroom and Chicken Soup

(Ready in about 10 minutes | Servings 8)

Ingredients

1 parsnip, peeled and finely chopped

4 carrots, peeled and grated

2 stalks celery, finely chopped

1 large-sized onion, peeled and diced

2 cloves garlic, peeled and minced

1 cup mushrooms, thinly sliced

3 teaspoons butter, melted

4 cups chicken stock

1 teaspoon dried thyme

1 teaspoon dried rosemary

Salt and freshly ground black pepper, to taste

8 chicken thighs, skin removed

1 cup frozen whole kernel corn, thawed

1 cup frozen baby peas, thawed

Directions

Add the parsnip, carrot, celery, onion, garlic, mushroom, and butter to your pressure cooker. Seal the cooker's lid and bring to LOW pressure; maintain the pressure for 1 to 2 minutes. Then, open the lid naturally.

Add the remaining ingredients, except for corn and peas. Cover with the lid and bring to HIGH pressure. Then, remove the lid according to manufacturer's directions.

Add corn and peas and cook for 5 minutes. Ladle into soup bowls and serve with croutons if desired.

White Fish and Potato Chowder

(Ready in about 15 minutes | Servings 6)

Ingredients

2 tablespoons butter

2 leeks, thinly sliced

2 cups water

4 cups clam juice

6 russet potatoes, peeled and diced

2 bay leaves

Salt and freshly ground black pepper, to taste

1 pound white fish, cut into bite-sized pieces

1 teaspoon dried rosemary

1/2 teaspoon dried thyme

1/2 cup heavy cream

Directions

Melt the butter in your pressure cooker over medium heat. Then, sauté the leeks for 2 minutes. Stir in the water, clam juice, and potatoes. Add the bay leaves, salt, and black pepper.

Then, bring to HIGH pressure and maintain pressure for about 4 minutes. Remove the lid according to the manufacturer's instructions.

Add the fish to your pressure cooker. Simmer for about 3 minutes or until the fish is opaque. Stir in the rosemary, thyme, and heavy cream. Taste and adjust the seasonings. Serve warm.

Creamed Chestnuts Soup

(Ready in about 25 minutes | Servings 8)

Ingredients

1/2 pound dried chestnuts

2 tablespoons butter

1 medium-sized carrot, chopped

1 stalk celery, roughly chopped

1 leek, roughly sliced

1 teaspoon dried rosemary

1 teaspoon dried thyme

1 teaspoon dried sage

1/2 teaspoon ground black pepper

1 medium potato, peeled and roughly chopped

4 cups chicken broth

2 tablespoons dark rum

Kosher salt, to taste

Directions

First, soak chestnuts in the refrigerator overnight. Drain, rinse, and reserve.

Melt butter in your cooker over medium heat. Stir in the carrot, celery, leek, rosemary, thyme, sage, and ground black pepper; sauté until the vegetables are soft.

Now stir in the potatoes, chicken broth, and soaked chestnuts. Close and lock the cooker's lid. Turn the heat up to HIGH and cook for 15 to 20 minutes at HIGH pressure.

Afterwards, open the cooker with the natural release method. Lastly, add the rum and kosher salt to taste. Purée your mixture with an immersion blender. Serve warm.

Cream of Mushroom Soup

(Ready in about 20 minutes | Servings 4)

Ingredients

1/4 cup butter

1 onion, diced

2 cloves garlic, minced

2 cups mushrooms, sliced

2 carrots, diced

1/4 cup white wine

3 cups milk

1 teaspoon dried rosemary

1/2 teaspoon dried marjoram

1 cup béchamel sauce

Salt and black pepper, to taste

Directions

Warm the butter in your pressure cooker; sauté the onions until translucent and golden.

Add the garlic, mushrooms, carrots, and continue sautéing for 5 minutes longer. Stir in the wine, milk, rosemary, marjoram, and béchamel sauce. Season with salt and pepper.

Cover and bring to high pressure. Then, turn the heat to LOW and cook for about 8 minutes. Lastly, allow pressure to release naturally.

Purée the soup and serve warm.

Creamed Asparagus Soup

(Ready in about 20 minutes | Servings 6)

Ingredients

2 tablespoons butter

1 onion, diced

2 pounds asparagus, trimmed and cut into pieces

1 teaspoon garlic powder

1 teaspoon salt

1/2 teaspoon black pepper

1/4 teaspoon cayenne pepper

6 cups vegetable stock

1/4 cup milk

1 teaspoon lemon juice

Directions

Melt the butter in your pressure cooker; sauté the onion until tender and translucent. Add the asparagus, garlic powder, salt, black pepper, and cayenne pepper; sauté for 5 to 6 minutes.

Pour in the vegetable stock. Then, bring to HIGH pressure and cook for about 5 minutes.

Remove from the heat and allow pressure to release naturally. Add the milk and lemon juice, and purée your soup in a food processor. Serve warm.

Lima Bean Soup

(Ready in about 20 minutes | Servings 6)

Ingredients

2 cups dried lima beans

2 tablespoons olive oil

1/2 cup shallots, diced

2 cloves garlic, minced

1/2 cup water

2 cups vegetable broth

Sea salt and ground black pepper, to taste

Directions

Pour water into medium-sized dish. Then, add lima beans and soak them overnight.

Warm olive oil in your pressure cooker; sauté the shallots until they are tender and golden brown. Then, add the garlic and cook for 1 minute longer.

Add the water, vegetable broth, and soaked lima beans to the cooker. Seal the lid and continue to cook for 6 minutes. Remove from the heat and allow pressure to release gradually.

Purée the soup in a food processor; sprinkle with sea salt and ground black pepper. Serve warm.

Potato Cheese Soup

(Ready in about 15 minutes | Servings 6)

Ingredients

2 tablespoons butter

1/2 cup red onion, chopped

4 cups chicken broth

3/4 teaspoon sea salt

1/2 teaspoon black pepper

1/4 teaspoon red pepper flakes, crushed

6 cups potatoes, peeled and cubed

2 tablespoons water

2 tablespoons cornstarch

1/2 cup Ricotta cheese, cut into cubes

1 cup Cheddar cheese, shredded

2 cups half and half

1 cup frozen corn

Directions

Warm the butter in the pressure cooking pot. Sauté red onion for about 5 minutes. Add 2 cups chicken broth, salt, pepper, and red pepper flakes.

Put the steamer basket into the pressure cooker. Add the potatoes to the basket. Lock the lid in place, cook 4 minutes at HIGH pressure. Carefully remove the steamer basket from the pot.

In a small-sized bowl, dissolve cornstarch in water. Now add cornstarch mixture to the cooker, stirring often.

Add Ricotta cheese and Cheddar cheese. Stir until cheese is melted. Add remaining chicken broth, half and half, and corn. Cook for a few minutes longer until the soup is heated through. Serve.

Garlicky Bean Soup

(Ready in about 15 minutes | Servings 8)

Ingredients

2 cups dried white beans

3 tablespoons olive oil

1 medium-sized leek, sliced

4 cloves garlic, minced

2 cups water

4 cups vegetable stock

2 bay leaves

1 teaspoon apple cider vinegar

Sea salt and freshly cracked black pepper, to taste

Directions

Soak your white beans for 8 hours or overnight in enough water to cover them; drain and rinse.

In your pressure cooker, bring olive oil to temperature over medium heat. Now sauté the leek until it is golden brown. Add the garlic; continue sautéing for 1 minute more.

Pour in the water and vegetable stock; add bay leaves. Seal the lid and bring to HIGH pressure. Cook for about 10 minutes.

Remove the bay leaves; lastly, purée the soup and stir in the vinegar, salt, and black pepper. Ladle into individual dishes and serve warm.

Curried Chickpea Bisque

(Ready in about 25 minutes | Servings 8)

Ingredients

2 cups dried chickpeas

3 tablespoons canola oil

1 yellow onion, diced

2 cloves garlic, minced

1 teaspoon garam masala

2 teaspoons curry powder

2 cups vegetable broth

2 cups unsweetened soy milk

Salt and ground black pepper, to taste

Directions

Soak the chickpeas overnight.

Add canola oil to the cooker and sauté yellow onion until tender and translucent. Add the garlic, garam masala, and curry powder; then, sauté for 1 minute more.

Pour in vegetable broth and soy milk. Cover and bring to HIGH pressure. Maintain for 20 minutes.

Season with salt and pepper according to your taste. Add the soup to a food processor and purée until smooth; work in batches. Divide puréed soup among soup bowls and serve warm.

Vegetable Egg Soup

(Ready in about 15 minutes | Servings 6)

Ingredients

1/2 teaspoon star anise

1 teaspoon ginger

2-3 garlic cloves, minced

1 teaspoon celery seeds

1 teaspoon fennel seed

Salt to taste

1 teaspoon freshly ground black pepper

2 ripe tomatoes, chopped

4 cups water

2 cups vegetable broth

4 eggs, whisked

2 scallions, chopped

Directions

Put all the ingredients, except for eggs and scallions, into your pressure cooking pot.

Turn the heat up to HIGH. Cook for about 7 minutes at HIGH pressure.

Open the pressure cooker following manufacturer's instructions. Then, pour in the eggs and gently stir to combine.

Serve sprinkled with the scallions. Enjoy!

Nutty Vegetable Stew

(Ready in about 20 minutes | Servings 4)

Ingredients

1 tablespoon peanut oil

1 shallot, diced

2 green garlics, finely minced

1 yellow bell pepper, chopped

2 tablespoons fresh ginger, minced

1 sweet potato, peeled and cubed

2 cups canned tomatoes, diced and drained

1 (4-ounce) can chickpeas, drained

1 cup water

2 cups vegetable broth

1/2 cup peanut butter

Kosher salt and ground black pepper, to taste

1/2 cup nut milk of choice

Directions

Bring the peanut oil to MEDIUM heat in the pressure cooker. Then, sauté the shallot, green garlics, and bell pepper for about 3 minutes. Add the ginger, and sauté for 30 seconds more.

Add the remaining ingredients, except for the milk, to the pressure cooker.

Cover and bring to HIGH pressure; maintain for 10 minutes. After that, allow pressure to release naturally. Stir in the nut milk just before serving. Ladle into individual bowls and serve. Enjoy!

Beer and Beef Stew

(Ready in about 25 minutes | Servings 8)

Ingredients

2 teaspoons olive oil

1 onion, diced

2 carrots, diced

2 celery stalks, diced

1 parsnip, diced

2 cloves garlic, minced

2 potatoes, peeled and diced

2 tablespoons fresh rosemary, minced

2 pounds lean beef meat, cubed

1 teaspoon sea salt

1/2 teaspoon black pepper

1/2 teaspoon cayenne pepper

1 teaspoon cocoa powder

1 cup beer

Directions

Warm the oil in a pressure cooker over medium heat. Now sauté the onion, carrots, celery, parsnip, garlic, potatoes, rosemary, and meat for 5 to 6 minutes.

Add sea salt, black pepper, cayenne pepper, cocoa powder, and the beer. Close and lock the cooker's lid.

Turn the heat up to HIGH; then, lower the heat to the minimum needed to maintain pressure. Cook approximately 15 minutes at HIGH pressure. Serve warm.

Zesty Beef Stew

(Ready in about 25 minutes | Servings 8)

Ingredients

2 teaspoons vegetable oil

2 medium-sized sweet onions, diced

2 carrots, diced

1 celery stalk, diced

1 bell pepper, seeded and diced

2 potatoes, peeled and diced

2 tablespoons fresh thyme, minced

2 pounds lean beef meat, cubed

Sea salt and ground black pepper, to taste

1/2 teaspoon red pepper flakes, crushed

1 ½ cups water

Directions

Warm vegetable oil in a pressure cooker over medium heat. When the oil is hot enough, sauté sweet onions, carrots, celery, and bell pepper, until all the ingredients are browned.

Add the remaining ingredients. Close and lock the cooker's lid.

Cook this stew for about 15 minutes at HIGH pressure. Ladle into serving dishes and enjoy!

Vegan Brunswick Stew

(Ready in about 25 minutes | Servings 4)

Ingredients

2 tablespoons canola oil

1 leek, chopped

1 carrot, chopped

2 stalks celery, sliced

1 green bell pepper, diced

1 red bell pepper, diced

2 cups mushroom, chopped

1 (28-ounce) can crushed tomatoes

2 cups corn kernels

1 cup tomato paste

1/2 cup barbecue sauce

1 teaspoon salt

1/2 teaspoon black pepper

1 teaspoon cayenne pepper

Directions

Heat canola oil in the pressure cooker over medium heat; sauté the leek, carrot, celery, and bell peppers until all the vegetables are soft, or about 5 minutes.

Add all remaining ingredients. Cover, bring to HIGH pressure and maintain for 30 minutes. Remove from the heat, open the lid naturally, and serve right away.

Sausage and Pea Soup

(Ready in about 25 minutes | Servings 8)

Ingredients

1 pound ground sausage

2 tablespoons margarine

1 medium-sized leek, finely chopped

2 cloves garlic, minced

1 cup carrots, diced

2 cups water

28 ounces vegetable stock

1 package (16-ounce) peas

1/2 cup half and half

1 teaspoon cayenne pepper

Salt and fresh ground black pepper to taste

Directions

In the preheated cooker, cook the sausage until browned.

Then, warm margarine in your pressure cooker pot. Sauté the leeks, garlic, and carrots until tender.

Stir in the remaining ingredients, except for half and half. Now choose 'HIGH' pressure and 10 minutes cook time. After that, wait 10 minutes, and open the lid naturally.

Puree the mixture with an immersion blender. Continue to simmer and add the reserved and browned sausage and half and half. Stir until it is heated through. Enjoy!

Chickpea and Navy Stew

(Ready in about 20 minutes | Servings 8)

Ingredients

1 ½ cups dried navy beans

1 cup dried chickpeas, soaked

2 cloves garlic, minced

2 tablespoons canola oil

4 cups water

Kosher salt and ground black pepper

1/4 cup sharp cheese, grated

Directions

Add all the above ingredients, except for cheese, to your pressure cooking pot. Close and lock the cooker's lid according to manufacturer's instructions.

Turn the heat up to HIGH; when the pot reaches pressure, lower the heat. Cook for 15 minutes at HIGH pressure.

Open the pressure cooker with the natural-release method.

Ladle the stew into serving dishes; top each serving with grated cheese. Serve.

Eggplant and Chickpea Stew

(Ready in about 30 minutes | Servings 4)

Ingredients

2 eggplants, cut into large cubes

1 large-sized carrot, diced

1 (14-ounce) can chickpeas, drained

2 cups water

4 cups vegetable stock

1 cup tomato paste

1 teaspoon cumin

1 teaspoon celery seeds

1/2 cup fresh parsley, chopped

1/4 teaspoon red pepper flakes, crushed

1/4 teaspoon ground black pepper

1 teaspoon salt

Directions

Add the ingredients to your pressure cooker; lock the cooker's lid into place.

Bring to LOW pressure and maintain for about 30 minutes. Turn off the heat and allow pressure to release according to manufacturer's directions.

Open the lid and ladle the stew into individual bowls. Serve warm.

Zucchini and Chickpea Stew

(Ready in about 30 minutes | Servings 4)

Ingredients

2 large-sized zucchinis, cut into bite-sized chunks

1 parsnip, chopped

1 large-sized carrot, diced

1 (14-ounce) can chickpeas, drained

4 cups chicken broth

3 cups water

2 tablespoons tomato ketchup

1 teaspoon dried thyme

1/2 cup fresh cilantro, chopped

1/4 teaspoon ground black pepper

1 teaspoon salt

Directions

Add all the above ingredients to a pressure cooker; cover with the lid.

Cook for about 30 minutes at LOW pressure. Turn off the heat; allow pressure to release according to manufacturer's instructions.

Turn off the heat and remove the cooker's lid. Taste and adjust the seasonings. Serve warm.

Vegan Sausage Stew

(Ready in about 15 minutes | Servings 6)

Ingredients

12 cups water

1 pound red potatoes, whole and unpeeled

6 ears corn on the cob, husked and halved

1 (14-ounce) package vegan sausage, sliced

Salt and black pepper, to taste

1 teaspoon cayenne pepper

1 teaspoon dried basil

2 heads garlic, peeled

Directions

Add the water and red potatoes to your pressure cooker. Now lock the cooker's lid into place; bring to HIGH pressure and maintain for 5 to 6 minutes. Then, quick-release the pressure.

Uncover the cooker and stir in all remaining ingredients. Cover and bring to HIGH pressure; maintain for 5 more minutes. Then, allow pressure to release naturally and gradually.

Remove the ingredients from the cooker with a slotted spoon. Serve and enjoy!

DINNER RECIPES
Bean and Chickpea Stew

(Ready in about 25 minutes | Servings 4)

Ingredients

1 ½ cups dried beans, soaked

1 cup dried chickpeas, soaked

2 cloves garlic, minced

2 tablespoons scallions, chopped

2 tablespoons olive oil

4 cups water

Kosher salt and ground black pepper

1/4 cup Cheddar cheese, grated

Directions

Simply drop all of the above ingredients, except for cheese, in the pressure cooker. Now close and lock the cooker's lid.

Turn the heat up to HIGH. Cook for about 15 minutes at HIGH pressure.

Open the pressure cooker using the Natural-release method.

Ladle the stew into individual dishes; top each serving with grated Cheddar cheese.

Greek-Style Eggplant Stew

(Ready in about 30 minutes | Servings 4)

Ingredients

2 eggplants, cut into cubes

1 parsnip, chopped

1 carrot, chopped

1 (14-ounce) can chickpeas, drained

2 cups water

4 cups vegetable broth

1/4 teaspoon cayenne pepper

1 cup tomato paste

1 teaspoon celery seeds

1/2 teaspoon fennel seeds

1 teaspoon cumin

1/4 teaspoon ground black pepper

1 teaspoon salt

Directions

Add all of the above ingredients to your pressure cooker; lock the lid into place.

Bring to LOW pressure, maintaining the pressure for about 30 minutes. Turn off the heat; allow pressure to release according to manufacturer's instructions.

Next, ladle the stew into individual serving dishes. Serve warm topped with grated sharp cheese if desired.

Barley and Cabbage Stew

(Ready in about 20 minutes | Servings 4)

Ingredients

2 tablespoons vegetable oil, divided

1 cup dry chickpeas, soaked

1 cup barley

2 cloves garlic, pressed

1 leek, diced

2 carrots, diced

2 parsnips, chopped

1/2 head cabbage, shredded

4 cups water

1 teaspoon sea salt

1/2 teaspoon ground black pepper

1/2 teaspoon red pepper, flakes

1 teaspoon dried thyme

Directions

Add all of the above ingredients to a pressure cooker. Close and lock the lid.

Turn the heat to HIGH; cook your stew for 15 minutes at HIGH pressure.

Use the Natural release method. Taste and adjust the seasonings; serve right away!

Cauliflower and Mushroom Stew

(Ready in about 15 minutes | Servings 4)

Ingredients

2 tablespoons olive oil

1 onion, sliced

2 cloves garlic, minced

1 cup cauliflower, chopped into florets

1 cup mushrooms, sliced

12 ounces soft silken tofu, drained and cubed

1 teaspoon soy sauce

3 cups vegetable broth

Fresh parsley, for garnish

Directions

Warm the oil over medium heat. Then, sauté the onion and garlic till they become tender.

Add the remaining ingredients, except for parsley, to the pressure cooker. Cover the cooker; bring to LOW pressure, maintaining it for 5 minutes. Remove from heat; now allow pressure to release naturally.

Remove the lid and serve sprinkled with chopped parsley. Enjoy!

Broccoli with Balsamic-Mustard Sauce

(Ready in about 10 minutes | Servings 6)

Ingredients

4 cups broccoli florets

1 teaspoon cayenne pepper

1/2 teaspoon kosher salt

1/2 teaspoon black pepper

1/2 teaspoon thyme, dried

1/2 teaspoon dried dill weed

1 cup water

1/2 cup vegetable broth

4 tablespoons butter

1/2 teaspoon mustard

1 tablespoon balsamic vinegar

Directions

Put the broccoli, cayenne pepper, kosher salt, black pepper, thyme, dried dill, water, and vegetable broth into your pressure cooker.

Cover the cooker with the lid; bring to LOW pressure and maintain the pressure for about 3 minutes. Turn off the heat and quick-release the pressure. Reserve.

To make the sauce: whisk together the butter, mustard, and balsamic vinegar. Drizzle the sauce over reserved broccoli. Serve.

Herbed Cabbage in Beer

(Ready in about 10 minutes | Servings 6)

Ingredients

2 tablespoons sesame oil

2 cloves garlic, minced

1 onion, sliced

1 medium-sized head cabbage, cut into strips

1/2 cup beer

Salt and ground black pepper, to your taste

1 teaspoon dried thyme

1 teaspoon dried sage

Directions

Heat sesame oil over medium heat. Then, sauté the garlic along with onion, stirring periodically, until they have softened.

Stir in cabbage and beer. Now set the temperature to HIGH; cook for 5 to 6 minutes at HIGH pressure.

Lastly, open the cooker. Add salt, black pepper, thyme, and sage. Enjoy!

Delicious Cabbage with Apples and Almonds

(Ready in about 10 minutes | Servings 8)

Ingredients

2 tablespoons sesame oil

1 onion, diced

2 apples, peeled, cored, and sliced

1/2 cup dry wine

1 head red cabbage, cut into strips

1 teaspoon salt

1/2 teaspoon freshly ground black pepper

1/2 teaspoon cayenne pepper

Toasted almonds, for garnish

Directions

First, warm sesame oil over medium heat. Then, sauté the onion until soft.

Stir in the apples and dry wine.

Stir red cabbage into the pressure cooking pot. Cover and cook for 5 minutes at HIGH pressure.

When time is up, open the pressure cooker. Season with salt, black pepper, and cayenne pepper. Sprinkle with toasted almonds and serve.

Saucy Baby Carrots

(Ready in about 10 minutes | Servings 4)

Ingredients

1 pound baby carrots, cut into halves lengthwise

2 tablespoons sesame oil

1 teaspoon fresh ginger, minced

1 cup water

Kosher salt and ground black pepper, to your liking

1/2 teaspoon garlic powder

1/2 teaspoon allspice

Directions

Stir the carrot, sesame oil, and fresh ginger into your cooker. Add the rest of the ingredients. Now stir to combine well. Then, lock the cooker's lid.

Cook for 1 minute at HIGH pressure. Open the pressure cooking pot according to manufacturer's directions.

Season with salt, black pepper, garlic powder, and allspice. Serve at room temperature.

Pork Chops with Squash

(Ready in about 15 minutes | Servings 4)

Ingredients

2 tablespoons unsalted butter

4 rib chops

1 teaspoon salt

1/2 teaspoon ground black pepper

1/2 teaspoon red pepper flakes, crushed

2 medium acorn squashes, peeled, seeded, and cut into eighths

2 tablespoons honey

1 teaspoon dried sage

1/2 teaspoon dried thyme

1/4 teaspoon allspice

1 cup chicken stock

Directions

Melt the butter in a pressure cooker; set over medium heat. Season the chops with the salt, black pepper, and red pepper. Then, brown the chops.

Add the squash to the cooker. Sprinkle the honey, sage, thyme, and allspice over the chops.

Then, pour in chicken stock. Lock the lid onto the cooking pot. Cook for 6 minutes at HIGH pressure. Use the Quick-release method to open your cooker.

Unlock and open the cooking pot. Transfer prepared chops to a serving platter. Ladle the sauce over the chops.

Tomato-Chili Pork Chops

(Ready in about 15 minutes | Servings 4)

Ingredients

2 tablespoons olive oil

4 rib chops

1 onion, chopped

2 cloves garlic, minced

1 (4 ½-ounce) can mild green chilli, chopped

1 teaspoon dried basil

1 teaspoon dried oregano

1 (14-ounce) can tomatoes, diced

1 cup basmati rice

1 ½ cups chicken broth

Directions

Warm olive oil in a pressure cooker over medium heat. Then, brown the chops.

Add the onion and garlic to the cooking pot. Then, cook, stirring frequently, until softened, about 5 minutes.

Stir in the chilies, basil, and oregano; cook until they are aromatic, stirring often. Stir in the canned tomatoes and rice; then, pour in the chicken broth.

Nestle the pork chops into the cooker. Lock the lid onto the cooker. Cook for 7 minutes at HIGH pressure.

Use the quick-release method. Set your cooker aside for 10 to 15 minutes to steam the rice. Serve warm.

Peppery Bulgur Salad

(Ready in about 20 minutes | Servings 6)

Ingredients

1 ¼ cups bulgur, rinsed and drained

1 teaspoon salt

1/2 teaspoon ground black pepper

1/2 teaspoon cayenne pepper

1/2 teaspoon rosemary

2 ½ cups water

2 tablespoons canola oil

1 cup scallions, minced

2 cloves garlic, minced

1 yellow bell pepper, seeded and chopped

1 red bell pepper, seeded and chopped

1/3 cup fresh lemon juice

1/3 cup extra-virgin olive oil

Sea salt and freshly cracked black pepper

Directions

Put the bulgur, salt, ground black pepper, cayenne pepper, rosemary into a pressure cooker. Stir in the water and canola oil.

Close the lid. Select HIGH pressure and 6 minutes cook time.

Open the cooker using the Natural Release method; allow it to stand for about 12 minutes.

Fluff the bulgur with a fork; add the remaining ingredients. Give it a good stir and serve.

Hominy and Pork Stew

(Ready in about 15 minutes | Servings 4)

Ingredients

2 tablespoons olive oil

1 onion, chopped

1 large yellow bell pepper, stemmed, cored, cut into strips

1 large red bell pepper, stemmed, cored, cut into strips

2 cloves garlic, minced

1 teaspoon dried basil

1 teaspoon dried oregano

1 teaspoon dried thyme

2 ½ cups canned hominy, drained and rinsed

1 (14-ounce) can diced tomatoes

1 cup chicken broth

1 pound pork loin chops, cut into strips

Directions

Heat the oil in a pressure cooker over medium heat. Stir in the onion and bell peppers; sauté, stirring often, until the onion softens, about 4 minutes.

Add the garlic, basil, oregano, and thyme. Add the hominy, tomatoes, broth, and pork; cook for 1 more minute. Lock the lid onto the cooker.

Raise the heat to HIGH. Cook for 8 minutes. Use the Quick-release method.

Unlock and open the cooker. Give it a good stir before serving.

Pork Loin Chops with Pears

(Ready in about 15 minutes | Servings 4)

Ingredients

2 tablespoons butter

4 loin chops

1 teaspoon salt

1 teaspoon ground black pepper

1 teaspoon cayenne pepper

2 spring onions, thinly sliced

2 large-sized firm pears, peeled, cored, and cut into 4 wedges

1/2 cup pear cider

Several dashes of hot red pepper sauce

Directions

Melt butter in a pressure cooker over medium heat. Season the chops with the salt, ground black pepper, and cayenne pepper. Transfer the chops to a large plate.

Add spring onions and pears; cook, stirring periodically, until the pears have softened and browned, about 3 minutes.

Pour in the pear cider and red pepper sauce. Nestle the chops into the sauce. Lock the lid onto the cooker.

Cook for 8 minutes, maintaining HIGH pressure. Set the pot off the heat for 5 to 7 minutes. Use the Quick-release method. Serve warm.

Pork Chops with Almonds

(Ready in about 15 minutes | Servings 4)

Ingredients

2 tablespoons olive oil

4 loin chops, trimmed

1 teaspoon salt

1/2 teaspoon ground black pepper

1/2 teaspoon red pepper flakes, crushed

1 teaspoon dried thyme

1/2 teaspoon dried sage

2 tablespoons toasted almonds, chopped

2 cloves garlic, minced

1 cup chicken broth

1 tablespoon balsamic vinegar

Directions

First, set a pressure cooking pot over medium heat; heat the oil. Season the chops with the salt, black pepper, red pepper, thyme, and sage.

Brown your chops on all sides, turning once or twice. Reserve.

Add the almonds, garlic, chicken broth and balsamic vinegar. Return reserved chops to the cooker. Lock the lid onto the pot.

Cook for 12 minutes using HIGH pressure. Allow the pressure to release naturally. Serve warm and enjoy.

Saucy Pork Chops with Carrots

(Ready in about 15 minutes | Servings 4)

Ingredients

2 tablespoons unsalted butter

2 tablespoons olive oil

4 loin chops, trimmed

1/2 teaspoon salt

1/2 teaspoon ground black pepper

1/2 teaspoon cayenne pepper

4 carrots, peeled and chopped

1/2 cup dry white wine

1/2 cup water

Directions

Melt the butter and olive oil in a pressure cooker over medium heat. Season the chops with the salt, black pepper, and cayenne pepper. Then, brown the chops for about 4 minutes. Reserve the chops.

Add the remaining ingredients. Return the chops to the cooker. Cook for 12 minutes using HIGH pressure.

Afterward, use the quick-release method. Serve and enjoy!

Beef and Bean Casserole

(Ready in about 12 minutes | Servings 4)

Ingredients

2 tablespoons olive oil

1 leek, thinly sliced

1 green bell pepper, stemmed, seeded, and chopped

1 red bell pepper, stemmed, seeded, and chopped

1 clove garlic, minced

1 pound lean ground beef

1 (28-ounce) can tomatoes, diced

2 cups fresh corn kernels

1 (15-ounce) can kidney beans, drained and rinsed

1 (12-ounce) bottle beer

1 tablespoon cayenne pepper

1 teaspoon ground cumin

1 teaspoon dried basil

1/2 teaspoon sea salt

8 ounces dried pasta

Directions

Heat the oil in a pressure cooker set over medium heat. Sauté the leeks, bell peppers, and garlic; cook, stirring frequently, until the vegetable become tender, or about 4 minutes. Add ground beef.

Cook, stirring often, until the beef has browned a bit. Stir in the remaining ingredients.

Cook for 5 minutes at HIGH pressure. Use the quick-release method and remove the lid. Give it a good stir and serve.

Herby Mashed Potatoes

(Ready in about 15 minutes | Servings 6)

Ingredients

2 ¼ pounds russet potatoes, peeled and cut into chunks

1 teaspoon kosher salt

1/2 teaspoon ground black pepper

1 teaspoon red pepper flakes, crushed

1 teaspoon dried rosemary

1 teaspoon dried thyme

1/2 teaspoon dried marjoram

3 tablespoons butter, cut into pieces

3/4 cup buttermilk

Directions

Simply drop the potatoes in a pressure cooker; then, fill the cooker with the water to cover the potatoes. Sprinkle with kosher salt. Close and lock the lid.

Set the burner heat to HIGH. Then, cook for 6 minutes.

Use the Quick Release method. Drain your potatoes in a colander.

Using a potato masher, mash the potatoes. Stir in black pepper, red pepper, rosemary, thyme, marjoram, butter and the buttermilk.

Beat the mixture to the desired consistency. Serve with your favorite cheese.

Rich Sausage and Vegetable Dinner

(Ready in about 20 minutes | Servings 6)

Ingredients

1 ½ pounds pork sausage

1 cup scallions, sliced

2 potatoes, peeled and sliced

1 carrot, thinly sliced

1 parsnip, thinly sliced

1 red bell pepper, seeded and sliced

1 green bell pepper, seeded and sliced

3/4 cup tomato paste

1/2 teaspoon cumin powder

Salt and black pepper, to your liking

Red pepper flakes, to your liking

Directions

Drop pork sausage in a pressure cooking pot; then, sauté the sausage for about 5 minutes. Reserve.

Place the scallions, potatoes, carrot, parsnip, and bell peppers in the bottom of your cooker. Top with the reserved sausage.

Pour the tomato paste into the pressure cooker. Sprinkle with ground cumin, salt, black pepper, and red pepper flakes. Cover and bring to HIGH pressure; cook for 7 minutes. Serve warm.

Colorful Wheat Berry Salad

(Ready in about 35 minutes | Servings 8)

Ingredients

2 tablespoons olive oil

6 ¾ cups water

1 ½ cups wheat berries

1 teaspoon sea salt

1/2 teaspoon freshly ground black pepper

1/4 cup apple cider vinegar

1/4 cup olive oil

1 cup scallions, peeled and diced

1 ½ cups frozen peas, thawed

1 parsnip, thinly sliced

1 large-sized carrot, chopped

2 stalks celery, finely diced

2 bell peppers, seeded and diced

1/4 cup sun-dried tomatoes, diced

1/4 cup fresh parsley, chopped

Directions

Add the olive, water and wheat berries to your pressure cooker. Lock the lid into place; bring to HIGH pressure and maintain pressure for 50 minutes. Now perform Quick-release.

Make the dressing by processing salt, black pepper, apple cider vinegar, olive oil, and scallions in a blender.

Toss prepared wheat berries with remaining ingredients. Dress the salad and serve chilled.

Wheat Berry Salad with Corn

(Ready in about 35 minutes | Servings 8)

Ingredients

1 ½ cups wheat berries

6 ¾ cups water

1 teaspoon sea salt

1/2 teaspoon freshly ground black pepper

2 tablespoons balsamic vinegar

1 tablespoon lime juice

1/3 cup extra-virgin olive oil

1 cup shallots, finely chopped

1 ½ cups frozen corn kernels, thawed

1 red bell pepper, seeded and diced

1 green bell pepper, seeded and diced

1 carrot, chopped

2 stalks celery, finely diced

1/4 cup sun-dried tomatoes, diced

1/4 cup fresh cilantro, chopped

1/4 cup olives, pitted and sliced

Directions

Add wheat berries to your pressure cooker. Fill the cooker with the water. Lock the lid into place; bring to HIGH pressure and maintain pressure for 50 minutes. Now quick-release the pressure. Reserve cooked white berries.

To make the dressing, process salt, black pepper, balsamic vinegar, lime juice, extra-virgin olive oil, and shallots in a blender.

Then, toss wheat berries with remaining ingredients. Dress the salad and serve well chilled.

Chili Bean Salad with Dried Cherries

(Ready in about 35 minutes + chilling time | Servings 12)

Ingredients

Water

2 cups dried cannellini beans

2 tablespoons soy sauce

1 teaspoon chili paste

2 cloves garlic, minced

2 teaspoons sesame oil

3 tablespoons sherry vinegar

2 cups frozen corn kernels, thawed

2 carrots, thinly sliced

3/4 cup dried cherries

3 green onions, peeled and diced

Salt and freshly cracked black pepper, to taste

1 teaspoon red pepper flakes, for garnish

Directions

Place water and cannellini beans in a bowl; let them soak overnight.

Next, prepare the dressing by whisking soy sauce, chili paste, minced garlic, sesame oil, and sherry vinegar. Refrigerate this dressing overnight.

Drain the beans; now cook them in a pressure cooker along with 3 cups of water for 25 minutes. Then, allow pressure to release.

Next, drain cooked beans; transfer them to a salad bowl. Add the remaining ingredients. Drizzle with reserved dressing and serve.

Refreshing Summer Salad

(Ready in about 35 minutes | Servings 8)

Ingredients

6 ¾ cups water

1 ½ cups wheat berries

1 teaspoon cayenne pepper

1/2 teaspoon freshly ground black pepper

1 teaspoon kosher salt

1 tablespoon orange juice

2 tablespoons balsamic vinegar

1/3 cup extra-virgin olive oil

1 cup green onions, finely chopped

1/2 cup frozen peas, thawed

1 cup green beans, sliced

2 red bell peppers, seeded and diced

2 stalks celery, finely diced

1/4 cup fresh cilantro, chopped

1/4 cup black olives, pitted and sliced

1/4 teaspoon dried cranberries

Directions

Simply throw the water and wheat berries in a pressure cooker. Cover and bring to HIGH pressure; maintain pressure for 50 minutes.

Now quick-release the pressure. Reserve.

To make the dressing, process cayenne pepper, black pepper, kosher salt, orange juice, balsamic vinegar, olive oil, and green onions in a food processor or a blender.

Afterward, add the rest of the ingredients. Dress the salad and serve well chilled.

Aromatic Tomato and Lentil Dinner

(Ready in about 15 minutes | Servings 6)

Ingredients

1 tablespoon olive oil

2 carrots, peeled and chopped

1 stalk celery, peeled and chopped

1 parsnip, chopped

2 red bell peppers, chopped

1 cup pearl onions, chopped

1 cup dried lentils

1 (14.5-ounce) can tomatoes, chopped

2 cups water

1 teaspoon cayenne pepper

1 sprig fresh rosemary

Kosher salt and ground black pepper, to taste

Directions

Heat olive oil in a pressure cooker over medium heat. Stir in the carrots, celery, parsnip, bell peppers, and pearl onions. Sauté till they have softened.

Then add dried lentils, tomatoes, and water; give it a good stir. Seal the lid and cook for 10 minutes at HIGH pressure.

Open the cooker according to manufacturer's directions. Season with cayenne pepper, kosher salt, and ground black pepper. Enjoy!

Asparagus Salad with Pearl Onions

(Ready in about 10 minutes | Servings 4)

Ingredients

1 ½ pounds fresh asparagus, snap off the ends

1 cup pearl onions, minced

1/2 cup water

3 tablespoons olive oil

2 tablespoons lime juice

1 teaspoon cayenne pepper

1/2 teaspoon cumin powder

Salt and freshly ground white pepper, to taste

Directions

Put the asparagus and pearl onions into a pressure cooker; fill the cooker with the water.

Cover and cook on HIGH for 3 minutes. Then, allow pressure to release naturally and gradually. Transfer the asparagus to a serving platter. Allow asparagus to cool.

In the meantime, make the dressing. In a measuring cup or a mixing bowl, combine the rest of the ingredients; whisk to combine well. Dress the asparagus salad and serve.

Mediterranean Eggplant Salad

(Ready in about 15 minutes | Servings 6)

Ingredients

1 eggplant, peeled and diced

1/2 cup water

3 tablespoons extra-virgin olive oil

2 cloves garlic, minced

2 cups tomatoes, chopped

1 tablespoon dry white wine

Sea salt and black pepper, to taste

1/2 teaspoon red pepper flakes

2 tablespoons fresh cilantro leaves, chopped

Directions

Throw the eggplant in a pressure cooker. Fill the cooker with the water. Cover the cooker; bring to HIGH pressure. Then, maintain pressure for 4 minutes. Quick release the pressure and remove the lid.

Add the remaining ingredients, except for cilantro. Bring to HIGH pressure and maintain pressure for 2 minutes longer.

Serve chilled and topped with fresh cilantro. Enjoy!

Beef and Tortilla Casserole with Cheese

(Ready in about 30 minutes | Servings 6)

Ingredients

2 tablespoons olive oil

1 shallot, chopped

1 (4 ½-ounce can) chopped mild green chili peppers

2 cloves garlic, minced

1 ¼ pounds lean ground beef

1 ½ tablespoons chili powder

1/2 teaspoon ground cumin

1 (14-ounce) can crushed tomatoes

1/4 cup loosely packed fresh cilantro leaves, chopped

6 corn tortillas

8 ounces Cheddar cheese, shredded

Directions

Set a large saucepan over medium heat. Then, heat the oil, and sauté the shallots approximately 3 minutes. Stir in the chili peppers and garlic; cook for 1 to 2 minutes.

Stir in the ground beef. Continue cooking, stirring frequently, until the beef has lightly browned, about 4 minutes.

Stir in the chili powder and ground cumin. Add the tomatoes and cilantro. Cook another 2 minutes and remove the saucepan from the heat.

Set the pressure cooker rack; pour in 2 cups water. Ladle a half of the beef sauce into a casserole dish. Add a tortilla, then, add 1/2 cup of the sauce, and 1/2 cup of Cheddar cheese. Repeat the layering five more times.

Next, cover the casserole with an aluminum foil. Set the casserole on an aluminum sling. Lock the lid onto the cooking pot.

Set the pot over HIGH heat. Cook for 20 minutes. Then, remove the lid. Serve warm.

Old-Fashioned Beef and Potato Stew

(Ready in about 55 minutes | Servings 4)

Ingredients

2 tablespoons olive oil

1 small-sized onion, thinly sliced

3 cloves garlic, peeled and minced

1 ¼ pounds beef, cubed

4 potatoes, peeled and diced

1 teaspoon dried basil

1 teaspoon dried oregano

1 teaspoon dried sage

1 teaspoon dried rosemary

1 cup tomato sauce

1 ¼ cups water

1/2 cup white wine

Salt and black pepper, to taste

1 teaspoon cayenne pepper

Directions

Place a cooker over medium heat. Swirl in the oil. Now sauté the onion, garlic, and beef until the meat has browned and the onion has softened.

Stir in the remaining ingredients; give it a good stir. Cook for 45 minutes at LOW pressure. Serve warm over cooked rice if desired.

Beef and Quinoa Delight

(Ready in about 25 minutes | Servings 6)

Ingredients

1 tablespoon olive oil

1 medium-sized leek, thinly sliced

2 cloves garlic, minced

1 pound top round, cut into strips

1 teaspoon ground coriander

1 teaspoon sea salt

1 teaspoon red pepper flakes, crushed

1/2 teaspoon freshly ground black pepper

1 cup plain yogurt

1 (28-ounce) can stewed tomatoes

2 cups cooked quinoa

Directions

Set a cooking pot over medium heat. Swirl in the oil. Now sauté the leeks until tender and fragrant. Add the remaining ingredients, except for quinoa, to your pressure cooker.

Turn the heat up to HIGH. Reduce the heat maintaining the pressure. Cook for 15 minutes at HIGH pressure.

Afterward, open your cooker by releasing pressure. Serve over prepared quinoa.

Meatballs with Pasta and Sauce

(Ready in about 10 minutes | Servings 4)

Ingredients

1 pound lean ground beef

1 teaspoon dried marjoram

1 tablespoon dried basil

1 teaspoon dried rosemary

2 tablespoons olive oil

1 large fennel bulb, trimmed and chopped

1 medium leek, chopped

1 red bell pepper, coarsely chopped

8 ounces dried pasta of choice

3 ½ cups tomatoes, diced

1/2 cup beef broth

1/2 cup water

1/2 cup dry white wine

Sea salt, to your liking

Directions

Mix the beef, marjoram, basil, and rosemary in a medium-sized mixing bowl. Form the mixture into 20 meatballs.

Heat olive oil in a pressure cooker set over medium heat. Add the fennel, leek, and bell pepper; cook, stirring frequently, for about 5 minutes.

Stir in the pasta, tomatoes, beef broth, water, wine, and salt. Add the meatballs and lock the lid.

Raise the heat to HIGH. When the pressure has been reached, reduce the heat while maintaining this pressure. Cook for 5 minutes.

Lastly, open your cooker by releasing pressure with the quick-release method. Stir gently before serving and enjoy!

Meatball and Cabbage Casserole

(Ready in about 15 minutes | Servings 4)

Ingredients

1 head cabbage, shredded

1 teaspoon fennel seeds

1 ½ pounds lean ground beef

3/4 cup cooked rice

1 medium onion, minced

1 large egg plus 1 large egg yolk

1/4 cup fresh parsley, chopped

2 cloves garlic, minced

1/2 teaspoon salt

1/2 teaspoon ground black pepper

1 (28-ounce) can tomatoes, crushed

2 tablespoons lemon juice

1/2 cup water

Directions

Stir the cabbage and fennel seeds in a mixing bowl. Use 1/2 of this mixture to make a bed in the bottom of a pressure cooker.

In another bowl, combine the beef, cooked rice, onion, egg, egg yolk, fresh parsley, garlic, salt, and ground black pepper. Mix to combine well.

Form the mixture into 20 meatballs. Lay half of these meatballs over the cabbage mixture; then, top with a layer of the remaining cabbage mixture. Nestle the remaining meatballs in this cabbage mixture.

Whisk the tomatoes, lemon juice, and water in a large-sized mixing bowl. Pour into the pressure cooker. Lock the lid onto the pot.

Set the pot over HIGH heat. Then, reduce the heat and maintain this pressure. Cook for 7 minutes. Use the quick-release method to release the pressure. Unlock and open the lid. Serve in individual serving bowls. Enjoy!

Meatballs with Cabbage and Cranberries

(Ready in about 15 minutes | Servings 4)

Ingredients

1 head cabbage, shredded

6 tablespoons cranberries

1/2 teaspoon cumin seeds

1 pound lean ground beef

1/2 pound ground pork

3/4 cup cooked rice

1 shallot, minced

1 large egg plus 1 large egg yolk

1/4 cup fresh cilantro, chopped

3 cloves garlic, minced

1/2 teaspoon salt

1/2 teaspoon ground black pepper

1 teaspoon cayenne pepper

1 (28-ounce) can tomatoes, crushed

2 tablespoons balsamic vinegar

1/2 cup water

Directions

Add the cabbage, cranberries, and cumin seeds to a pressure cooker.

In a bowl, combine ground beef, ground pork, cooked rice, shallot, egg, egg yolk, fresh cilantro, garlic, salt, black pepper, and cayenne pepper. Mix to combine well.

Form the mixture into 20 meatballs. Nestle the meatballs in the cabbage mixture.

Whisk the tomatoes, balsamic vinegar and water in a measuring cup or a bowl. Pour the mixture into the pressure cooker. Lock the lid onto the pot.

Set the pot over HIGH heat. Cook for 7 minutes. Use the quick-release method to release the pressure. Unlock and open the lid. Serve warm.

Pork with Yogurt Sauce

(Ready in about 30 minutes | Servings 6)

Ingredients

1 tablespoon olive oil

1 onion, diced

2 cloves garlic, minced

1 pound pork, cubed

1 tablespoon coriander

1 teaspoon chili powder

Salt and black pepper, to taste

1 teaspoon cayenne pepper

2 medium-sized tomatoes, chopped

1 cup yogurt

Directions

Start by melting the oil over medium heat in a pressure cooking pot. Sauté the onion and minced garlic until they have softened.

Add the remaining ingredients, except the yogurt, to the pressure cooker.

Cook for 15 minutes at HIGH pressure. Next, open the cooker by releasing pressure.

Afterward, add the yogurt; simmer until it has thickened, approximately 10 minutes. Serve warm.

Holiday Beef Roast

(Ready in about 45 minutes | Servings 8)

Ingredients

1/2 pound carrots

2 stalks celery, diced

2 medium-sized turnips, chopped

2 parsnips, diced

2 bell peppers, seeded and thinly sliced

1 onion, peeled and sliced

2 cloves garlic, peeled and minced

1 boneless chuck roast, into serving-sized portions

1 envelope onion soup mix

Salt and ground black pepper, to taste

1 teaspoon cayenne pepper

1 teaspoon dried rosemary

1 cup water

1 cup tomato juice

Directions

Lay the vegetables in the bottom of your pressure cooker. Place the chuck roast on the vegetable layer.

In a mixing bowl, combine the remaining ingredients; mix well to combine. Now pour the mixture into the pressure cooking pot.

Then, bring to LOW pressure; maintain pressure for 45 minutes. Transfer the roast and vegetables to a serving platter. Serve and enjoy!

Mom's Gourmet Sauerkraut

(Ready in about 20 minutes | Servings 6)

Ingredients

1 pounds lean ground beef

1/2 pound ground pork

1 leek, thinly sliced

3 cloves garlic, minced

1 (5-ounce) can tomatoes, diced

1 cup tomato juice

3 cups sauerkraut, shredded

Salt and freshly ground black pepper, to taste

2 bay leaves

1 teaspoon red pepper, crushed

Directions

Add the ground beef, pork, leek and garlic to the pressure cooker. Cook over medium-high heat until the meat becomes lightly browned; drain off any rendered fat.

Stir in the remaining ingredients. Cover the cooker.

Now bring to LOW pressure and maintain pressure for 8 minutes.

Afterward, allow pressure to release gradually. Discard the bay leaves and serve warm.

Halibut Fillets with Artichokes

(Ready in about 10 minutes | Servings 4)

Ingredients

Non-stick cooking spray

4 skinless halibut fillets

1 lemon, sliced

20 olives, pitted

2 (6-ounce) jars marinated artichoke hearts, drained

4 tablespoons dry white wine

Salt and ground black pepper, to taste

2 cups water

Directions

Brush 4 (13-inch-square) sheets parchment paper with some nonstick cooking spray. Place a fish fillet on the parchment.

Top each fillet with a few lemon slices, five olives, and a few artichoke hearts; drizzle each fillet with one tablespoon of dry wine. Season with salt and black pepper to your liking. Make the fish packages.

Place a trivet and steamer basket in your pressure cooker. Pour in the water. Stack the fish packages in the steamer basket.

Close and lock the lid. Cook for 5 minutes, maintaining HIGH pressure. Remove the pot from the heat.

Open the cooker using the Quick Release method. Serve warm.

Flavorful Trout with Lemon Mayonnaise

(Ready in about 10 minutes | Servings 4)

Ingredients

1 cup mayonnaise

1 teaspoon grated lemon zest

1 tablespoon low-sodium soy sauce

2 teaspoons hot sauce, or to taste

1 head butter lettuce, torn into large pieces

3/4 cup chicken stock

2 tablespoons dry white wine

4 (6- to 8-ounce) trout, cleaned and boned

Sea salt and freshly ground black, to taste

1 teaspoon dried rosemary

4 tablespoons olive oil

2 lemons, thinly sliced

Directions

Make the lemon mayonnaise by mixing first four ingredients; whisk to combine well. Transfer in a refrigerator.

In a pressure cooker, arrange about 2/3 of the lettuce leaves to make a bed. Pour in the chicken stock and dry white wine.

Season each trout with salt, black pepper, and rosemary. Drizzle with the olive oil. Stuff each trout with the lemon slices. Set the trout on top of the lettuce bad. Cover everything with the remaining lettuce leaves.

Close and lock the lid. Now cook for 3 minutes at HIGH pressure. Open the cooker with the Quick Release method. Serve warm with the lemon mayonnaise on the side. Enjoy!

Vegetarian Chickpea Stew

(Ready in about 30 minutes | Servings 4)

Ingredients

1 (14-ounce) can chickpeas, drained

2 eggplants, cut into large cubes

1 carrot, diced

1 celery stalk, chopped

1 parsnip, chopped

6 cups vegetable stock

1 cup tomato paste

1 teaspoon celery seeds

1/2 teaspoon fennel seeds

1/2 cup fresh cilantro, chopped

1 teaspoon salt

1/4 teaspoon ground black pepper

Directions

Add all of the above ingredients to your pressure cooker; lock the cooker's lid into place.

Bring to LOW pressure and cook for about 30 minutes. Next, allow pressure to release according to manufacturer's instructions.

To serve, ladle the stew into individual bowls. Enjoy!

The Best Vegan Gumbo Ever

(Ready in about 1 hour 35 minutes | Servings 6)

Ingredients

1/2 cup olive oil

1/2 cup flour

1 red onion, diced

1 red bell pepper, diced

1 green bell pepper, diced

1 carrot, diced

1 stalk celery, diced

2 parsnips, chopped

4 cloves garlic, minced

2 cups water

4 cups vegetable stock

1 tablespoon vegan Worcestershire sauce

1 (16-ounce) package frozen okra, chopped

2 bay leaves

1 teaspoon cayenne pepper

Sea salt and black pepper, to taste

1 pound vegan chicken, chopped

1/4 cup fresh cilantro, chopped

1/4 cup fresh parsley, chopped

6 cups hot cooked rice

Directions

To make the roux: Heat olive oil over medium heat. Now add the flour and cook, stirring often, until the roux gets a brown rich color, approximately 25 minutes.

Add the onion, bell peppers, carrot, celery, parsnips, and garlic to the roux; sauté for 5 minutes. Add the water and stock, bringing to a boil over HIGH heat.

Add the remaining ingredients, except for rice. Now bring to LOW pressure; maintain the pressure for 1 hour 10 minutes.

Allow the pressure to release naturally and gradually. Serve over cooked rice.

Yummy Sauerkraut with Pork and Bacon

(Ready in about 20 minutes | Servings 6)

Ingredients

1/2 pound ground pork

6 slices bacon, cut into pieces

2 cloves garlic, minced

1 red onion, thinly sliced

1 cup beef stock

3 cups sauerkraut, shredded

Salt and freshly ground black pepper, to taste

1 tablespoon brown sugar

2 bay leaves

Directions

Add the pork, bacon, garlic and onion to a pressure cooking pot. Cook over medium-high heat until the pork has lightly browned; drain off any excess fat.

Stir in the rest of the above ingredients. Cover and bring to LOW pressure, maintaining pressure for 10 minutes.

Afterward, allow pressure to release naturally. Serve right now.

Roasted Cod Fillets with Vegetables

(Ready in about 10 minutes | Servings 4)

Ingredients

Non-stick cooking spray

4 skinless cod fillets

1 lime, sliced

2 red bell peppers, thinly sliced

1 red onion, thinly sliced

4 tablespoons dry white wine

Salt and ground black pepper, to taste

1 teaspoon dried rosemary

1/2 teaspoon dried marjoram

1/2 teaspoon dried thyme

2 cups water

Directions

Coat 4 (13-inch-square) sheets of parchment paper with nonstick cooking spray. Place a cod fillet on the parchment.

To make the fish packages, top each fillet with a few lime slices, a few slices of pepper, and a few slices of red onion; drizzle each fillet with one tablespoon of dry wine. Season with salt, black pepper, rosemary, marjoram, and thyme.

Place a trivet and steamer basket in the pressure cooker. Pour in 2 cups of water. Arrange the fish packages in the steamer basket.

Cook for 5 minutes at HIGH pressure. Remove the cooking pot from the heat.

Open the cooker using the Quick Release method. Serve on four individual plates.

Herbed Braised Cauliflower

(Ready in about 10 minutes | Servings 6)

Ingredients

2 tablespoons olive oil

1/2 cup scallions, chopped

2 cloves garlic, crushed

1 pound cauliflower, cut into florets

1/2 teaspoon salt

1/4 teaspoon ground black pepper

1 teaspoon cayenne pepper

1/2 teaspoon dried basil

3/4 cups water

Directions

Heat olive oil in a pressure cooker over medium heat. Add scallions and garlic; sauté, stirring often, about 2 minutes. Add the cauliflower florets and continue to cook for about 5 minutes.

Sprinkle with salt, ground black pepper, cayenne pepper, dried basil, and water.

Cook for 3 minutes at HIGH pressure. Afterward, open the cooker by following the manufacturer's directions. Serve over rice if desired.

Steaks in Coconut Milk Sauce

(Ready in about 10 minutes | Servings 4)

Ingredients

1 tablespoon olive oil

2 onions, finely minced

2 tablespoons fresh ginger, peeled and grated

1/2 cup fresh cilantro, coarsely chopped

1 stalk lemongrass, chopped into pieces

1 tablespoon soy sauce

1 (14-ounce) can coconut milk

4 mahi-mahi steaks

Sea salt and ground black pepper

4 green onions, sliced

2 lemons, sliced

Directions

In a pressure cooker, heat the olive oil over medium heat. Cook the onions until soft, about 2 minutes. Add the ginger, cilantro, lemongrass, soy sauce, and coconut milk. Bring to a simmer.

Add steaks, salt, black pepper, and green onions. Close and lock the lid. Set the burner heat to HIGH. Set a timer to cook for 3 minutes.

Open the cooker with the Natural Release method; let stand for 10 minutes. Serve immediately garnished with lemon slices.

Brussels Sprouts with Pine Nuts

(Ready in about 10 minutes | Servings 6)

Ingredients

1 cup water

1 pound Brussels sprouts, outer leaves removed and halved

2 tablespoons sesame oil

1 teaspoon salt

1/2 teaspoon black pepper

1 teaspoon cayenne pepper

1/2 cup pine nuts, toasted and chopped

Dried cranberries, for garnish

Directions

Start by pouring the water into a pressure cooker. Now place the steamer basket in the pressure cooker.

Then, throw Brussels sprouts in the steamer basket. Drizzle them with sesame oil. Sprinkle with salt, black pepper, and cayenne pepper. Close and lock the lid according to manufacturer's instructions.

Turn the heat up to HIGH. Cook for about 4 minutes at HIGH pressure.

Transfer the sprouts to a serving dish. Sprinkle with toasted pine nuts and dried cranberries. Serve.

Braised Cabbage in Beer

(Ready in about 10 minutes | Servings 6)

Ingredients

2 tablespoons butter

1 onion, sliced

2 cloves garlic, minced

1 medium head cabbage, cut into strips

3⁄4 cup beer

Salt and black pepper, to your taste

1 teaspoon cayenne pepper

Directions

Start by melting the butter in a cooker over medium heat. Then, sauté the onion and garlic, stirring periodically, until they have softened.

Stir in cabbage and beer. Now set the temperature to HIGH; cook for 5 minutes at HIGH pressure.

Lastly, open the cooker by releasing pressure. Then, sprinkle with salt, black pepper, and cayenne pepper; serve and enjoy.

Saucy Cabbage with Soy Sauce

(Ready in about 10 minutes | Servings 4)

Ingredients

4 cups cabbage, cut into strips

2 carrots, grated

2 cloves garlic, minced

1 medium-sized red onion, chopped

1 jalapeño pepper, finely minced

1⁄2 cup vegetable stock

1⁄4 cup soy sauce

Directions

Add the cabbage, carrots, garlic, red onion, and jalapeño pepper to a pressure cooker. Then, stir in the vegetable stock and soy sauce; give it a good stir.

Cover the cooker and bring to HIGH pressure; maintain pressure for 3 minutes.

Afterward, remove the lid according to manufacturer's directions. Transfer to a large-sized platter and serve.

Easy Rice Pilaf

(Ready in about 10 minutes | Servings 6)

Ingredients

2 tablespoons olive oil

1/3 cup shallots, minced

1 ½ cups long-grain white rice

1/2 teaspoon sea salt

1/4 teaspoon ground black pepper

2 ¼ cups vegetable broth

Directions

In a pressure cooker, heat olive oil over medium heat. Add the shallots and rice; then, cook, stirring periodically, until the onion is translucent. Add the salt, black pepper, and broth.

Close and lock the lid. Set the burner heat to HIGH. After that reduce the heat, maintaining HIGH pressure. Set a timer to cook for 4 minutes.

Open the cooker with the Natural Release method. Serve as a light, healthy dinner.

Spring Mushroom Risotto

(Ready in about 10 minutes | Servings 4)

Ingredients

2 tablespoons olive oil

1/3 cup green onions, finely chopped

1/4 cup green garlic, minced

1 cup mushrooms, chopped

1/2 cup carrots, julienned

1 cup jasmine rice

1/2 teaspoon paprika

1/2 teaspoon sea salt

1/4 teaspoon ground black pepper

2 ¼ cups chicken stock

Directions

Heat a pressure cooking pot over medium heat. Swirl olive oil in the cooker until hot. Add green onion, green garlic, mushroom, carrots, and jasmine rice.

Cook, stirring occasionally, until the onion is translucent. Add the paprika, sea salt, black pepper, and chicken stock.

Set the burner heat to HIGH. After that, reduce the heat, maintaining HIGH pressure. Cook for 4 minutes.

Open the cooker using the Natural Release method. Serve warm.

Yummy Vegan Gumbo

(Ready in about 2 hours | Servings 6)

Ingredients

1/2 cup canola oil

1/2 cup all-purpose flour

1 onion, diced

1 red bell pepper, diced

1 carrot, diced

1 stalk celery, diced

4 cloves garlic, minced

2 cups vegetable broth

4 cups water

1 tablespoon Vegan Worcestershire sauce

1 (16-ounce) package frozen chopped okra

2 bay leaves

Sea salt and black pepper, to taste

1 pound vegan chicken, chopped

1/2 cup parsley, chopped

6 cups hot cooked rice

Directions

Warm canola oil over medium heat in your pressure cooker. To make the roux: add the flour and cook, stirring frequently, until your roux gets a rich brown color, or for about 25 minutes.

Add the onion, bell pepper, carrot, celery, and garlic to the roux; continue to sauté for 5 minutes. Add the broth and water, bringing to a boil over HIGH heat for 20 minutes.

Add the rest of the above ingredients, except for rice. Cover, bring to LOW pressure and maintain for 1 hour 10 minutes. Afterwards, allow pressure to release naturally.

Serve over prepared rice and enjoy!

Barley and Chickpea Stew

(Ready in about 20 minutes | Servings 4)

Ingredients

1 cup barley

1 cup dry chickpeas, soaked

2 tablespoons olive oil, divided

2 cloves garlic, pressed

1 onion, diced

2 carrots, diced

1 parsnip, chopped

2 celery stalks, diced

1/2 head red cabbage, shredded

4 cups water

1 teaspoon sea salt

1/2 teaspoon ground black pepper

1/2 teaspoon cayenne pepper

Directions

Simply throw all of the above ingredients in the pressure cooker. Close and lock the lid.

Turn the heat to HIGH and cook your stew for 15 minutes at HIGH pressure.

Open with a natural release method. Release the rest of the pressure with the cooker's valve.

Season to taste and serve right away!

Asian-Style Tofu Stew

(Ready in about 15 minutes | Servings 4)

Ingredients

2 tablespoons sesame oil

1 small-sized onion, sliced

2 cloves garlic, minced

1 cup broccoli, chopped into florets

1 cup mushrooms, sliced

12 ounces soft silken tofu, drained and cubed

1 tablespoon red pepper, crushed

1 teaspoon tamari sauce

3 cups vegetable stock

Fresh chives, for garnish

Directions

Warm the sesame oil over medium heat in your pressure cooker. Then, sauté the onion and garlic for 3 to 4 minutes.

Add the rest of your ingredients, except for chives, to the pressure cooker. Cover with the lid; bring to LOW pressure and maintain for 5 minutes. Remove from heat and allow pressure to release naturally.

Remove the lid and serve in individual bowls. Sprinkle with chives. Enjoy!

Beef and Mushroom Stew

(Ready in about 35 minutes | Servings 8)

Ingredients

1 (3-pound) chuck roast, cut into bite-sized pieces

2 (4-ounce) cans mushrooms, drained and sliced

2 (10 3/4-ounce) cans cream of mushroom soup

2 cups water

1 tablespoon Worcestershire sauce

3 (24-ounce) bags frozen vegetables, thawed

Salt and freshly ground black pepper, to taste

1 teaspoon red pepper flakes, crushed

Directions

Add chuck roast, mushroom, mushroom soup, water, and Worcestershire sauce to the pressure cooker.

Then, bring to LOW pressure; maintain pressure for 30 minutes. Stir in frozen vegetables. Bring to a simmer and maintain pressure for 5 minutes.

Sprinkle with salt, black pepper, and red pepper. Taste for seasoning and serve warm.

Veggies in Lime-Butter Sauce

(Ready in about 10 minutes | Servings 6)

Ingredients

2 cups cauliflower florets

2 cups broccoli florets

1/2 teaspoon salt

1/2 teaspoon black pepper

1/2 teaspoon dried dill weed

1 cup water

4 tablespoons butter

1 tablespoon lime juice

1/2 teaspoon yellow mustard

Directions

Put the cauliflower, broccoli, salt, black pepper, dried dill, and water into your pressure cooker. Cover and bring to LOW pressure; maintain pressure for 2 to 3 minutes.

Turn off the heat; quick-release the pressure; remove the cooker's lid.

To make the sauce: whisk together the butter, lime juice, and yellow mustard. Drizzle the sauce over the cooked cauliflower and broccoli. Serve.

Delicious Braised Cauliflower

(Ready in about 10 minutes | Servings 6)

Ingredients

2 tablespoons sesame oil

1/2 cup sweet onion, chopped

2 cloves garlic, crushed

1/4 teaspoon pepper flakes, crushed

1 pound cauliflower, cut into florets

1/2 teaspoon salt

1/4 teaspoon ground black pepper

1/2 teaspoon dried basil

3/4 cups water

Directions

Heat sesame oil in your pressure cooker over medium heat. Add sweet onion, garlic, and red pepper flakes; cook, stirring continuously, for about 2 minutes. Add the cauliflower florets and continue cooking for about 5 minutes.

Sprinkle with salt, black pepper, and dried basil; add the water.

Cook for 2 to 3 minutes at HIGH pressure. Lastly, open the cooker by following the manufacturer's instructions. Serve over rice.

Seared Brussels Sprouts

(Ready in about 10 minutes | Servings 6)

Ingredients

2 tablespoons butter, at room temperature

1 pound Brussels sprouts, outer leaves removed and halved

1/4 cup water

Salt and ground black pepper, to taste

1 teaspoon red pepper flakes, to taste

Directions

Add butter to your pressure cooker and melt it over medium-high heat. When the butter is melted, cook your Brussels sprouts for a few minutes or until tender.

Add the water, and lock on the lid. Bring to HIGH pressure, and maintain pressure for about 1 minute. Season with salt, black pepper, and red pepper to taste. Serve as a perfect light dinner.

Brussel Sprout Salad with Walnuts

(Ready in about 10 minutes | Servings 6)

Ingredients

1 cup water

1 pound Brussels sprouts, outer leaves removed and halved

2 tablespoons olive oil

1 teaspoon salt

1/4 teaspoon black pepper

1/2 cup walnuts, toasted and chopped

Dried cranberries, for garnish

Directions

Begin by pouring the water into your pressure cooker. Then, add the steamer basket to the cooker.

Throw Brussels sprouts in the steamer basket. Close and lock the cooker's lid according to manufacturer's instructions.

Turn the heat up to HIGH; when the pressure is reached, lower the heat to the minimum that is needed to maintain pressure. Cook for about 4 minutes at HIGH pressure.

Replace the sprouts to a serving dish. Drizzle your Brussels sprouts with olive oil; season with salt and black pepper. Sprinkle with walnuts and cranberries. Enjoy!

Aunt's Savoy Cabbage

(Ready in about 10 minutes | Servings 6)

Ingredients

2 tablespoons ghee or butter

1 yellow onion, sliced

1 clove garlic, minced

1 medium Savoy cabbage, cut into strips

3⁄4 cup beer

Salt and black pepper, to your taste

1/2 teaspoon smoked paprika

Directions

Begin by melting ghee (butter) in an uncovered cooker over medium heat. Then, sauté the onions and garlic, stirring occasionally, until they are fragrant and softened.

Stir in Savoy cabbage and beer. Cover and set the temperature to HIGH; cook for 5 minutes at HIGH pressure.

Afterwards, open the cooker by releasing pressure. Replace the cabbage to a nice serving platter; sprinkle with salt, black pepper, and smoked paprika; serve.

Tangy Red Cabbage

(Ready in about 10 minutes | Servings 4)

Ingredients

2 cloves garlic, minced

1 bunch scallions, sliced

1 chili pepper, finely minced

1⁄2 cup water

1⁄4 cup tamari sauce

4 cups red cabbage, cut into strips

2 carrots, julienned

Directions

Add the garlic, scallions, chili pepper, water, and tamari sauce to your pressure cooker; stir well. Stir in the cabbage and carrots.

Cover and bring to HIGH pressure; maintain pressure for 2 minutes.

Afterwards, remove the lid according to manufacturer's instructions. Transfer to a large platter and serve.

Red Cabbage with Pine Nuts

(Ready in about 10 minutes | Servings 8)

Ingredients

2 tablespoons olive oil

1 onion, diced

2 apples, peeled, cored, and sliced

1/2 cup white wine

1 head red cabbage, cut into strips

1 teaspoon kosher salt

1/2 teaspoon freshly ground black pepper

Pine nuts, for garnish

Directions

Heat olive oil in your pressure cooker over medium heat. Sauté the onion until translucent and soft.

Add the apples and wine.

Stir the cabbage into the pressure cooker. Cover and cook for 2 to 4 minutes at HIGH pressure.

When time is up, open the pressure cooker according to manufacturer's instructions. Season with salt and black pepper. Sprinkle with pine nuts and serve immediately.

Delicious Carrots in Milk Sauce

(Ready in about 10 minutes | Servings 4)

Ingredients

1 pound carrots, cut into 1-inch chunks

1/4 cup water

3/4 cup milk

Sea salt and white pepper, to taste

2 tablespoons olive oil

1 tablespoon flour

Directions

Fill your cooker with carrots, water, milk, salt, white pepper, and olive oil. Cover with the lid.

Turn the heat up to HIGH. Cook approximately 4 minutes at HIGH pressure. Afterwards, open the pressure cooker by releasing pressure.

Next, remove carrots to serving dish using a slotted spoon.

To make the sauce: Place the pressure cooker over medium heat. Add flour and cook until the sauce has thickened, stirring continuously. Serve the sauce over prepared carrots and enjoy!

Flavorful Ginger Carrots

(Ready in about 5 minutes | Servings 4)

Ingredients

1 pound carrots, peeled and cut into matchsticks

2 tablespoons olive oil

1 teaspoon fresh ginger, minced

1 cup water

Kosher salt and ground black pepper, to your taste

1/2 teaspoon allspice

Directions

Add the carrot matchsticks, olive oil, ginger, and water to your cooker. Stir to combine well. Close and lock the cooker's lid.

Cook for 1 minute at HIGH pressure. Open the pressure cooker according to manufacturer's directions.

Season with salt, black pepper and allspice; serve right away!

Butter Corn Evening Treat

(Ready in about 10 minutes | Servings 4)

Ingredients

4 ears sweet corn, shucked

1/2 cup water

1 tablespoon butter

1/2 teaspoon cinnamon

Salt and white pepper, to taste

Directions

Place a rack in your pressure cooker; arrange the corn on the rack. Pour in the water.

Then, bring to LOW pressure; maintain pressure for about 3 minutes. Remove the lid according to manufacturer's directions.

Spread softened butter over each ear of corn; sprinkle with cinnamon, salt and white pepper. Serve.

Cilantro and Orange Sweet Corn

(Ready in about 10 minutes | Servings 4)

Ingredients

4 ears sweet corn, shucked

1/2 cup water

2 tablespoons butter

2 tablespoons fresh cilantro, chopped

2 teaspoons fresh orange juice

1/2 teaspoon orange rind, grated

Kosher salt and white pepper, to taste

1/2 teaspoon paprika

1/4 teaspoon grated nutmeg

Directions

Put a rack into your pressure cooking pot; lay the ears of corn on the rack. Pour the water into the cooker.

Cook for 3 minutes at LOW pressure.

In a small-sized bowl, combine the rest of the ingredients until they are well blended. Afterwards, spread this mixture on prepared ears of corn. Serve.

Tomato and Eggplant Salad

(Ready in about 15 minutes | Servings 6)

Ingredients

1 eggplant, peeled and diced

1/2 cup water

3 tablespoons vegetable oil

2 cloves garlic, minced

2 cups tomatoes, chopped

1 tablespoon white wine

1 teaspoon cayenne pepper

Sea salt and black pepper, to taste

2 tablespoons fresh parsley

Directions

Throw the eggplant and water in your pressure cooker. Cover and bring to HIGH pressure; maintain pressure for 4 minutes. Quick release the pressure, remove the lid and set aside.

Add the rest of the above ingredients, except for parsley. Bring to HIGH pressure and maintain pressure for about 2 minutes.

Sprinkle with fresh parsley and serve chilled.

Country Beef and Potato Stew

(Ready in about 55 minutes | Servings 4)

Ingredients

2 tablespoons olive oil

1 pound beef, cubed

1 small-sized onion, thinly sliced

3 cloves garlic, peeled and minced

4 potatoes, peeled and diced

1 teaspoon dried oregano

1/2 teaspoon dried basil

1 cup tomato sauce

1 cup water

3/4 cup white wine

Salt and black pepper, to taste

Directions

Warm olive oil in a cooking pot. Sauté the beef, onion, and garlic until the meat has browned and the onion becomes translucent.

Add the remaining ingredients; stir to combine ingredients well. Cover and cook for 45 minutes at LOW pressure. Serve over cooked rice and enjoy!

Creamed Beef with Quinoa

(Ready in about 25 minutes | Servings 6)

Ingredients

1 tablespoon olive oil

1 yellow onion, thinly sliced

2 cloves garlic, minced

1 pound top round, cut into strips

1/2 teaspoon cloves, ground

1 teaspoon ground coriander

3/4 teaspoon salt

1/2 teaspoon freshly ground black pepper

1 cup plain yogurt

1 (28-ounce) can whole stewed tomatoes

2 cups prepared quinoa

Directions

Heat olive oil in a cooking pot over medium heat. Sauté the onion until tender and translucent. Add the rest of the ingredients, except for quinoa, to your pressure cooker.

Turn the heat up to HIGH; when the cooker reaches pressure, lower the heat. Cook for about 15 minutes at HIGH pressure.

Afterwards, open the pressure cooker by releasing pressure. Serve over prepared quinoa.

Saucy Beef in Yogurt

(Ready in about 30 minutes | Servings 6)

Ingredients

1 tablespoon butter, at room temperature

1 red onion, diced

5 green garlics, minced

1 pound bottom round, cubed

1 tablespoon cumin

1 tablespoon coriander

1/2 teaspoon cardamom

1 teaspoon chili powder

Salt and black pepper, to taste

2 ripe tomatoes, chopped

1 cup whole milk yogurt

Directions

Start by melting the butter over medium heat in your cooker. Sauté the onion and green garlic until they are softened.

Add the remaining ingredients, except for the yogurt, to your pressure cooker.

Cook for 13 to 15 minutes at HIGH pressure. Lastly, open the cooker by releasing pressure.

Pour in the yogurt; simmer until it has thickened, or 10 to 12 minutes. Serve warm.

Corned Beef and Cabbage

(Ready in about 1 hour | Servings 6)

Ingredients

Non-stick cooking spray

2 onions, peeled and sliced

1 corned beef brisket

1 cup apple juice

2 teaspoons orange zest, finely grated

2 teaspoons yellow mustard

1/2 head cabbage, diced

Sea salt and ground black pepper, to taste

Directions

Treat the inside of the cooker with non-stick cooking spray. Arrange the onions on the bottom of your cooker.

Add the beef, apple juice, orange zest, and yellow mustard. Lock the lid into place; bring to LOW pressure; maintain for 45 minutes. Afterwards, remove the lid.

Place the cabbage on top of the ingredients. Then, bring to LOW pressure; maintain pressure for 8 minutes. Season with salt and black pepper to taste.

Carve the brisket and serve.

Old-Fashioned Beef Roast

(Ready in about 45 minutes | Servings 8)

Ingredients

1/2 pound carrots

2 parsnips, diced

2 stalks celery, diced

1 red bell pepper, seeded and thinly sliced

1 green bell pepper, seeded and thinly sliced

1 onion, peeled and sliced

2 cloves garlic, peeled and minced

1 boneless chuck roast, into serving-sized portions

1 envelope onion soup mix

Salt and ground black pepper, to taste

1 cup water

1 cup tomato juice

Directions

Arrange the vegetables in the bottom of your pressure cooker. Lay the chuck roast on the vegetable layer.

In a mixing bowl, combine the rest of the ingredients; mix well to combine; pour the mixture into the pressure cooker.

Then, bring to LOW pressure; maintain pressure for 45 minutes. Serve warm.

Burger and Cabbage

(Ready in about 20 minutes | Servings 6)

Ingredients

1 ½ pounds lean ground beef

1 leek, diced

1 1(5-ounce) can tomatoes, diced

1 cup tomato juice

3 cups cabbage, shredded

Salt and freshly ground black pepper, to taste

1 teaspoon cayenne pepper

Directions

Add the ground beef and leek to the pressure cooker. Cook over medium-high heat until your beef is lightly browned; drain off any rendered fat.

Stir in the rest of the ingredients.

Lock the lid into place; bring to LOW pressure and maintain pressure for about 8 minutes. Then, allow pressure to release gradually and naturally. Uncover, taste and adjust for seasonings. Serve.

Chicken in Orange Sauce with Walnuts

(Ready in about 20 minutes | Servings 8)

Ingredients

2 tablespoons margarine

3 pounds chicken thighs, boneless and skinless

1 teaspoon dried dill

1/2 teaspoon salt

1/4 teaspoon black pepper, ground

1/4 teaspoon fresh or dried ginger

1/2 cup white raisins

1/2 cup chopped walnuts

1 ½ cups orange juice

1 tablespoon cornstarch

1/4 cup cold water

Directions

Begin by melting margarine in the pressure cooker over MEDIUM heat. Then, fry the chicken thighs for 2 to 3 minutes, turning once. Add the remaining ingredients, except for cornstarch and water.

Lock the cooker's lid into place. Bring to LOW pressure; maintain pressure for about 10 minutes. Afterwards, remove the lid according to the manufacturer's instructions.

In a small-sized bowl, while whisking vigorously, combine the cornstarch with the water. Slowly stir into the cooker.

Continue to cook for 3 minutes or until the sauce has thickened and the mixture is thoroughly warmed. Serve.

Chicken and Baby Carrots in Tomato Sauce

(Ready in about 20 minutes | Servings 8)

Ingredients

2 tablespoons sesame oil

2 pounds chicken breasts, cubed

1 onion, peeled and finely chopped

1 pound baby carrots

Kosher salt ground black pepper, to taste

1/2 teaspoon curry powder

1 ½ cups tomato juice

1 tablespoon cornstarch

1/4 cup cold water

Directions

Heat sesame oil in the pressure cooker over MEDIUM heat. Sauté the chicken and onion for about 3 minutes, stirring periodically. Add the rest of the above ingredients, except for cornstarch and water.

Lock the cooker's lid into place. Bring to LOW pressure; maintain pressure for about 10 minutes. Uncover and quick-release the pressure.

In a small-sized bowl, combine together the cornstarch and the water. Gradually stir the cornstarch mixture into the pressure cooker.

Cook for 3 minutes or until everything is thoroughly heated. Serve right away.

Traditional Chicken Paprikash

(Ready in about 20 minutes | Servings 8)

Ingredients

2 tablespoons vegetable oil

1 medium-sized leek, peeled and diced

4 cloves garlic, finely minced

1 bell pepper, peeled and sliced

4 chicken breast halves

1/4 cup tomato sauce

2 tablespoons paprika

1 ½ cup chicken broth

1 tablespoon flour

3/4 cup sour cream

Salt and freshly ground black pepper, to taste

Directions

Bring the vegetable oil to temperature in the pressure cooker over medium-high heat. Add the leek, garlic, and bell pepper; then, sauté for about 3 minutes. Add the chicken and continue cooking until it is browned.

In a bowl, combine together the tomato sauce, paprika, and chicken broth. Pour this tomato mixture over the chicken in the cooker. Cover and bring to LOW pressure; maintain pressure approximately 10 minutes.

Remove the chicken from the pot by using a slotted spoon. Divide the chicken among serving plates. Combine together flour and sour cream.

Return the cooker to the heat; stir in the flour mixture. Simmer for 5 minutes, stirring continuously, or until the cooker juices have thickened. Salt and pepper to taste; spoon the sauce over the chicken.

Saucy Collard Greens

(Ready in about 20 minutes | Servings 6)

Ingredients

1 tablespoon canola oil

1 small-sized onion, diced

2 cloves garlic, minced

1 chipotle pepper, minced

4 cups vegetable broth

1 teaspoon liquid smoke

1 tablespoon tamari sauce

1 teaspoon white vinegar

Salt and black pepper, to taste

1 pound collard greens, tough stalks and stems removed, chopped

Directions

Warm the canola oil in your pressure cooker over MEDIUM heat. Add the onion, garlic, and chipotle pepper; sauté until the vegetables begin to soften, or 4 to 5 minutes.

Add all remaining ingredients, except for collard greens; stir well to combine. Lock the lid onto the pressure cooker. Bring the cooker up to HIGH pressure.

Then, maintain pressure for 10 minutes. Remove from the heat and quick-release the pressure. Carefully remove the lid. Add collard greens and simmer until they are completely wilted. Serve warm.

Herbed Fennel in Wine Sauce

(Ready in about 20 minutes | Servings 4)

Ingredients

2 tablespoons butter

1 large-sized sweet onion, diced

4 fennel bulbs, outer leaves removed, diced

1 cup white wine

1/2 teaspoon dried dill weed

1/2 teaspoon celery seeds

Salt and black pepper, to taste

Directions

Begin by bringing the butter to temperature in the pressure cooker over medium heat. Then, sauté sweet onion for about 3 minutes.

Stir in the fennel bulbs and continue sautéing for about 3 minutes. Stir in the wine, dill weed, and celery seeds. Lock the lid onto the pressure cooker, and bring to LOW pressure; maintain for 8 minutes.

Afterwards, remove the lid. Let it simmer until the fennel is thoroughly cooked. Salt and pepper; serve.

Green Beans with Sesame and Dill

(Ready in about 10 minutes | Servings 4)

Ingredients

2 cups water

1 pound green beans, trimmed

1/2 teaspoon cumin

1 teaspoon dill weed

1 tablespoon sesame oil

2 tablespoons sesame seeds, toasted

Salt and freshly cracked black pepper, to taste

Directions

Fill the bottom of your cooker with two cups of water. Place the steamer basket in the cooker.

Then, throw green beans in your steamer basket. Sprinkle the cumin and dill over green beans.

Secure the lid and allow to cook on HIGH; cook until the pressure indicator rises. Now decrease the heat and cook for 5 minutes.

Toss prepared green beans in the sesame oil. Sprinkle with sesame seeds, salt, and black pepper. Toss to combine and serve.

Easy and Yummy Fennel Purée

(Ready in about 20 minutes | Servings 4)

Ingredients

2 tablespoons butter

1 medium-sized leek, sliced

4 fennel bulbs, outer leaves removed, diced

1 cup vegetable broth

1 teaspoon red pepper flakes, crushed

Sea salt and black pepper, to taste

Directions

Melt the butter in the pressure cooker over medium heat. When the butter is melted, sauté the leeks for 3 to 4 minutes.

Add the fennel bulbs and continue sautéing for 3 to 4 minutes. Pour in the vegetable broth. Lock the lid onto the cooker, and bring to LOW pressure; maintain for 8 minutes.

Remove the lid. Then, simmer until the fennel bulbs are thoroughly cooked. Sprinkle with red pepper flakes.

To make a purée: transfer the cooked fennel to the food processor. Pulse until uniform and creamy; add some cooking liquid if necessary. Salt and pepper to your taste. Replace to the serving dish and serve.

Nutty Green Bean Salad

(Ready in about 10 minutes | Servings 4)

Ingredients

1 pound green beans, fresh or frozen

1 cup water

1/4 cup pine nuts, toasted

2 teaspoons lemon juice

1 tablespoon extra-virgin olive oil

Salt and black pepper, to taste

Directions

Arrange green beans in a steamer basket.

Pour the water into the pressure cooker; add the steamer basket. Cover with the lid.

Cook for about 7 minutes at HIGH pressure.

Afterwards, open the cooker by releasing pressure. Dress with pine nuts, lemon juice, and olive oil. Salt and pepper to taste. Serve.

Delicious Spicy Kale

(Ready in about 15 minutes | Servings 4)

Ingredients

2 cups water

1 teaspoon kosher salt

8 cups kale leaves, chopped

2 tablespoon sesame oil

2 cloves garlic, minced

1/2 teaspoon dried dill weed

1 teaspoon dried red pepper flakes

1/2 cup vegetable stock

1/2 teaspoon ground white pepper

Directions

Pour the water into a pressure cooker. Add salt and bring water to a boil. Blanch kale for 1 minute; drain and reserve.

Warm the sesame oil in your pressure cooker over MEDIUM heat. Add the garlic, dill weed, and red pepper flakes; cook for 30 seconds to 1 minute. Add the vegetable stock, white pepper, and reserved kale. Gently stir to combine well.

Cover the cooker, and bring to HIGH pressure; maintain pressure for about 6 minutes. Remove from the heat and carefully remove the lid by following the manufacturer's instructions; serve right now.

Parsnip and Carrot Purée

(Ready in about 20 minutes | Servings 4)

Ingredients

1/2 pound parsnips, peeled and diced

1/2 pound carrots, peeled and diced

3 tablespoons butter or ghee

1 heaping teaspoon salt

1/2 teaspoon freshly cracked black pepper

Fresh chopped parsley, as garnish

Directions

Place the parsnips and carrots in the pressure cooker; add enough water to cover them.

Lock on the cooker's lid. Bring to HIGH pressure; maintain pressure for 3 minutes. Remove the vegetables with a slotted spoon and reserve the cooking water.

Add the parsnips, carrots, and about 1/4 cup of cooking water to a food processor. Mix until it is uniform and smooth, adding more water as needed.

Add the purée back to the cleaned pressure cooker. Add the butter (ghee), salt, and black pepper; cook over LOW heat for 10 minutes, stirring continuously. Transfer to a serving dish and sprinkle with fresh parsley. Enjoy!

Apple Cider Pork

(Ready in about 1 hour 10 minutes | Servings 8)

Ingredients

2 tablespoons butter

1 pork roast

Salt and black pepper, to taste

3 cups apple cider

2 apples, cored and quartered

2 bay leaves

1/4 teaspoon allspice

Directions

Warm the butter on HIGH until melted.

Generously season the pork roast with salt and black pepper; lay pork roast in the cooker and cook until it is browned on each side.

Add the apple cider, apples, bay leaves, and allspice to the pressure cooker; securely lock the cooker's lid. Set to 1 hour on HIGH.

Allow the cooker's pressure to release naturally for about 10 minutes. Carve the pork roast and drizzle with the cooking liquid.

BBQ Back Ribs

(Ready in about 35 minutes | Servings 6)

Ingredients

1 teaspoon garlic powder

1 teaspoon salt

3/4 teaspoon ground black pepper

1 tablespoon cayenne pepper

2 ribs, cut to fit into cooker

1 onion, sliced into rings

1 ½ cups chicken broth

2 tablespoons tomato paste

1 (18-ounce) bottle BBQ sauce

Directions

In a small-sized mixing bowl, combine garlic powder, salt, black pepper, and cayenne pepper. Rub the mixture over the surface of your ribs.

Lay rubbed ribs at the bottom of your cooker; place the onion rings on the ribs; add chicken broth and tomato paste to the pressure cooker. Set the cooker to 15 minutes on HIGH.

Lastly, grill cooked ribs for about 15 minutes, turning once or twice, basting with BBQ sauce.

Creamed Shrimp with Pasta

(Ready in about 20 minutes | Servings 4)

Ingredients

2 tablespoons olive oil

2/3 cup red onion, diced

1 cup dried pasta of choice

12 ounces frozen shrimp

2 ½ cups chicken broth

2-3 cloves garlic, minced

1 teaspoon dried basil

1/2 teaspoon dried oregano

1/2 cup heavy cream

1 cup Parmesan cheese, grated

3/4 teaspoon salt

1/4 teaspoon ground black pepper

Directions

Warm olive oil over medium-high heat; sauté red onion for about 3 minutes, or until it is translucent.

Add pasta, shrimp, chicken broth, garlic, basil, and oregano to the pressure cooker. Securely lock the lid and set for 7 minutes on HIGH.

Use a quick release to release the pressure. Set the pressure cooker to HIGH; stir in heavy cream, Parmesan cheese, salt, and black pepper. Then, simmer for about 2 minutes. Serve right away.

Poached Salmon Fillets

(Ready in about 10 minutes | Servings 4)

Ingredients

3 tablespoons butter

2 pounds salmon fillets

1 cup chicken broth

1 cup scallions, chopped

2 cloves garlic, minced

Juice of 1 lime

1 tablespoon fresh tarragon, chopped

Kosher salt and ground black pepper, to taste

Directions

Simply throw all the above ingredients in your pressure cooker.

Securely lock the pressure cooker's lid; set to 6 minutes on HIGH.

Then, release the cooker's pressure. Serve right now.

Spiced Lemony Scallops

(Ready in about 10 minutes | Servings 4)

Ingredients

2 tablespoons olive oil

1 onion, thinly sliced

1 red bell pepper, seeded and sliced

1 jalapeño pepper, seeded and chopped

2 tomatoes, diced

1 tablespoon chopped fresh oregano

1 teaspoon granulated garlic

1/3 cup chicken stock

1 ½ pounds sea scallops

1 small-sized lemon, freshly squeezed

Salt and ground black pepper, to taste

Directions

Warm olive oil over medium-high heat. Then, sauté the onion, bell pepper, and jalapeño pepper until they are tender.

Add tomatoes, oregano, granulated garlic, and chicken stock to the cooker; stir to combine.

Top with the scallops. Drizzle with lemon juice; salt and pepper to taste.

Cover the cooker and set for 2 minutes on HIGH. Serve immediately.

Flaky Tilapia Fillets

(Ready in about 10 minutes | Servings 2)

Ingredients

2 tilapia fillets

Salt and black pepper, to taste

1 teaspoon garlic powder

2 sprigs thyme

1 sprig rosemary

2 slices lemon

2 tablespoons butter, softened

Directions

Prepare 2 squares of parchment paper.

Lay a fillet in the center of each square of parchment paper. Sprinkle with salt, black pepper, and garlic powder.

Sprinkle with thyme and rosemary. Drizzle with lemon and butter. Close up parchment paper around the tilapia fillets in order to form two packets.

Next, place a trivet at the bottom of the cooker. Pour 1 cup of water into the cooker. Lay the packets on the trivet.

Cover the cooker with the lid and set for 5 minutes on HIGH. Serve right away!

Tuna Steaks in Buttery Sauce

(Ready in about 10 minutes | Servings 4)

Ingredients

2 pounds tuna steaks

1/4 cup white wine

1/4 cup chicken broth

2 cloves garlic, minced

2 sprigs fresh rosemary

1 sprig fresh thyme

6 tablespoons butter

2 tablespoons capers

1 teaspoon cayenne pepper

Salt and black pepper, to taste

Directions

Add tuna steaks to your pressure cooker. Then, add white wine, chicken broth, garlic, rosemary, and thyme to the pressure cooker.

Cover and cook on HIGH for 4 minutes. Then, let the cooker's pressure release naturally.

Stir in butter, capers, cayenne pepper, salt and black pepper. Serve.

Pressure Cooker Mac and Cheese

(Ready in about 20 minutes | Servings 6)

Ingredients

3 cups macaroni of choice

1 cup water

2 cups vegetable broth

2 tablespoons butter

Sea salt and ground white pepper, to taste

1 cup Ricotta cheese

2 cups Cheddar cheese, shredded

Directions

Add macaroni, water, vegetable broth, butter, salt, and white pepper to your pressure cooker.

Then, cook for 6 minutes on HIGH. Perform a quick release to release the pressure.

Stir in Ricotta cheese and Cheddar cheese. Stir to combine and let stand for 5 to 10 minutes to thicken. Serve.

Sausage and Veggie Risotto

(Ready in about 10 minutes | Servings 4)

Ingredients

2 tablespoons canola oil

8 ounces ground pork sausage

2 garlic cloves, minced

1 onion, diced

1 green bell pepper, diced

1 carrot, chopped

2 stalks celery, diced

2 cups white rice

1 teaspoon chili powder

1 teaspoon cayenne pepper

1/4 teaspoon black pepper

Sea salt to taste

2 ¼ cups chicken stock

Directions

Heat canola oil until sizzling.

Then, cook the sausage, garlic, onion, bell pepper, carrot, and celery in the pressure cooker, for about 6 minutes.

Stir in the rest of the above ingredients. Cook for 4 minutes on HIGH.

Let the pressure release naturally for a few minutes. Serve warm and enjoy!

Mushroom and Sausage Risotto

(Ready in about 10 minutes | Servings 4)

Ingredients

2 tablespoons vegetable oil

8 ounces chicken sausage

2 garlic cloves, minced

1 onion, diced

1 cup mushrooms, chopped

2 carrots, trimmed and chopped

2 cups rice

1 teaspoon paprika

Sea salt and ground black pepper, to taste

2 ¼ cups chicken stock

Directions

In your pressure cooker, heat vegetable oil until sizzling.

Then, sauté the sausage, garlic, onion, mushrooms, and carrot, until the sausage is lightly browned and the mushrooms are tender and fragrant.

Stir in the remaining ingredients. Cook on HIGH for 4 minutes.

Let the pressure release gradually and naturally for a few minutes. Serve right away.

Pea Risotto with Cream Cheese

(Ready in about 15 minutes | Servings 8)

Ingredients

2 tablespoons olive oil

1 leek, finely chopped

2 cloves garlic, minced

2 cups Arborio rice

5 cups vegetable stock

1/4 cup dry white wine

1 bay leaf

2 cups frozen peas, thawed

Salt and ground black pepper, to taste

1 cup cream cheese

Directions

First, heat olive oil in your pressure cooker over medium heat. Sauté the leek and garlic until tender, or about 5 minutes.

Add rice, and sauté for 1 minute more.

Add the remaining ingredients, except for cream cheese. Securely lock the lid; cook for 6 minutes on HIGH.

Stir the peas into the prepared risotto; taste and adjust the seasonings. Divide the risotto among serving dishes and top with a dollop of the cream cheese. Enjoy!

Collard Greens with Bacon

(Ready in about 20 minutes | Servings 4)

Ingredients

4 strips bacon, diced

1 small-sized onion, peeled and chopped

2-3 cloves garlic, minced

2 bunches collard greens, coarsely chopped

2 cups vegetable broth

2 teaspoons minced

Sea salt and ground black pepper, to taste

Directions

In your pressure cooker, fry the bacon strips until they are nearly crisp, or about 5 minutes.

Add remaining ingredients and lock the lid. Set for 15 minutes on HIGH.

Let the pressure release naturally for 5 to 10 minutes. Serve warm and enjoy!

Sugar Snap Peas with Corn and Ricotta

(Ready in about 10 minutes | Servings 6)

Ingredients

2 tablespoons olive oil

1 white onion, diced

4 cups corn kernels

3 cups sugar snap peas

1/2 cup vegetable broth

1 teaspoon dried thyme

1/2 teaspoon onion powder

1/2 teaspoon garlic powder

Sea salt and ground black pepper

3/4 cup Ricotta cheese, cubed

Directions

Heat olive oil over medium-high heat. Then, sauté white onion until it is tender, fragrant, and translucent, or for 3 to 4 minutes.

Add the remaining ingredients, except for Ricotta cheese. Securely lock the cooker's lid; cook for about 3 minutes on HIGH.

Stir in Ricotta cheese just before serving. Enjoy!

Penne Pasta with Smoked Salmon

(Ready in about 10 minutes | Servings 6)

Ingredients

1/4 cup vegetable oil

2 cups penne pasta

2 cups water

2 cups chicken stock

Sea salt and freshly ground black pepper, to taste

1 teaspoon dried thyme

1/2 teaspoon dried rosemary

3 tablespoons butter

1/2 cup Ricotta cheese

2 green garlics, finely minced

1 pound smoked salmon, cut into bite-sized pieces

1/3 cup Parmesan cheese, grated

Directions

Heat the oil over medium heat. Stir in the pasta, water, stock, salt, black pepper, thyme, and rosemary. Cook at HIGH pressure for 8 minutes.

Quick-release the pressure; remove the lid according to manufacturer's directions.

Cut in the butter. Add Ricotta cheese, green garlic, and smoked salmon; toss to combine well. Top with Parmesan cheese and serve immediately.

Fettuccine with Bacon and Cheese

(Ready in about 10 minutes | Servings 6)

Ingredients

2 tablespoons canola oil

2 cups fettuccine pasta

3 cups beef broth

1 cup water

Salt and freshly ground black pepper, to taste

1/2 teaspoon dried rosemary

1 teaspoon mustard seeds

3 tablespoons butter

1/2 cup cream cheese

1/2 cup scallions, finely chopped

2 garlic cloves, finely minced

1/2 pound crisp fried bacon, crushed

1/3 cup Parmigiano-Reggiano cheese, grated

Directions

In your pressure cooker, warm the oil over medium heat. When the oil is warm enough, stir in the fettuccine, broth, water, salt, black pepper, rosemary, and mustard seeds. Cook at HIGH pressure approximately 8 minutes.

Next, remove the lid according to manufacturer's directions.

Add the remaining ingredients; gently toss until everything is well incorporated. Serve and enjoy.

Saucy Bulgur with Mushrooms

(Ready in about 20 minutes | Servings 4)

Ingredients

1 cup bulgur

3 cups chicken broth

2 tablespoons butter

1 yellow onion, sliced

2 carrots, peeled and chopped

2 celery ribs, peeled and chopped

1/2 cup mushrooms, chopped

1/2 teaspoon dried sage

1/2 teaspoon salt

1/2 teaspoon ground black pepper

Directions

Add the bulgur and broth to your pressure cooker.

Lock the lid into place; cook under HIGH pressure for 9 minutes. Then, allow pressure to release gradually and naturally. Reserve cooked bulgur.

In a large-sized sauté pan, over medium heat, warm the butter; when the butter is melted, sauté the onion, carrot, and celery for 6 to 7 minutes.

Add the remaining ingredients; sauté for an additional 2 minutes.

Combine the vegetable mixture with the cooked bulgur. Serve right away.

Couscous-Stuffed Peppers with Walnuts

(Ready in about 25 minutes | Servings 4)

Ingredients

2 cups water

1 cup couscous

2 tablespoons toasted walnuts, chopped

4 ounces feta cheese, crumbled

1/2 teaspoon dried dill weed

1/2 teaspoon dried basil

1 teaspoon dried oregano

1 teaspoon salt

1/2 teaspoon ground black pepper

4 large-sized red bell peppers, seeded and stemmed

Directions

Preheat your oven to 350 degrees F. Add the water and couscous to your pressure cooker.

Cover with the lid and bring to HIGH pressure, and maintain for 2 minutes. Turn off the heat, and allow pressure to release.

Next, remove the lid and fluff your couscous; add the walnuts, feta cheese, dill, basil, oregano, salt, and black pepper. Stir to combine well.

Stuff the peppers with prepared couscous mixture; place the stuffed peppers in a baking dish. Bake in the preheated oven for 15 minutes. Serve warm and enjoy!

Couscous with Kalamata Olives and Peppers

(Ready in about 10 minutes + chilling time | Servings 4)

Ingredients

2 cups water

1 cup couscous

1/2 cup Kalamata olives, pitted and chopped

1/2 cup scallions, chopped

1 red bell pepper, seeded and diced

1 yellow bell pepper, seeded and diced

2 cloves garlic, minced

2 teaspoons extra-virgin olive oil

1 teaspoon wine vinegar

1/4 teaspoon ground white pepper

1 teaspoon salt

Directions

Stir the water and couscous into a pressure cooker. Lock the lid into place; cook on HIGH pressure for 2 minutes.

Remove from the heat and allow pressure to release according to manufacturer's directions. Carefully remove the cooker's lid.

Fluff the couscous and stir in all remaining ingredients. Taste and adjust the seasonings. Refrigerate at least 2 hours before serving. Enjoy!

FAST SNACKS RECIPES

Roasted Baby Potatoes

(Ready in about 10 minutes | Servings 4)

Ingredients

6 tablespoons grapeseed oil

2 pounds baby new potatoes

1/2 cup vegetable stock

1 teaspoon cayenne pepper

1 teaspoon kosher salt

Parmesan cheese, grated

Directions

In a pressure cooker over medium-high heat, heat grapeseed oil. Add the potatoes and cook until they have all been browned. Pour in the vegetable stock.

Close and lock the lid. Set the burner heat to HIGH. Set a timer to cook for 5 minutes.

Remove the pot from the heat. Open the cooker with the Natural Release method.

Sprinkle the potatoes with cayenne pepper, kosher salt and grated Parmesan cheese; serve immediately.

Fingerling Potatoes with Cheese

(Ready in about 10 minutes | Servings 4)

Ingredients

1 pound fingerling potatoes

2 teaspoons salt

12 ounces Gruyère cheese, thinly sliced

Sea salt and freshly ground black pepper, to taste

3 green onions, trimmed and sliced diagonally in 1/8-inch strips

Pickled cauliflower, for serving

Directions

Place the potatoes in a pressure cooker pot; fill the cooker with water. Add the salt.

Close and lock the lid. Cook for 6 minutes at HIGH pressure. Remove the pot from the heat and open the cooker with the Quick release method.

Meanwhile, preheat your oven to 250 degrees F.

Next, cut the potatoes in half lengthwise. Bake the potatoes covered with cheese and sprinkled with salt and black pepper.

Divide the warm potatoes among serving plates. Bake for 10 to 12 minutes in the oven. Serve the potatoes warm with the green onions and pickled cauliflower. Enjoy!

Candied Jewel Yams

(Ready in about 10 minutes | Servings 6)

Ingredients

6 medium-sized Jewel yams, pierced in several places

2/3 cup firmly packed light brown sugar

1 teaspoon sea salt

5 tablespoons unsalted butter

1/2 cup water

Directions

Place the yams in a pressure cooker pot; fill with the water to cover.

Close and lock the lid. Set the burner heat to high. Set a timer to cook for 9 minutes.

Remove the pot from the heat and open the cooker with the Quick Release method. Drain the yams in a colander. Then, slip off the skins and cut into slices. Reserve.

In a saucepan, cook the sugar, sea salt, butter, and water over medium-low heat. Add the sliced yams; gently stir until they're glazed, about 3 minutes. Serve warm.

Braised Escarole with Garlic and Paprika

(Ready in about 10 minutes | Servings 4)

Ingredients

1 head escarole

1/4 cup extra-virgin olive oil

2 cloves garlic, to taste, chopped

1/2 teaspoon paprika

1/2 cup vegetable broth

Sea salt and freshly ground black pepper, to your liking

Directions

Cut the root ends off the escarole and discard the core. Rinse in a colander; cut the leaves into bite-size pieces.

Warm the oil and garlic in a pressure cooker over medium-high. Add the paprika, broth, and reserved escarole. Sprinkle with salt and black pepper.

Close and lock the lid. Set the burner heat to HIGH. Set a timer to cook for 1 minute.

Afterward, open the cooker with the Quick release method. Taste and adjust the seasonings.

Kale in Almond Milk Sauce

(Ready in about 10 minutes | Servings 4)

Ingredients

2 tablespoons olive oil

1 onion, thinly sliced

2 bunches kale, stemmed and roughly chopped

1 cup almond milk

2 tablespoons fresh lime juice

Sea salt and freshly ground black pepper

1 teaspoon paprika

Directions

Place the oil along with onion in a pressure cooker. Turn the heat to MEDIUM-HIGH. Then, cook until the onion is translucent, about 5 minutes.

Add the kale, almond milk, and lime juice. Close and lock the lid.

Set the burner heat to HIGH. Set a timer to cook for 4 minutes.

Lastly, open the cooker according to manufacturer's directions. Season with salt, black pepper, and paprika. Serve at room temperature.

Yummy Butter Corn

(Ready in about 10 minutes | Servings 4)

Ingredients

4 ears sweet corn, shucked

1/2 cup water

1/4 stick butter, softened

1/2 teaspoon allspice

Salt and white pepper, to your liking

Directions

Set a rack in a pressure cooker; lay the ears of corn on the rack. Pour in the water.

Then, bring to LOW pressure; cook for 3 minutes. Remove the cooker's lid according to manufacturer's instructions.

Spread the butter over each ear of corn; sprinkle with allspice, salt, and white pepper. Serve.

Sesame and Cumin Green Beans

(Ready in about 10 minutes | Servings 4)

Ingredients

2 cups water

1 pound green beans, trimmed

1/2 teaspoon cumin seeds

2 tablespoons grapeseed oil

2 tablespoons sesame seeds, toasted

Salt and white pepper, to taste

Directions

Fill the bottom of a pressure cooker with the water. Place the steamer basket in the pressure cooker.

Then, throw green beans in the steamer basket. Sprinkle the cumin seeds over green beans.

Secure the cooker's lid; cook on HIGH. Then, decrease the heat and cook for 5 minutes.

Toss prepared green beans in the grapeseed oil. Sprinkle with toasted sesame seeds, salt, and white pepper. Toss to combine well and serve.

Spiced Kale Snack with Walnuts

(Ready in about 10 minutes | Servings 4)

Ingredients

2 cups water

1 teaspoon sea salt

8 cups kale leaves, chopped

2 tablespoons grapeseed oil

2 cloves garlic, minced

1 teaspoon paprika

1 teaspoon dried rosemary

1 teaspoon dried thyme

1/2 cup vegetable broth

Ground white pepper, to your liking

Chopped walnuts, for garnish

Directions

Fill the pressure cooker with the water. Add sea salt and bring it to a boil. Blanch kale leaves for 1 minute; reserve.

Warm the grapeseed oil in the pressure cooker over MEDIUM heat. Add the garlic, paprika, rosemary, thyme; cook for 1 minute. Add the broth and white pepper; stir in the reserved kale.

Cover the cooker and bring to HIGH pressure; maintain pressure for 6 minutes. Lastly, remove the lid by following the manufacturer's directions.

Transfer prepared kale to a serving bowl. Scatter chopped walnuts over the top; serve right away.

Lemony Baby Artichokes

(Ready in about 10 minutes | Servings 6)

Ingredients

1/4 cup fresh lemon juice

3 cups cold water

2 pounds baby artichokes

Salt and ground white pepper, to taste

Directions

Combine the lemon juice and cold water in a large-sized bowl.

Trim baby artichokes with a paring knife. Toss artichokes into the lemon bath.

Pour the lemon water into a pressure cooker. Set a trivet on the bottom and pile the prepared artichokes on top.

Close and lock the lid. Set the burner heat to HIGH. Set a timer to cook for 6 minutes. Remove the cooker from the heat.

Lastly, open the cooker with the Quick Release method. Season with salt and white pepper and serve.

Fastest-Ever Baba Ghanoush

(Ready in about 15 minutes | Servings 16)

Ingredients

1 tablespoon grapeseed oil

1 large-sized eggplant, peeled and diced

4 cloves garlic, finely minced

1/2 cup water

3 tablespoons fresh parsley

3/4 teaspoon salt

1/4 teaspoon black pepper, to taste

2 tablespoons tahini

1 tablespoon olive oil

Directions

Add the grapeseed oil to the pressure cooker; heat the oil over medium heat. Stir in the eggplant. Sauté the eggplant until it is tender. Add the garlic and continue to sauté for 30 seconds more.

Pour in the water; lock the cooker's lid. Bring to HIGH pressure; maintain pressure for 5 minutes. Then, quick-release the pressure and uncover.

Spoon prepared mixture into a food processor along with the remaining ingredients (except the olive oil).

Transfer to a serving bowl. Drizzle with the olive oil. Serve with pita wedges and enjoy.

Baby Artichokes with Mayonnaise

(Ready in about 10 minutes | Servings 6)

Ingredients

3 cups cold water

1/4 cup fresh lemon juice

2 pounds baby artichokes

Sea salt and red pepper flakes, to taste

Plain mayonnaise, for serving

Directions

Combine the water and lemon juice in a mixing bowl.

Trim baby artichokes using a paring knife. Toss artichokes into the lemon water.

Pour the lemon water into a pressure cooker. Set a trivet on the bottom and add the prepared artichokes to the top.

Close and lock the cooker's lid. Set the burner heat to HIGH. Cook for 6 minutes.

Lastly, open the cooker with the Quick release method. Sprinkle with salt and red pepper flakes; serve with plain mayonnaise.

Asparagus with Hollandaise Sauce

(Ready in about 5 minutes | Servings 6)

Ingredients

For the Asparagus:

2 pounds asparagus, bottom 2 inches snapped off with a vegetable peeler

1 cup water

For the Sauce:

4 egg yolks

1 tablespoon fresh lime juice

1 teaspoon lime zest grated

1/2 sea salt

1/4 teaspoon ground black pepper

1 cup butter, melted

1/3 cup sour cream

Directions

In a pressure cooker, lay the asparagus spears on the steamer plate. Add the water.

Close and lock the cooker's lid. Set the burner heat to HIGH. Cook for 3 minutes.

Open the pressure cooker with the Quick release method.

To make the sauce, add the egg yolks, lime juice and zest, salt, and black pepper to a food processor. Process until everything is well combined. With the motor running, add the melted butter in a slow stream.

Whisk in the sour cream. Drizzle the asparagus with the sauce. Serve right now.

Spinach and Artichoke Dip

(Ready in about 15 minutes | Servings 12)

Ingredients

1 ½ cups frozen chopped spinach, thawed and well drained

2 cups canned artichoke hearts, coarsely chopped

1/2 cup mayonnaise

1/2 cup sour cream

1 ½ cups cream cheese, shredded

1/2 teaspoon cayenne pepper

Sea salt and ground black pepper, to taste

Directions

Combine all of the above ingredients in a baking dish that fits in the pressure cooker. Cover it with an aluminum foil. Then, prepare a foil sling.

Place the rack at the bottom of the cooker. Pour about 2 cups of water into the pressure cooker. Place the baking dish on the rack.

Seal the lid and select HIGH pressure and 10 minutes cooking time. Then, use a quick pressure release; remove the lid.

Serve warm with your favorite dippers.

Rich Christmas Relish

(Ready in about 30 minutes | Servings 12)

Ingredients

7 cups water

1 ½ cups red kidney beans

2 teaspoons grapeseed oil

Salt and ground black pepper, to taste

2 tablespoons tahini paste

1/4 cup pineapple, drained and crushed

1/2 teaspoon garlic powder

1/2 teaspoon onion powder

1/2 cup fresh parsley, finely minced

Directions

Add 3 cups of water and red kidney beans to a pressure cooking pot; then, let it soak overnight. Drain the beans and replace them to your pressure cooker. Pour in the remaining 4 cups of water.

Add the grapeseed oil; lock the lid into place. Bring to HIGH pressure, maintaining the pressure for 15 minutes. Then, quick release any remaining pressure.

Next, drop the cooked beans in the bowl of your blender. Stir in the remaining ingredients; pulse until everything is well incorporated but still a little chunky.

Serve chilled with your favorite dippers.

Glazed Baby Carrots with Dried Cherries

(Ready in about 10 minutes | Servings 6)

Ingredients

1 cup water

2 pounds baby carrots, sliced diagonally

1/4 cup dried cherries

A pinch of salt

3/4 teaspoon allspice

2 tablespoons butter, softened

2 tablespoons maple syrup

Directions

Put the water, baby carrots, and dried cherries into a pressure cooking pot. Close the lid and cook for 4 minutes at LOW pressure.

Next, add the remaining ingredients to the warm baby carrots. Give it a good stir. Serve at room temperature.

Rich Winter Meat Dip

(Ready in about 10 minutes | Servings 24)

Ingredients

2 tablespoons lard, softened

3 bacon slices, cut into strips

2 cloves garlic, peeled and minced

1 shallot, coarsely chopped

1 bell pepper, cut into strips

1/2 cup salsa

1/4 cup tomato paste

1/2 cup water

1 pound chicken breasts, boneless and diced

1/2 cup sour cream

1 cup Ricotta cheese, grated

Salt and freshly ground black pepper, to taste

Dried rosemary, chopped

Directions

Add the lard and bacon to a pressure cooking pot. Then, sauté the garlic, shallot, and bell pepper for 3 minutes.

Next, stir in the salsa, tomato paste, water, and chicken breasts. Lock the lid into place; bring to LOW pressure, maintaining pressure for 6 minutes.

Next, uncover and continue to simmer over MEDIUM heat.

Reduce the heat; fold in the sour cream and cheese. Give it a good stir. Season with salt, black pepper, and dried rosemary. Serve with tortilla chips.

Buttery Haricots Verts

(Ready in about 10 minutes | Servings 6)

Ingredients

1/2 stick butter, room temperature

1 large shallot, diced

1 ½ pounds haricots verts, cut into pieces on the diagonal

1 teaspoon salt

Freshly ground black pepper, to taste

1 cup water

1 cup sour cream

1 teaspoon paprika

Chopped green garlic, for serving

Directions

Melt the butter in a pressure cooker over medium-high heat. Sauté the shallot until soft, about 3 minutes. Add the haricots verts, salt, black pepper, and the water.

Close and lock the lid. Set the burner heat to HIGH. Set a timer to cook for 2 minutes.

Remove the cooker from the heat. Use the Quick release method. Drain the haricots verts in a colander. Add the sour cream and paprika. Serve sprinkled with green garlic.

Soft Braised Green Beans

(Ready in about 15 minutes | Servings 6)

Ingredients

2 tablespoons sesame oil

1 onion, diced

2 cloves garlic, minced

2 pounds green beans, ends trimmed

2 medium-sized tomatoes, seeded and diced

1 cup water

2 tablespoons dry rosé wine

Sea salt and freshly ground black pepper, to your liking

Smoked paprika, to your liking

Directions

In a pressure cooker over medium-high heat, heat the sesame oil. Add the onion and garlic; cook, stirring occasionally for about 3 minutes.

Add the green beans, tomatoes, water, and rosé wine. Close and lock the lid. Set the burner heat to HIGH. Set a timer to cook for 4 minutes.

Open the cooker with the Quick Release method. Season green beans with salt, black pepper, and paprika. Serve and enjoy!

Christmas Party Green Bean Appetizer

(Ready in about 10 minutes | Servings 6)

Ingredients

2 tablespoons extra-virgin olive oil

2 white onions, chopped

1 ½ cups fresh shiitake mushrooms, chopped

1 ½ pounds green beans, cut into pieces

1/2 cup water

2 tablespoons tamari sauce

1 tablespoon rice vinegar

Directions

In a pressure cooking pot, heat the oil over medium-high heat. Add the onions and cook, stirring a few times. Stir in the shiitake mushrooms and cook for two more minutes.

Add the green beans, water, tamari sauce, and rice vinegar.

Close and lock the lid. Set the burner heat to HIGH. Set a timer to cook for 2 minutes.

Open your cooking pot with the Quick release method. Serve on a nice serving platter.

Lima Beans Appetizer

(Ready in about 10 minutes | Servings 4)

Ingredients

1 (10-ounce) package baby lima beans, frozen

2 tablespoons fresh cilantro, chopped

2 cloves garlic, minced

1/2 teaspoon sea salt

Freshly cracked black pepper, to your liking

1 cup vegetable broth

3 tablespoons olive oil

1 lemon, cut into wedges

Directions

Place the lima beans, cilantro, garlic, and salt in a pressure cooker. Add black pepper, vegetable broth, and olive oil. Bring to a boil.

Close and lock the lid. Set the burner heat to HIGH. Set a timer to cook for 3 minutes.

Open the cooker with the Quick release method. Taste and adjust the seasonings; serve immediately garnished with lemon wedges.

Black-Eyed Pea Dipping Sauce

(Ready in about 15 minutes + chilling time | Servings 16)

Ingredients

8 cups water

2 cups dried black-eyed peas

1 shallot, diced

1 pickled jalapeño, finely chopped

1 medium-sized tomato, seeded and diced

2 tablespoons fresh cilantro

2 tablespoons balsamic vinegar

1 tablespoon lemon juice

2 tablespoons olive oil

1/2 teaspoon fennel seeds

Kosher salt and ground black pepper

Directions

Place 4 cups of water in a deep bowl along with the black-eyed peas; let it soak at least 1 hour. Drain and rinse the peas and transfer them to the pressure cooker.

Add the remaining 4 cups of water to the cooker. Lock the lid and bring to HIGH pressure; maintain the pressure for 12 minutes.

Remove the cooker from the heat; release pressure according to manufacturer's instructions. Transfer the black-eyed peas to a nice serving bowl.

Stir in the remaining ingredients; give it a good stir. Serve chilled.

Cheesy Lima Beans

(Ready in about 10 minutes | Servings 4)

Ingredients

1 (10-ounce) package baby lima beans, frozen

2 tablespoons fresh parsley, chopped

2 cloves garlic, minced

Kosher salt and ground black pepper, to taste

1 cup vegetable stock

3 tablespoons sesame oil

1 tablespoon fresh lime juice

1/3 cup Cheddar cheese, shaved

Directions

Put the lima beans, fresh parsley, garlic, and kosher salt into your pressure cooker. Add black pepper, stock, and sesame oil. Bring to a boil.

Close and lock the lid. Set the burner heat to HIGH. Set a timer to cook for 3 minutes.

Open the cooker with the Quick release method. Drizzle lima beans with lime juice. Add Cheddar cheese and serve.

Petit Pea and Onion Appetizer

(Ready in about 5 minutes | Servings 6)

Ingredients

3 tablespoons olive oil

1 white onion, finely diced

1 teaspoon dried thyme

1 teaspoon dried dill weed

2 pounds frozen petit peas

1/2 cup water

Sea salt, to taste

Directions

In a pressure cooker over medium-high heat, warm the olive oil. Add the onion and sauté, stirring a few times, until soft.

Stir in the remaining ingredients. Cover and set the burner heat to HIGH. Set a timer to cook for 4 minutes.

Remove the pot from the heat. Open the cooking pot using the Quick release method. Serve immediately.

Pearl Onion Appetizer

(Ready in about 10 minutes | Servings 6)

Ingredients

1/2 cup water

1 pound pearl onions, outer layer removed

1/2 teaspoon sea salt

3/4 teaspoon black pepper, freshly ground

1 tablespoon lemon juice

3 tablespoons balsamic vinegar

2 tablespoons maple syrup

1 tablespoon flour

Directions

Put the water and pearl onions into your pressure cooker along with the salt and black pepper. Lock the cooker's lid.

Turn the heat up to HIGH. When the cooker reaches pressure, cook for 5 minutes at LOW pressure. Transfer pearl onions to the bowl.

In a saucepan, combine the remaining ingredients. Cook on LOW heat one more minute. Spoon the sauce over the pearl onions and serve.

Chipotle and Cheese Dip

(Ready in about 10 minutes | Servings 12)

Ingredients

2 tablespoons margarine

2 tablespoons flour

1 cup milk

16 ounces Colby cheese, shredded

1 chipotle pepper, finely minced

1/2 cup tomatoes, canned

1 teaspoon kosher salt

1 teaspoon garlic powder

1/4 teaspoon black pepper

1/4 teaspoon cayenne pepper

1 teaspoon dried basil

Directions

In a pressure cooker, warm the margarine over medium heat; slowly and gradually add the flour; stir until you have a paste.

Then, add the milk and stir until the mixture has thickened. Bring it to a boil.

Fold in shredded Colby cheese; stir again. Add the remaining ingredients; seal the lid. Cook on MEDIUM heat for 3 minutes. Serve warm.

Pressure-Steamed Cauliflower Appetizer

(Ready in about 5 minutes | Servings 6)

Ingredients

2 cups water

1 head cauliflower, leaves trimmed and cored

Directions

Place the water in a pressure cooker. Position a trivet and steamer basket in the cooking pot. Lay the cauliflower in the steamer basket.

Close and lock the lid. Set the burner heat to HIGH. Set a timer to cook for 5 minutes.

Remove the pot from the heat. Open the cooker with the Quick release method.

Cut the cauliflower into florets and serve with your favorite dipping sauce.

Hot Chicken Wings

(Ready in about 20 minutes | Servings 6)

Ingredients

1 cup water

2 pounds chicken wings

4 tablespoons hot sauce

1/4 cup tomato paste

1/4 cup honey

1 teaspoon cumin seeds

1 teaspoon dried basil

2 teaspoons sea salt

1 teaspoon ground black pepper

3/4 teaspoon smoked paprika

Directions

Pour the water into a pressure cooker; place a steamer basket in the pressure cooker.

Arrange the chicken wings in the steamer basket. Close and lock the cooker's lid. Cook for 10 minutes at HIGH pressure.

In the meantime, prepare the dipping sauce by mixing the rest of the ingredients.

Next, open the cooker by releasing the pressure. Cook chicken wings under the broiler for about 5 minutes. Serve hot.

Beet Salad with Pine Nuts

(Ready in about 15 minutes | Servings 6)

Ingredients

6 medium-sized beets

2 ½ cups water

1 tablespoon balsamic vinegar

1 teaspoon lime juice

1 teaspoon lime zest, grated

1 tablespoon honey

1/2 teaspoon cayenne pepper

1/2 teaspoon ground black pepper

3/4 teaspoon salt

3 tablespoons extra-virgin olive oil

2 tablespoons toasted pine nuts, finely chopped

Directions

Scrub the beets. Transfer them to your pressure cooker; fill the pot with the water. Close the cooker's lid; bring to HIGH pressure. Reduce heat to medium; cook for 10 minutes.

Release pressure and remove the lid. Drain the beets and allow them to cool completely. Then, rub off skins; cut the beets into wedges. Transfer the beets to a nice serving bowl.

To make the vinaigrette, whisk the remaining ingredients in a small mixing bowl. Drizzle the vinaigrette over the beets. Scatter toasted pine nuts over the top and serve.

Party Classic Bean Spread

(Ready in about 30 minutes | Servings 6)

Ingredients

2 tablespoons olive oil

1/2 cup scallions, thinly sliced

1 ½ cups dried beans, rinsed

3 cups water

1 tablespoon balsamic vinegar

Salt and black pepper, to taste

1 teaspoon paprika

1/2 teaspoon garlic powder

1 thyme sprig, chopped

1 rosemary sprig, chopped

Directions

Heat olive oil in the pressure cooker; then, sauté the scallions. Stir in the beans and water; seal the cooker's lid.

Turn the heat up to HIGH; maintain pressure for 30 minutes.

Open the cooker according to manufacturer's directions. Drain the beans; allow them to cool completely. Purée cooked beans in a food processor. Add the remaining ingredients.

Purée until it is smooth. Serve with dippers of choice.

Aromatic Garlic and Dill Dip

(Ready in about 10 minutes | Servings 10)

Ingredients

1 cup water

2 whole heads garlic, peeled

1/2 cup butter, softened

1 teaspoon dill weed

1 teaspoon sea salt

3/4 teaspoon black pepper, to taste

Directions

Pour water into a pressure cooker; place the steamer basket in the pressure cooker. Add the garlic.

Seal the lid and bring to HIGH pressure; maintain the pressure for about 2 minutes. Remove from the heat and allow the pressure to release according to manufacturer's instructions.

Next, mash the garlic cloves; add the remaining ingredients. Serve chilled.

Yams with Orange and Garam Masala

(Ready in about 10 minutes | Servings 4)

Ingredients

1 cup water

4 medium-large Jewel yams, peeled and cut into chunks

2 tablespoons butter, to taste

1/3 cup orange juice

1 teaspoon garam masala

Salt and ground white pepper, to your liking

Directions

Place a trivet in a pressure cooker; add the water. Pile the yams in a steamer basket.

Close and lock the lid. Set the burner heat to HIGH. Set a timer to cook for 7 minutes. Open the cooker with the Natural Release method. Remove the basket from the pot.

Melt the butter in a saucepan; stir in the yams and mash them with a fork, gradually adding the orange juice and garam masala. Season with salt and white pepper. Serve at room temperature.

Maple Mashed Jewel Yams

(Ready in about 10 minutes | Servings 4)

Ingredients

4 medium-large Jewel yams, peeled and cut into chunks

Sea salt

3 tablespoons butter, melted

3 tablespoons maple syrup

1/2 teaspoon allspice

1/4 cup half-and-half

Directions

Place the Jewel yams in a pressure cooker; fill with the water to cover.

Close and lock the cooker's lid. Set the burner heat to HIGH. Set a timer to cook for 7 minutes.

Remove the pot from the heat. Open the cooker with the Quick Release method. Drain the yams in a colander.

Use a handheld electric mixer and mash the yams. Slowly add the salt, melted butter, maple syrup, allspice, and half-and-half. Taste and adjust the seasonings. Serve right now.

Maple Apple Jewel Yams

(Ready in about 10 minutes | Servings 6)

Ingredients

4 Jewel yams, peeled and cut into chunks

3 apples, cored, peeled and diced

A pinch of salt

1 teaspoon brown sugar

3 tablespoons butter, melted

3 tablespoons maple syrup

1/4 teaspoon cinnamon

1/4 teaspoon cardamom

1/4 teaspoon grated nutmeg

1/4 cup sour cream

Directions

Put the yams and apples into a pressure cooker; fill the cooker with the water to cover the ingredients.

Close and lock the cooker's lid. Set the burner heat to HIGH. Now cook for 7 minutes.

Remove the pot from the heat. Uncover your cooker using the Quick Release method. Drain the yams and apples in a colander and transfer them to a serving dish.

Add the remaining ingredients. Give it a gentle stir. Serve and enjoy!

Sweet Potato Appetizer with Mandarins and Walnuts

(Ready in about 10 minutes | Servings 6)

Ingredients

1 ½ cups water

2 pounds large sweet potatoes, peeled and cubed

Juice of 1 lemon

1 ¼ cups mayonnaise

1 tablespoon orange juice

1 teaspoon orange zest, grated

2 teaspoons fresh ginger, peeled and grated

1/2 teaspoon kosher salt

1/2 teaspoon white pepper, ground

1/4 teaspoon allspice

1/4 teaspoon ground nutmeg

1 cup walnuts, coarsely chopped

3 mandarins, peeled and sectioned

Raisins, for garnish

Directions

Place a trivet in your pressure cooker. Add the water and sweet potato cubes in a steamer basket; place it in the pot. Sprinkle with the lemon juice.

Cover and set the burner heat to HIGH. Set a timer to cook for 4 minutes.

Remove the pot from the heat and open the cooker according to manufacturer's directions; let rest for 15 minutes. Transfer boiled sweet potatoes to a serving dish.

In a bowl, whisk together the mayonnaise, orange juice and zest, ginger, kosher salt, white pepper, allspice, and nutmeg; whisk till everything is well incorporated. Add this mixture to the serving dish with potatoes. Add walnuts and mandarins.

Stir to combine and sprinkle with raisins. Serve and enjoy!

Sweet Zesty Cabbage Appetizer

(Ready in about 10 minutes | Servings 4)

Ingredients

2 tablespoons olive oil

1 sweet onion, chopped

1 head red cabbage, coarsely shredded

1/3 cup chicken broth

1/3 cup sweet red vermouth

1 tablespoon maple syrup

1/2 teaspoon sea salt

1 ½ cups green grapes, seedless and halved

Juice of 1/2 lemon

1 tablespoon orange juice

Directions

In a pressure cooker, heat olive oil over medium-high. Stir in the sweet onion and sauté until soft, about 3 minutes.

Add the shredded cabbage and toss to combine with the oil. Stir in the chicken broth, vermouth, maple syrup, and sea salt; bring to a boil.

Close and lock the lid. Set the burner heat to HIGH. Now cook for 4 minutes.

Remove the pot from the heat and open the cooker according to manufacturer's instructions. Add the grapes, lemon juice, and orange juice. Taste and adjust the seasonings.

Yummy Sauerkraut with Bacon

(Ready in about 10 minutes | Servings 8)

Ingredients

2 tablespoons butter

3 slices bacon, chopped

1 red onion, thinly sliced

1 teaspoon caraway seeds

6 cups sauerkraut, rinsed and drained

1 cup vegetable stock

3/4 cup dry white wine

Directions

In a pressure cooker over medium heat, melt the butter. Add the bacon and onion; cook, stirring a few times until softened.

Stir in the caraway seeds and sauerkraut; stir to combine. Pour in the vegetable stock and white wine. Bring to a boil.

Then, cook for 8 minutes at HIGH pressure. Remove the pot from the heat.

Open the cooker with the Natural Release method. Replace to a serving dish and enjoy!

Saucy Fennel Under Pressure

(Ready in about 10 minutes | Servings 4)

Ingredients

3 medium fennel bulbs

2 tablespoons butter

1 teaspoon rice flour

1 teaspoon kosher salt

1/4 teaspoon freshly grated nutmeg

1/4 teaspoon ground cinnamon

2 cups half-and-half

Mozzarella cheese, for serving

Directions

Trim the fennel bulbs and cut them in half lengthwise from the top.

In a pressure cooker, melt the butter over medium heat. Add the fennel pieces, cut side down; cook for about 2 minutes.

Add the remaining ingredients, except for Mozzarella cheese. Bring to a simmer. Close and lock the lid. Then, cook for 4 minutes at HIGH pressure.

Remove the pot from the heat. Open the cooker according to manufacturer's directions. Serve immediately garnished with Mozzarella cheese.

Braised Leeks with Vinaigrette

(Ready in about 10 minutes | Servings 4)

Ingredients

12 baby leeks, trimmed

1/2 cup water

1/2 cup vegetable broth

1 bay leaf

1 teaspoon caraway seeds

3 sprigs fresh parsley

1 rib celery, sliced

For the Vinaigrette:

2 tablespoons sherry vinegar

1 medium shallot, minced

1 tablespoon capers, rinsed

1/2 teaspoon salt

1 tablespoon mustard

2 tablespoons sour cream

1/3 cup olive oil

1/2 freshly ground black pepper

Directions

Using a knife, cut the leeks in half lengthwise. Pour the water into a pressure cooker. Add vegetable broth and bay leaf. Lay the leeks in the pot; place the caraway seeds, parsley, and celery on top of them.

Set the burner heat to HIGH. Set a timer to cook for 3 minutes.

Remove the pot from the heat. Open the cooker with the Quick Release method. Transfer the leeks to a serving platter.

In a small-sized mixing dish, combine all the ingredients for the vinaigrette. Pour the vinaigrette over the leeks. Serve immediately at room temperature.

Aromatic Red Potatoes

(Ready in about 10 minutes | Servings 12)

Ingredients

1 cup water

1 tablespoon extra-virgin olive oil

3 pounds unpeeled red potatoes, washed and cubed

Salt and ground black pepper, to taste

1 teaspoon dried thyme

1/2 teaspoon dried rosemary

1/2 teaspoon cayenne pepper

Directions

Put the water and olive oil into a pressure cooker. Place a rack in the pressure cooker; load the cooker with potato cubes.

Close the lid and bring to pressure over HIGH heat. Cook for 3 minutes; turn off the heat; use quick release method to depressurize your cooker.

Season prepared potatoes with salt, black pepper, thyme, rosemary, cayenne pepper. Enjoy!

Herbed Bean Spread

(Ready in about 30 minutes | Servings 6)

Ingredients

2 tablespoons grapeseed oil

1/2 cup scallions, thinly sliced

1 ½ cups dried beans, rinsed

1 cup vegetable broth

2 cups water

1 tablespoon apple cider vinegar

Salt and black pepper, to taste

1 teaspoon paprika

1/2 teaspoon fennel seeds

1 teaspoon cumin seeds

1 rosemary sprig, chopped

Directions

Warm grapeseed oil in the preheated pressure cooker; then, sauté scallions. Stir in dried beans, vegetable broth, and water; lock the cooker's lid.

Turn the heat up to HIGH; maintain pressure approximately 30 minutes.

Open the cooker according to manufacturer's directions. Drain the beans; allow the beans to cool. Purée the beans in a food processor. Add the remaining ingredients.

Purée until smooth. Transfer to a serving dish and serve.

Artichoke, Yogurt and Bean Dip

(Ready in about 20 minutes | Servings 20)

Ingredients

1/2 cup dry kidney beans, soaked overnight

1 cup water

6 medium-sized artichokes, outer leaves removed

1 small-sized lime, freshly squeezed

2 cloves of garlic, smashed

1 cup plain yogurt

1 tablespoon mayonnaise

1/2 teaspoon salt

1/4 teaspoon ground black pepper

1 cup Colby cheese, grated

Directions

Simply drop the kidney beans and water in a pressure cooker.

Then, cut off the top about 1/3 of each artichoke. Slice your artichokes in half lengthwise. Drizzle them with fresh lime juice; put into the cooker cut-side up.

Close and lock the cooker's lid. Cook approximately 20 minutes at HIGH pressure. When time is up, open the pressure cooker according to manufacturer's instructions.

Add the remaining ingredients. Lastly, blend the ingredients with an immersion blender. Serve at room temperature with dippers of choice.

Braised Aromatic Zucchini

(Ready in about 10 minutes | Servings 6)

Ingredients

2 tablespoons olive oil

1 cup white, finely chopped

2 cloves garlic, crushed

4 medium-sized zucchini, cut into thick rounds

1 cup fresh tomatoes, diced

1/4 cup vegetable broth

1 tablespoon pesto sauce

Sea salt and freshly ground black pepper

1 tablespoon sherry vinegar

Directions

In a pressure cooking pot, warm the oil over medium-high heat. Sauté the onion until just soft, about 3 minutes.

Add the crushed garlic and stir for 30 seconds. Add the zucchini, tomatoes, vegetable broth, and pesto sauce. Bring to a boil.

Close and lock the lid. Set the burner heat to HIGH. Set a timer to cook for 2 minutes.

Remove the pot from the heat. Open the cooker with the Quick release method. Season to taste with salt and black pepper. Serve drizzled with sherry vinegar.

Prosciutto-Wrapped Asparagus

(Ready in about 15 minutes | Servings 4)

Ingredients

2 cups water

1 pound asparagus spears

Salt and black pepper, to your

8 ounces Prosciutto, thinly sliced

Directions

Add the water to a pressure cooker. Sprinkle asparagus spears with salt and black pepper. Next, wrap the asparagus spears in prosciutto slices.

Then, place the prosciutto-wrapped asparagus in a steamer basket in the cooker. Insert the steamer basket in the pressure cooker; close the lid according to manufacturer's directions.

Cook for 3 minutes at HIGH pressure. Then, open the cooker using the Normal release method.

Transfer the prosciutto-wrapped asparagus spears to the serving platter. Enjoy!

Egg and Ham Dipping Sauce

(Ready in about 10 minutes | Servings 4)

Ingredients

1/2 cups water

1 tablespoon grapeseed oil

4 slices ham

4 large-sized eggs

4 slices Cheddar cheese

1 tablespoon fresh parsley, chopped

Directions

Prepare a pressure cooker by adding the water and the trivet.

Brush the bottom and sides of the ramekins with grapeseed oil. Then, lay the ham slices at the bottom. Now break an egg into each ramekin.

Top with Cheddar cheese. Lay ramekins in the steamer basket.

Close the cooker's lid. Cook for 5 minutes at LOW pressure. After that, release pressure. Sprinkle with fresh parsley. Serve immediately and enjoy!

Marsala Baby Carrots

(Ready in about 5 minutes | Servings 4)

Ingredients

3 tablespoons butter

1/3 cup dry Marsala

1/2 cup chicken broth

2 teaspoons mustard

1/2 teaspoon sugar

Freshly grated nutmeg

1 ½ pounds whole baby carrots

Dash sea salt, plus more to taste

2 tablespoons olive oil

Freshly ground black pepper

1/3 cup chopped fresh basil

Directions

Melt the butter in a pressure cooker over medium-high heat. Add the Marsala, broth, mustard, sugar, and nutmeg; stir until everything is well combined.

Add the baby carrots; stir to coat. Sprinkle with the salt and bring to a boil.

Close and lock the cooker's lid. Set the burner heat to HIGH. Set a timer to cook for 4 minutes.

Remove the pot from the heat. Open the cooker with the Quick Release method.

Sprinkle with olive oil, black pepper, and basil. Serve hot.

Potato and Bacon Appetizer

(Ready in about 15 minutes | Servings 6)

Ingredients

4 slices bacon

2 cups water

5 potatoes, peeled and diced

1 cup sour cream

1/4 cup Colby-Jack cheese, grated

3 tablespoons butter

1 clove garlic, minced

1/2 teaspoon cayenne pepper

1/2 teaspoon dried rosemary, crushed

Sea salt and freshly ground black pepper, to taste

1/2 cup green garlic, for garnish

Directions

Cook the bacon on HIGH until it has browned. Then, crush the bacon and reserve; discard any excess fat, reserving one tablespoon of the bacon grease.

Pour the water into the pot; add the potatoes and securely lock the cooker's lid; set for 6 minutes on HIGH.

Afterward, release the cooker's pressure. Drain the potatoes. Then, mash the potatoes, gradually adding the rest of the ingredients, except for green garlic; add reserved bacon grease. Taste and adjust the seasonings.

Top with crushed bacon; garnish with fresh green garlic and serve.

Cheesy Polenta Cubes

(Ready in about 10 minutes | Servings 6)

Ingredients

4 tablespoons butter, melted

1/2 cup scallions, chopped

3 ½ cups vegetable stock

1 cup water

1 ½ cups coarse cornmeal

1 teaspoon salt

½ teaspoon ground black pepper

⅓ cup Parmigiano-Reggiano cheese, grated

Directions

Warm two tablespoons of butter on HIGH setting. Then, sauté the scallions until they're softened and translucent.

Add the vegetable broth, water, coarse cornmeal, salt, and black pepper. Now lock the lid and cook for 9 minutes under HIGH pressure.

Stir in cheese; add the remaining two tablespoons of butter; give it a good stir and serve.

Bacon and Kale Appetizer

(Ready in about 20 minutes | Servings 4)

Ingredients

4 strips bacon, diced

2 cloves garlic, crushed

1 onion, chopped

2 bunches kale, chopped

2 cups vegetable broth

1 teaspoon dried rosemary, crushed

Sea salt and black pepper, to your liking

Directions

In a pressure cooker, sauté the bacon strips over HIGH heat; cook for about 5 minutes or until they have browned.

Stir in the remaining ingredients; seal the pressure cooker's lid. Set for 15 minutes at HIGH pressure.

Let the pressure release naturally. Serve.

Hummus with Pita Chips

(Ready in about 1 hour | Servings 16)

Ingredients

1 cup chickpeas

2 teaspoons canola oil

4 cups water

1 tablespoon fresh cilantro

1 teaspoon dried parsley

2 cloves garlic, peeled and minced

2 tablespoons tahini

1/4 teaspoon dried spearmint

3/4 teaspoon salt, to taste

2 tablespoons lemon juice

1/4 cup sesame oil

Pita chips, for garnish

Directions

Add the chickpeas, canola oil, and 4 cups of water to your cooker. Cover and bring to HIGH pressure; maintain for 40 minutes. Then, allow pressure to release naturally.

Uncover, drain the chickpeas and cook on HIGH pressure for an additional 10 minutes.

Add the prepared chickpeas to your food processor (or a blender). Now stir in cilantro, parsley, garlic, tahini, spearmint, salt, and lemon juice. Pulse until everything is well combined. Make sure to scrape down the sides of the food processor bowl.

Lastly, add the sesame oil with the machine running and pulse until it is smooth. Serve with pita chips and enjoy!

Fastest-Ever Corn Cobs

(Ready in about 10 minutes | Servings 6)

Ingredients

3 cups water

6 ears sweet corn cobs, halved

Directions

Pour the water into your pressure cooker; insert the steamer basket.

Place the corn cobs in the steamer basket.

Seal the lid. Set the timer to 2 minutes under HIGH pressure. Run the cooker under cold water. Serve warm.

Traditional Baba Ghanoush

(Ready in about 15 minutes | Servings 16)

Ingredients

1 tablespoon sesame oil

1 large-sized eggplant, peeled and diced

5 cloves garlic, finely minced

1/2 cup water

3 tablespoons fresh cilantro

3/4 teaspoon salt

Cracked black pepper, to taste

1 tablespoon lemon juice

2 tablespoons tahini

1 tablespoon olive oil

Directions

Add the sesame oil to the pressure cooker; heat over medium heat. Stir in the eggplant. Sauté the eggplant until it is tender. Add the garlic; sauté for 30 seconds more.

Pour in the water, and lock the lid. Bring to HIGH pressure; maintain pressure for 4 to 5 minutes. Then, quick-release the pressure, and uncover.

Add the eggplant mixture to a food processor along with the cilantro, salt, black pepper, lemon juice, and tahini. Process it, scraping down the sides of the container.

Add the olive oil and process until smooth. Transfer to a serving bowl. Serve with your favorite pita wedges or veggie sticks.

Artichoke and Spinach Dip

(Ready in about 15 minutes | Servings 12)

Ingredients

2 cups canned artichoke hearts, coarsely chopped

1 ½ cups frozen chopped spinach, thawed and well drained

1/2 cup sour cream

1/2 cup mayonnaise

1 ½ cups mozzarella cheese, shredded

1/2 teaspoon paprika

Sea salt and ground black pepper, to taste

Directions

Combine all the ingredients together in a baking dish that fits in the pressure cooking pot. Cover it tightly with a foil. Make sure to prepare a foil sling.

Place the rack at the bottom of the cooker. Pour about 2 cups of water into the cooker. Place the baking dish on the rack.

Seal the lid and select HIGH pressure for 10 minutes. After that, turn off the cooker; use a quick pressure release; then, carefully remove the lid.

Serve warm with tortilla chips if desired. Enjoy!

Amazing Steamed Artichokes

(Ready in about 10 minutes | Servings 6)

Ingredients

3 medium artichokes

1 medium-sized lemon, halved

1 teaspoon yellow mustard

3 tablespoons mayonnaise

1/2 teaspoon cayenne pepper

Salt and ground black pepper, to taste

Directions

Pour 1 cup of water into the pressure cooker. Now place the steamer basket in your cooker. Add the artichokes; drizzle with lemon.

Close the lid and turn the heat to HIGH; Cook for 10 minutes at high pressure.

Then, open the pressure cooker with the natural release method. Check for the doneness. If it is not done, cook for an additional few minutes.

Then, make the sauce. In a mixing bowl, combine the mustard together with mayonnaise, cayenne pepper, salt, and black pepper. Serve with prepared artichokes. Serve warm.

Bacon and Bean Dip

(Ready in about 30 minutes | Servings 12)

Ingredients

2 cups water

1 cup dried beans

4 slices bacon, finely diced

2 cloves garlic, peeled and minced

1 onion, peeled and diced

1 (14 ½-ounce) can tomatoes, diced

2 teaspoons chili powder

1/2 teaspoon dried basil

Sea salt and black pepper, to taste

1/4 cup fresh parsley, finely chopped

1 cup sharp cheese, grated

Avocado slices, for garnish

Directions

Add the water and beans to a container and let it soak overnight. Drain the beans and set aside.

Throw the bacon, garlic, and onion into your cooker. Sauté for 3 to 4 minutes or until the onions are translucent.

Then, stir the beans into the pressure cooker together with the tomatoes, chili powder, and basil. Lock the lid into place. Bring to HIGH pressure and maintain pressure for 12 minutes.

Turn off the heat and allow pressure to release for 10 minutes. Uncover and transfer the prepared bean mixture to your food processor. Add the sea salt, black pepper, and parsley and blend until smooth.

Transfer the dip to a fondue pot and add cheese. Stir to combine and garnish with avocado. Serve immediately with your favorite dippers.

Caribbean-Style Relish

(Ready in about 30 minutes | Servings 12)

Ingredients

7 cups water

1 ½ cups kidney beans

2 teaspoons olive oil

Salt and ground black pepper, to taste

2 tablespoons tahini paste

1/4 cup pineapple, drained and crushed

1/2 teaspoon dried cumin

1 teaspoon garlic powder

1/2 cup fresh cilantro, finely minced

Directions

Add 3 cups of water and kidney beans to your cooker; let it soak overnight. Drain and replace to the pressure cooker. Pour in the remaining 4 cups of water. Add the olive oil and lock the lid into place.

Bring to HIGH pressure and maintain this pressure for 10 to 15 minutes. Remove from the heat. Then, quick release any remaining pressure.

Add the cooked beans to the bowl of your blender or a food processor. Stir in the rest of the above ingredients and pulse until it is well combined but still a little chunky.

Place in a refrigerator to chill, and serve as a dip for chips if desired.

Glazed Carrots with Cranberries

(Ready in about 5 minutes | Servings 6)

Ingredients

1 cup water

2 pounds carrots, sliced diagonally

1/4 cup dried cranberries

A pinch of kosher salt

3/4 teaspoon black pepper

2 tablespoons butter

2 tablespoons maple syrup

Directions

Put the water, carrots, and cranberries into the pressure cooker. Close the lid of the cooker. Cook for 3 to 4 minutes at LOW pressure.

While the carrots are still warm, add the salt, black pepper, butter, and maple syrup. Gently stir to combine. Serve right now.

Bacon and Chicken Dip

(Ready in about 10 minutes | Servings 24)

Ingredients

3 bacon slices, cut into strips

2 tablespoons lard, softened

3 cloves garlic, peeled and minced

1 onion, peeled and diced

1 red bell pepper, cut into strips

1/2 cup salsa

1/4 cup tomato paste

1/2 cup vegetable stock

1 pound chicken breast, boneless and diced

1/2 cup sour cream

1 cup Mozzarella cheese, grated

1/2 teaspoon dried dill

Salt and freshly ground black pepper, to taste

Directions

Add the bacon strips and lard to the pressure cooker. Then, sauté the garlic, onion, and bell pepper for 3 minutes or until they are tender.

Next, stir in the salsa, tomato paste, vegetable stock, and chicken. Lock the lid into place; bring to LOW pressure; maintain pressure for 6 minutes.

In order to thicken the sauce, uncover and continue to simmer over MEDIUM heat.

Reduce the heat; fold in the sour cream and Mozzarella cheese; stir to combine well. Lastly, sprinkle with dill, salt, and black pepper to taste. Serve warm with tortilla chips.

Asparagus with Yogurt Crème

(Ready in about 10 minutes + chilling time | Servings 4)

Ingredients

2 cups plain yogurt

1 cup water

1 pound asparagus, trimmed

1 teaspoon dried basil

Kosher salt, to taste

Black pepper, to taste

Directions

To prepare yogurt crème: Put the yogurt into a fine mesh strainer over a bowl; transfer it to the refrigerator for about 4 hours.

Add the water to the pressure cooker; place the steamer basket.

Place the asparagus in the steamer basket. Sprinkle with basil, kosher salt, and black pepper. Close the lid.

Turn the heat to HIGH; when your cooker reaches pressure, lower the temperature to the minimum. Allow to cook for 3 minutes at HIGH pressure.

Afterwards, open the pressure cooker by releasing pressure. Serve with prepared yogurt crème.

Amazing Red Potatoes

(Ready in about 10 minutes | Servings 12)

Ingredients

1 cup water

1 teaspoon vegetable oil

3 pounds whole and unpeeled red potatoes, washed and cubed

Salt and black pepper, to taste

Paprika, to taste

Directions

Put the water and vegetable oil into your pressure cooker. Place a rack in your cooker; load the cooker with potato cubes.

Close the lid and bring to pressure over HIGH heat. Cook for 3 minutes; turn off the heat; use quick release method to depressurize your cooker.

Season prepared potatoes with salt, black pepper, and paprika. Enjoy!

Party Eggplant Dip

(Ready in about 10 minutes | Servings 12)

Ingredients

1 tablespoon sesame oil

3 cloves garlic, minced

1 large eggplant, peeled and diced

1/2 cup water

3 tablespoons fresh cilantro

1/2 teaspoon salt

1/4 teaspoon ground black pepper

2 tablespoons fresh lemon juice

2 tablespoons tahini

1 tablespoon extra-virgin olive oil

Directions

Warm the sesame oil in the pressure cooker over medium heat. Add garlic and eggplant and sauté until they begin to get soft. Pour in the water.

Lock the cooker's lid and bring to HIGH pressure. Now maintain pressure for 4 minutes. After that, quick release the pressure and remove the lid.

Pulse the eggplant-garlic mixture in your food processor along with the cilantro, salt, black pepper, lemon juice, and tahini.

Then, pour in the extra-virgin olive oil and process until the mixture is smooth. Garnish with fresh chopped chives if desired and serve.

Stuffed Potato Shells

(Ready in about 40 minutes | Servings 6)

Ingredients

2 cups water

6 Idaho potatoes, washed

2 tablespoons olive oil

1/4 cup bacon bits

1 cup Cheddar cheese, shredded

1 teaspoon garlic powder

1 teaspoon onion powder

1/4 cup sour cream

Directions

Preheat your oven to 400 degrees F. Pour the water into your pressure cooker.

Slice the potatoes in half lengthwise. Place the steamer basket in the cooker. Then, arrange the potatoes in two layers in the steamer basket.

Then, lock the lid into place. Bring to HIGH pressure and cook for 10 minutes. Next, quick-release the pressure, and uncover the cooker. Then, scoop out the inside of the potatoes, leaving 1/4-thick shells.

Grease the scooped-out shell of each potato with olive oil. Layer them on a baking sheet. Bake them for 15 minutes; remove from the oven.

Stuff prepared potato skins with the bacon bits and cheese. Sprinkle with garlic powder and onion powder; then, bake for 10 minutes longer. Serve with sour cream.

Spicy Pea Dip

(Ready in about 15 minutes + chilling time | Servings 16)

Ingredients

8 cups water

2 cups dried black-eyed peas

1 red onion, diced

2 cloves garlic, minced

1 pickled jalapeño, finely chopped

1 ripe tomato, seeded and diced

2 tablespoons fresh parsley

1 tablespoon fresh cilantro

1/4 cup wine vinegar

2 tablespoons vegetable oil

1/2 teaspoon celery seed

1 teaspoon sea salt

1/2 teaspoon ground black pepper

Directions

Place 4 cups of water in a deep container along with the black-eyed peas; let it soak for 1 hour. Drain, rinse the black-eyed peas and add them to the pressure cooker.

Add the remaining 4 cups of water to the cooker. Lock the lid and bring to HIGH pressure; maintain for 11 minutes.

Remove the cooker from the heat; allow pressure to release gradually. Drain the black-eyed peas and transfer them to the large bowl.

Stir in all remaining ingredients; stir to combine well. Refrigerate your dip at least 2 hours before serving.

Zesty Pearl Onions

(Ready in about 10 minutes + chilling time | Servings 6)

Ingredients

1/2 cup water

1 pound pearl onions, outer layer removed

1 bay leaf

3/4 teaspoon black pepper, freshly ground

1/4 teaspoon salt

4 tablespoons balsamic vinegar

2 tablespoons maple syrup

1 tablespoon all-purpose flour

Directions

Throw the water and pearl onions in your pressure cooker along with the bay leaf, black pepper, and salt. Now lock the cooker's lid.

Turn the heat up to HIGH. When your cooker reaches pressure, cook for about 6 minutes at low pressure. Afterwards, open your cooker by releasing pressure. Transfer pearl onions to the bowl.

In a saucepan, combine the rest of the above ingredients. Cook over low heat about 1 minute. Pour the sauce over the pearl onions in the bowl. Serve chilled and enjoy.

Jalapeño and Cheese Dip

(Ready in about 10 minutes | Servings 12)

Ingredients

2 tablespoons butter

2 tablespoons all-purpose flour

1 cup milk

16 ounces Monterey Jack cheese, shredded

2 pickled jalapeños, minced

1/2 cup tomatoes, canned

1/4 teaspoon black pepper

1/4 teaspoon cayenne pepper

1 teaspoon basil

Sea salt, to taste

Directions

In your cooker, warm the butter over medium flame; slowly stir in the flour and stir until you have a paste. Pour in the milk and stir until the mixture has thickened. Bring it to a boil.

Add the cheese; vigorously stir until it is smooth. Add the rest of your ingredients; secure the lid on your cooker. Cook on medium; lower heat and cook for about 3 minutes.

Afterwards, remove the lid and serve right away.

BBQ Chicken Wings

(Ready in about 25 minutes | Servings 6)

Ingredients

12-15 chicken wings (about 2 pounds)

1/2 teaspoon ground black pepper

1 teaspoon cayenne pepper

1 ¼ teaspoons salt

2 tablespoons olive oil

3 cloves garlic, minced

1 yellow onion, chopped

1/4 cup flour

1/2 cup BBQ Sauce

Directions

Season chicken wings with black pepper, cayenne pepper, and salt.

Warm olive oil and sauté the garlic and yellow onion. Stir in seasoned chicken wings and cook until they are browned.

Then, dust the chicken wings with flour. Pour in the BBQ sauce. Place the lid on your cooker and lock the lid. Press the "Soup/Stew", and cook for 15 minutes. Release the pressure value to open.

Lastly, test the chicken wings for the doneness. Taste and adjust the seasonings. Serve warm.

Hot Party Wings

(Ready in about 20 minutes | Servings 6)

Ingredients

1 cup water

2 pounds chicken wings

4 tablespoons hot sauce

1/4 cup honey

1/4 cup tomato paste

1 teaspoon ground black pepper

1 teaspoon dried basil

2 teaspoons sea salt

Directions

Pour the water into your pressure cooker; place a steamer basket in the cooker.

Place the wings in the steamer basket. Close and lock the cooker's lid. Cook for 10 minutes at HIGH pressure.

While the chicken wings are cooking, prepare the dipping sauce by mixing the hot sauce, honey, tomato paste, black pepper, basil, and salt.

Then, open the cooker by releasing the pressure. Transfer the prepared wings to the bowl with sauce and coat them evenly. Cook under the broiler for about 5 minutes, until they become crisp. Enjoy!

Beets with Walnuts

(Ready in about 15 minutes | Servings 6)

Ingredients

6 medium-sized beets

2 ½ cups water

1 tablespoon apple cider vinegar

1 tablespoon honey

1/2 teaspoon paprika

1 teaspoon dried basil

1/2 teaspoon freshly ground black pepper

3/4 teaspoon salt

3 tablespoons extra-virgin olive oil

2 tablespoons walnuts, finely chopped

Directions

Scrub your beets. Transfer them to a pressure cooker; pour in the water. Close the cooker's lid and bring to HIGH pressure. Reduce heat to medium; cook for 10 minutes.

Remove from heat and release pressure through the steam vent. Remove the lid. Drain the beets and let them cool. Then, rub off skins and cut into wedges. Transfer them to a serving bowl.

Whisk the vinegar, honey, paprika, basil, black pepper, salt, and olive oil in a small-sized bowl. Drizzle the vinaigrette over the beets in the serving bowl. Scatter chopped walnuts over the top and serve.

Beets and Carrots with Pecans

(Ready in about 15 minutes | Servings 6)

Ingredients

2 ½ cups water

4 medium-sized beets, peeled

4 carrots, trimmed

1 tablespoon fresh lemon juice

1 tablespoon maple syrup

1 teaspoon cumin

1 teaspoon dried dill weed

1 teaspoon salt

1/2 teaspoon freshly ground black pepper

3 tablespoons extra-virgin olive oil

2 tablespoons pecans, finely chopped

2 tablespoons golden raisins

Directions

Place water, beets, and carrots in your pressure cooker. Close the lid and bring to HIGH pressure. Now cook for 10 minutes.

Turn off the heat and release pressure through steam vent. Drain and rinse beets and carrots. Cut them into wedges and replace to a bowl in order to cool completely.

In a mixing bowl or a measuring cup, whisk the lemon juice, maple syrup, cumin, dill, salt, black pepper, and olive oil.

Drizzle the dressing over the vegetables. Scatter pecans and raisins over the top and serve.

Herbed Bean Spread

(Ready in about 30 minutes | Servings 6)

Ingredients

2 tablespoons olive oil

2 green onions, thinly sliced

1 ½ cups dried beans, rinsed

3 cups water

1 tablespoon apple cider vinegar

Salt and black pepper, to taste

1 teaspoon cumin

1 thyme sprig, chopped

1 rosemary sprig, chopped

Directions

Warm olive oil in the preheated pressure cooker; then, sauté green onions. Stir in the beans and water; lock the lid.

Turn the heat up to HIGH; maintain pressure approximately 30 minutes.

Open with the natural release method. Drain the beans and allow them to cool. Purée them in your food processor. Add the rest of the above ingredients.

Purée until it is uniform and smooth. Transfer to a serving bowl and drizzle with some extra olive oil if desired.

Amazing Garlic Dipping Sauce

(Ready in about 10 minutes | Servings 10)

Ingredients

1 cup water

2 whole heads garlic, peeled

1/2 cup butter, softened

1 tablespoon fresh oregano

1 teaspoon dill weed

Ground black pepper, to taste

1 teaspoon salt

Directions

Pour water into your cooker; then, place the steamer basket in the cooker. Add the garlic.

Cover and bring to HIGH pressure; maintain for about 2 minutes. Remove from the heat; allow pressure to quick-release.

Then, mash the garlic cloves; add the rest of the ingredients. Serve chilled.

Artichoke Bean Dipping Sauce

(Ready in about 20 minutes | Servings 20)

Ingredients

1/2 cup dry kidney beans, soaked overnight

1 cup water

6 medium-sized artichokes, outer leaves removed

1 small-sized lemon, freshly squeezed

2 cloves of garlic, smashed

1 cup non-fat yogurt

1/4 teaspoon pepper

1 teaspoon salt, or to taste

1 cup Cheddar cheese, grated

Directions

Throw the beans and water in your cooker.

Then, cut off the top about 1/3 of each artichoke. Slice your artichokes in half lengthwise; remove the "choke". Drizzle with fresh lemon juice and put into the cooker cut-side up.

Close and lock the cooker's lid. Turn the heat up to HIGH; when your cooker reaches desired pressure, maintain pressure.

Cook approximately 20 minutes at high pressure. When time is up, open the pressure cooker and wait for the pressure to come down.

Add the rest of the ingredients. Lastly, mix the content by using an immersion blender. Serve warm or at room temperature with dippers of choice.

Favorite Prosciutto-Wrapped Asparagus

(Ready in about 5 minutes | Servings 4)

Ingredients

2 cups water

1 pound asparagus spears

8 ounces Prosciutto, thinly sliced

Directions

Add the water to your cooker.

Then, wrap the asparagus spears in prosciutto slices.

Next, place the prosciutto-wrapped asparagus in a steamer basket. Insert the steamer basket into the pressure cooker; close the cooker's lid.

Cook for 2 to 3 minutes at HIGH pressure. Then, open your cooker with the Normal release method.

Transfer your prosciutto-wrapped asparagus spears to the serving platter, serve and enjoy!

Egg and Ham Appetizer

(Ready in about 5 minutes | Servings 4)

Ingredients

1 ½ cups water

1 tablespoon olive oil

4 slices ham

4 large-sized eggs

4 slices Gruyere cheese

1 tablespoon fresh cilantro, chopped

Directions

Prepare your cooker by adding the water and the trivet.

Coat the bottom and sides of your ramekins with olive oil. Then, lay the ham slices at the bottom. Break an egg into each ramekin.

Top with Gruyere cheese. Lay ramekins in the steamer basket in your pressure cooker.

Close the lid and set the pressure level to LOW. Cook for 4 minutes at LOW pressure. After that, release pressure. Sprinkle with fresh cilantro. Serve right away!

Mustard Baked Beans

(Ready in about 1 hour | Servings 6)

Ingredients

2 cups white beans

6 strips bacon, diced

3 cloves garlic, minced

1 onion, diced

3 cups water

2 tablespoons olive oil

1/2 teaspoon cumin

1/3 cup ketchup

1/3 cup molasses

3 tablespoons Dijon mustard

Directions

Soak white beans for 30 minutes. Drain and rinse your beans and reserve.

Then, cook the bacon, garlic, and onion until bacon is crisp and the onion is tender, or 4 to 5 minutes.

Add the soaked beans, along with the water, olive oil, and cumin; now lock the cooker's lid. Cook for 20 minutes under HIGH pressure.

Let the pressure release naturally. Set the cooker to HIGH, and stir in ketchup, molasses, and Dijon mustard. Continue to cook at least 5 minutes. Serve warm.

Cheesy Potato and Bacon Appetizer

(Ready in about 15 minutes | Servings 6)

Ingredients

4 slices bacon

2 cups water

6 potatoes, peeled and quartered

1/2 cup sour cream

1/4 cup Parmigiano-Reggiano cheese, grated

3 tablespoons butter

Sea salt and freshly ground black pepper, to taste

1/2 cup Colby-Jack cheese, shredded

Fresh sliced chives, for garnish

Directions

Sauté bacon on HIGH until it is browned and crisp. Crush the bacon, and set it aside; make sure to reserve 1 tablespoon of the bacon grease.

Place the water and potatoes in the pot; now securely lock the cooker's lid; set for 6 minutes on HIGH.

Then, release the cooker's pressure. Drain the potatoes and add them back to the pot. Then, mash potatoes, adding the rest of the ingredients and reserved bacon grease, except for chives. Taste and adjust the seasonings.

Top with crushed bacon; garnish with fresh chives and serve.

Parmesan and Polenta Appetizer

(Ready in about 10 minutes | Servings 6)

Ingredients

4 tablespoons butter, melted

1 sweet onion, finely chopped

4 ½ cups vegetable broth

1 ½ cups coarse cornmeal

3/4 teaspoon kosher salt

1/2 teaspoon cayenne pepper

1/2 teaspoon ground black pepper

1/3 cup Parmesan cheese, grated

Directions

Melt 2 tablespoons of butter on HIGH. Then, sauté sweet onion for about 1 minute, until it is translucent.

Add the vegetable broth, cornmeal, salt, cayenne pepper, and black pepper. Now lock the cooker's lid and cook for 9 minutes under HIGH pressure.

Stir in Parmesan cheese and the remaining 2 tablespoons of butter before serving.

Bacon and Collard Greens Appetizer

(Ready in about 20 minutes | Servings 4)

Ingredients

4 strips bacon, diced

3 cloves garlic

1 onion

2 bunches collard greens, chopped

2 cups chicken stock

Sea salt and black pepper to taste

1 teaspoon cayenne pepper

Directions

In your pressure cooker, sauté the bacon over HIGH heat for about 5 minutes.

Stir in the remaining ingredients; lock the pressure cooker's lid. Set for 15 minutes over HIGH pressure.

Let the pressure release naturally and serve right away.

Bacon and Polenta Appetizer

(Ready in about 10 minutes | Servings 6)

Ingredients

2 tablespoons olive oil

2-3 cloves garlic, finely minced

1 cup green onions, finely chopped

4 strips bacon, chopped

4 ½ cups chicken stock

1 ½ cups coarse cornmeal

Sea salt and black pepper, to taste

1 teaspoon dried rosemary

1/2 teaspoon dried thyme

1/3 cup Parmesan cheese, grated

Directions

Warm the oil over HIGH heat. Sauté the garlic, onion and bacon for about 2 minutes.

Add the rest of your ingredients, except for Parmesan cheese. Now lock the lid and cook for 9 minutes on HIGH pressure. Gradually release the pressure.

While the polenta is still hot, stir in Parmesan; stir until Parmesan cheese has melted and serve immediately.

Broccoli and Potato Appetizer

(Ready in about 20 minutes | Servings 6)

Ingredients

2 cups water

6 potatoes, peeled and quartered

2 cups broccoli, broken into florets

3 tablespoons extra-virgin olive oil

1/4 cup half-and-half

1/2 cup sharp cheese, shredded

1/2 teaspoon dried dill weed

1/2 teaspoon cumin powder

Sea salt and ground black pepper, to taste

Directions

Add the water, potatoes, and broccoli to the pot. Securely lock the lid and set on HIGH for 6 minutes. Use a quick release to release the pressure.

Drain the vegetables, and add them back to the cooker. Now, mash them with a potato masher; add the remaining ingredients and mash until smooth and uniform.

Taste and adjust the seasonings. Serve right now or as a cold appetizer.

Brussels Sprouts with Bacon

(Ready in about 10 minutes | Servings 4)

Ingredients

1/4 pound bacon, diced

1 pound Brussels sprouts, trimmed and halved

1 tablespoon mustard

1 cup chicken stock

Salt and ground black pepper, to taste

1 teaspoon dried sage

1 teaspoon dried basil

2 tablespoons butter

Directions

Set your pressure cooker over medium-high heat; add the bacon and cook for 2 minutes, stirring periodically. Now add the Brussels sprouts, mustard, and chicken stock; cover the cooker.

Bring the pressure to HIGH and cook for 4 more minutes. Then, release pressure using cold water method.

Uncover the cooker and add the rest of the above ingredients. Taste, adjust the seasonings and replace to a serving platter. Enjoy!

Easiest Salsa Ever

(Ready in about 10 minutes | Servings 8)

Ingredients

1 pound tomato, quartered

2 poblano chili peppers, chopped

1 medium-sized leek, chopped

1/2 cup cold water

1/4 cup fresh basil, chopped

1/4 cup fresh cilantro, chopped

1 tablespoon fresh sage, chopped

Freshly cracked black pepper, to taste

1 teaspoon kosher salt

Directions

First, place the tomatoes in your pressure cooker. Pour in enough water to cover them. Lock the cooker's lid into place. Bring to HIGH pressure and maintain for 2 minutes.

Turn off the heat; use a quick release to release the pressure.

Add the drained and cooked tomatoes to your food processor. Now add poblano peppers, leek, cold water, basil, cilantro, sage, black pepper, and salt to your food processor. Mix until everything is well combined.

Serve chilled with corn tortilla chips.

Yummy Cayenne Peanuts

(Ready in about 50 minutes | Servings 16)

Ingredients

2 pounds raw peanuts

12 cups water

1 teaspoon cayenne pepper

1/3 cup sea salt

Directions

First, place raw peanuts in the pressure cooker. Add the water, cayenne pepper, and sea salt.

Close the lid; bring to a medium setting and cook for 45 minutes. Turn off the heat; allow pressure to release gradually.

Allow the peanuts to cool. Drain and transfer them to a serving bowl.

Cajun Garlic Peanuts

(Ready in about 50 minutes | Servings 16)

Ingredients

2 pounds raw peanuts

12 cups water

1 teaspoon Cajun seasoning

1 teaspoon garlic powder

1/3 cup sea salt

Directions

Throw green peanuts in the pressure cooker. Add the remaining ingredients; stir to combine.

Cover and bring to a medium setting; let it cook for 45 minutes. Afterwards, allow the pressure to release gradually.

Allow the peanuts to cool. Drain and serve.

Butternut Squash with Pine Nuts

(Ready in about 1 hour 15 minutes | Servings 6)

Ingredients

1 butternut squash, peeled and sliced

2 tablespoons extra-virgin olive oil

Salt and freshly ground pepper

3 ½ ounces pine nuts

1/2 cup green onions, chopped

2 tablespoons tomato paste

1 cup vegetable broth

1 teaspoon grated lemon rind

1/2 cup wine

1/2 cup sharp cheese shavings

Directions

Begin by preheating your oven to 350 degrees F. Now spread the butternut squash slices on a baking sheet; drizzle with 1 tablespoon of olive oil; sprinkle with salt and black pepper.

Cover with an aluminum foil; roast butternut squash slices until they are tender, or about 45 minutes. Add the squash to a food processor; puree until it's smooth.

In the meantime, toast the pine nuts on a baking sheet for about 4 minutes.

Then, warm the remaining 1 tablespoon of olive oil in a pressure cooker. Add green onions and sauté until they are softened, 4 minutes. Add the roasted pine nuts and tomato paste; cook, stirring constantly, for about 2 minutes.

Add the vegetable broth, lemon rind, and wine; cover and cook for 7 minutes. Remove the lid and release the pressure.

Add the cooker back to medium heat; bring the contents to a boil. Cook for about 4 minutes. Add the reserved squash puree; cook until it is warmed through. Serve with cheese shavings.

Meatballs in Herbed Sauce

(Ready in about 15 minutes | Servings 12)

Ingredients

2 tablespoons pineapple juice

1 tablespoon maple syrup

1 tablespoon dried thyme

1 cup water

2 tablespoons soy sauce

1/2 pound ground pork

1 pound extra lean ground beef

2 cloves garlic, minced

1 cup shallots, diced

1/2 cup bread crumbs

Fresh parsley, for garnish

Directions

In your cooker, place pineapple juice, maple syrup, thyme, water, soy sauce; stir to combine. Bring to a boil over HIGH heat.

Cook until the sauce has thickened; turn off the heat.

In a bowl, combine ground pork, ground beef, garlic, shallots, and bread crumbs; mix until everything is incorporated.

Now shape the mixture into 12 equal meatballs; carefully transfer meatballs to the pressure cooker. Lock the lid into place and bring to HIGH pressure; maintain pressure for about 5 minutes.

Release pressure quickly. Transfer to a large serving platter. Sprinkle with fresh chopped parsley and serve warm.

Fast and Easy Carrot Coins

(Ready in about 5 minutes | Servings 6)

Ingredients

1 cup water

1 pound carrots, peeled and sliced into thick coins

Directions

Fill the cooker's base with water. Place the carrot coins in the steamer basket; put the basket into the pressure cooker. Close the lid.

Turn the heat up to HIGH and maintain the pressure for 1 to 2 minutes at HIGH.

Afterwards, open the pressure cooker by releasing pressure. Replace to a serving platter and serve.

Butter and Maple Carrot Coins

(Ready in about 10 minutes | Servings 4)

Ingredients

1 cup water

1 pound carrots, trimmed and cut into thick coins

2 tablespoons butter, softened

1 tablespoon maple syrup

1 teaspoon balsamic vinegar

Sea salt and freshly ground black pepper

2 tablespoons fresh cilantro, chopped

Directions

Pour the water into your pressure cooker. Throw the carrots into the steamer basket and lay it in your pressure cooker.

Cover and maintain the pressure for 1 to 2 minutes at HIGH. Then, open the pressure cooker by releasing pressure.

Warn butter in a saucepan over medium heat. Then, add carrots, and cook stirring occasionally, for about 3 minutes. Add maple syrup, balsamic vinegar, salt, and black pepper; cook for 1 more minute.

Remove to a serving platter and serve sprinkled with fresh cilantro. Enjoy!

Cabbage and Mushroom Spring Rolls

(Ready in about 10 minutes | Servings 12)

Ingredients

1/2 pound cabbage, shredded

1 cup bamboo shoots, sliced

1/4 cup fresh parsley, chopped

3 cloves garlic, minced

1 cup mushrooms, sliced

1 onion, finely chopped

1 tablespoon rice wine vinegar

12 spring roll wrappers

2 cups water

Directions

In a bowl, mix together the cabbage, bamboo shoots, parsley, garlic, mushrooms, onion, and rice wine vinegar; stir to combine.

Lay the wrappers on a flat surface. Then, divide the cabbage mixture among wrappers. Roll up the wrappers, and transfer them to the pressure cooker steamer basket.

Pour the water into the bottom of the cooker. Place the steamer basket in the cooker. Lock the lid into place. Bring to HIGH pressure and maintain pressure for about 3 minutes. Serve warm with your favorite dipping sauce.

Herby Tomato Sauce

(Ready in about 15 minutes | Servings 16)

Ingredients

2 tablespoons olive oil

1/2 cup green onions, sliced

3 cloves garlic, peeled and minced

2 ½ pounds tomatoes, peeled and diced

1 teaspoon dried oregano

1 teaspoon dried basil

1 teaspoon dried sage

1 teaspoon granulated sugar

Salt and freshly ground black pepper, to taste

Directions

Warm the olive oil in your pressure cooker over medium heat. Then, sauté green onions and garlic for about 30 seconds.

Add the tomatoes to the pressure cooker along with the remaining ingredients.

Lock the lid into place; bring to LOW pressure and maintain for 10 minutes. Turn off the heat and let pressure release naturally. Use immediately or refrigerate for up to a week. Enjoy!

Old-Fashioned Peanuts in Shells

(Ready in about 1 hour | Servings 6)

Ingredients

1 pound raw peanuts in shells

8 cups of water

1/4 cup salt

Directions

Rinse the peanuts in cold water. Transfer them to a pressure cooker and add the water.

Seal the cooker's lid and turn the heat to HIGH.

When the pressure comes up to pressure, reduce the heat to LOW. Cook for about 30 minutes.

Turn off the heat; allow the pressure to release gradually, or for about 20 minutes. Add the salt and serve.

Spiced Artichokes in Wine

(Ready in about 15 minutes | Servings 4)

Ingredients

4 fresh artichokes, tops and stems removed

2 tablespoons canola oil

2 large-sized garlic cloves, minced

1 white onion, peeled and finely minced

Sea salt and freshly cracked black pepper, to taste

1 teaspoon cayenne pepper

1 cup white wine, best you can afford

Directions

Put the prepared artichokes into your pressure cooker. Drizzle with canola oil.

Sprinkle the artichokes with garlic, onion, salt, black pepper, and cayenne pepper. Pour white wine over the artichokes.

Cook in your pressure cooker approximately 10 minutes. Serve mayonnaise on the side for dipping if desired.

Artichokes with Hot Hollandaise Sauce

(Ready in about 15 minutes | Servings 4)

Ingredients

6 artichokes, tops and stems removed

2 tablespoons extra-virgin olive oil

1 cup scallions, finely minced

1 teaspoon salt

1/4 teaspoon freshly cracked black pepper

1 teaspoon dried dill weed

2 tablespoons lemon juice

1 cup water

Hot hollandaise sauce, for garnish

Directions

Lay the artichokes in your pressure cooker. Drizzle the artichokes with the olive oil.

Sprinkle them with scallions, salt, black pepper, and dill weed. Drizzle the lemon juice over the artichokes. Pour in the water.

Cook the artichokes in the pressure cooker for about 10 minutes. Serve with hot hollandaise sauce and enjoy!

Yummy Healthy Caponata

(Ready in about 10 minutes | Servings 8)

Ingredients

1 large-sized zucchini, cut into thick slices

1 medium-sized eggplant, cut into thick slices

1 leek, sliced

1 red bell pepper, seeded and sliced

1 yellow bell pepper, seeded and sliced

1 green bell pepper, seeded and sliced

Salt and black pepper, to taste

1 teaspoon dried basil

1/2 teaspoon dried oregano

1/2 teaspoon garlic powder

1/2 teaspoon onion powder

Extra-virgin olive oil, to taste

Directions

Add all the ingredients to your pressure cooker, except for olive oil. Cook for about 5 minutes.

Transfer to a serving platter. Drizzle with olive oil and serve. Enjoy!

Easy Veggie Appetizer

(Ready in about 10 minutes | Servings 6)

Ingredients

1 large-sized zucchini, cut into thick slices

2 bell peppers, sliced

1 red onion, sliced

2-3 cloves garlic, peeled

Salt and black pepper, to taste

1 teaspoon paprika

A few drops of smoked liquid

Salt and black pepper, to taste

1/2 teaspoon dried basil

Extra-virgin olive oil, to taste

Directions

Throw all the ingredients in your pressure cooker, except for olive oil. Cook for about 5 minutes.

Drizzle with extra-virgin olive oil and serve.

Sesame and Honey Chicken Wings

(Ready in about 20 minutes | Servings 6)

Ingredients

12 chicken wings, cut apart at joints

1/2 cup chicken stock

1/2 cup honey

3 tablespoons sesame oil

2 tablespoons tamari sauce

2 garlic cloves, crushed

1 teaspoon cayenne pepper

1 teaspoon grated ginger

1/4 cup sesame seeds

Directions

Add 1 cup of water to your pressure cooker. Then, place a steamer basket in the cooker. Lay the chicken wings in the steamer basket.

Close and lock the cooker's lid. Cook for 10 minutes at HIGH pressure.

Meanwhile, in a mixing bowl, combine the rest of the above ingredients. Coat the chicken wings with this honey mixture.

After that, place the wings under the broiler for about 5 minutes. Serve and enjoy!

Kale and Cheese Dipping Sauce

(Ready in about 10 minutes | Servings 16)

Ingredients

1 ½ cups kale leaves, torn

1 (14-ounce) can artichoke hearts, drained and coarsely chopped

1 cup light mayonnaise

1/2 cup Ricotta cheese

1 cup Mozzarella cheese, shredded

Sea salt and ground black pepper, to taste

1/2 teaspoon dried dill weed

1 teaspoon paprika

Directions

Pour 2 cups of water into your pressure cooker; place a rack in the bottom.

Mix all the above ingredients; transfer them to a baking dish that fits in your pressure cooking pot. Then, cover the baking dish with a foil. Place the baking dish onto the rack.

Lock the cooker's lid into place; cook on HIGH pressure for 10 minutes. After that, use a quick pressure release. Serve with pita wedges of choice. Enjoy!

50.Cheesy Rainbow Dip

(Ready in about 10 minutes | Servings 16)

Ingredients

1 (14-ounce) can artichoke hearts, drained and coarsely chopped

1 red bell pepper, chopped

1 yellow bell pepper, chopped

1 ½ cups Cottage cheese

1 cup Colby cheese, shredded

1/2 teaspoon dried basil

Sea salt and ground black pepper, to taste

1 teaspoon red pepper flakes, crushed

Directions

Add about 2 cups of water to a pressure cooker; lay a rack in the bottom of the cooker.

Combine together all the above ingredients in a baking dish. Then, cover the baking dish with an aluminum foil. Transfer the baking dish to the pressure cooker.

Cover and cook on HIGH pressure for about 10 minutes. Afterwards, use a quick pressure release. Serve.

Zesty Carrots with Almonds

(Ready in about 15 minutes | Servings 4)

Ingredients

1/4 cup rendered duck fat

1 ½ pounds carrots, peeled and cut into rounds

1/3 cup dried cherries

3/4 cup water

1 sea salt

2 tablespoons sherry vinegar

Freshly ground black pepper

3 tablespoons almonds, toasted and chopped

Directions

In a pressure cooker over medium-high heat, heat the duck fat. Stir in the carrots, dried cherries, and water. Sprinkle with the salt.

Close and lock the lid. Set the burner heat to high. Set a timer to cook for 2 ½ minutes. Open the cooker with the Quick release method.

Stir in sherry vinegar and ground black pepper. Stir to combine well. Scatter the almonds over the top. Serve hot and enjoy.

Mashed Veggie Appetizer

(Ready in about 20 minutes | Servings 6)

Ingredients

2 cups water

6 potatoes, peeled and quartered

2 cups cauliflower, broken into florets

3 tablespoons grapeseed oil

1/4 cup half-and-half

1/2 cup Cheddar cheese, shredded

1/2 teaspoon cumin powder

1 teaspoon paprika

Sea salt and ground black pepper, to taste

Directions

Add the water, potatoes, and cauliflower to the cooking pot. Securely lock the cooker's lid; cook for 6 minutes under HIGH pressure. Then, release the pressure according to manufacturer's instructions.

Drain the vegetables using a colander and return them to the cooker. Now, mash your veggies with a potato masher; add the rest of the ingredients; mash again until smooth. Serve as a cold appetizer.

DESSERT RECIPES

Classic Chocolate Pudding
(Ready in about 15 minutes | Servings 6)

Ingredients

1/2 ounce unsweetened chocolate, shaved

6 ounces semisweet chocolate, chopped

6 tablespoons sugar

1 ½ cups light cream

4 egg yolks, whisked

1/4 teaspoon pure almond extract

1 tablespoon vanilla extract

A pinch of salt

Directions

Place the chocolate and the sugar in a large-sized bowl.

Then, heat the cream in a saucepan over low heat until it is thoroughly warmed. Pour the warmed light cream over the chocolate; whisk until the chocolate has melted.

Then, whisk in the yolks, almond extract, vanilla extract, and salt. Pour the mixture into 6 heat-safe ramekins; fill each ramekin. Cover each ramekin with foil.

Set the rack in a pressure cooker; pour in 2 cups water. Place the ramekins on the rack.

Lock the lid onto the pot. Cook for 10 minutes under HIGH pressure. Reduce the pressure. Serve chilled and enjoy!

Yummy Chocolate Treat
(Ready in about 40 minutes | Servings 8)

Ingredients

2 cups milk

2 ½ cups cream

1/2 cup white sugar

1/2 cinnamon powder

1/4 teaspoon grated nutmeg

1/2 teaspoon vanilla essence

3 cups chocolate, shaved

6 large-sized egg yolks

4 cups water

Directions

In a saucepan, heat the milk, cream, sugar, cinnamon powder, nutmeg, and vanilla over medium heat.

Turn off the heat; add the chocolate; stir until the chocolate has completely melted. Whisk in the egg yolks.

Prepare the pressure cooker by adding the water. Pour the mixture into a heat-safe dish; lay the dish on a prepared trivet in the pressure cooker.

Cook for about 30 minutes under HIGH pressure. Serve at room temperature.

Lemony White Chocolate Pudding

(Ready in about 15 minutes | Servings 6)

Ingredients

6 ounces white chocolate, chopped

1 cup half-and-half

1 cup heavy cream

4 egg yolks, whisked

1 tablespoon sugar

1 tablespoon lemon zest, finely grated

1/4 teaspoon vanilla extract

1/4 teaspoon lemon extract

Gingersnaps, for serving

Directions

Put the chocolate into a large bowl. In a pan, combine the half-and-half and cream; heat over low heat until bubbles fizz around the edges.

Next, pour the warm mixture over the chocolate; whisk until the mixture has completely melted. Whisk in the egg yolks, sugar, lemon zest, vanilla extract, and lemon extract. Pour the mixture into six heat-safe ramekins; cover each ramekin with an aluminum foil.

Set the pressure cooker rack in the pressure cooker; pour in 2 cups of water. Set the ramekins on the rack and seal the lid onto the cooker.

Set the pot over HIGH heat. Cook for 10 minutes. Reduce the pressure according to manufacturer's directions. Serve garnished with gingersnaps and enjoy.

Coffee Pudding for Sunday Brunch

(Ready in about 15 minutes | Servings 6)

Ingredients

1 cup half-and-half

1 cup heavy cream

1 tablespoon espresso instant powder

1/2 cup sugar

1 egg plus 4 egg yolks, whisked

1 teaspoon hazelnut extract

Directions

In a mixing bowl, whisk the half-and-half, heavy cream, and espresso powder.

Stir in the sugar and mix until it has dissolved; now fold in the egg and egg yolks. Afterward, add the hazelnut extract; mix again to combine. Divide the mixture among six heat-safe ramekins; cover them with foil.

Set the pressure cooker rack in a pressure cooker; pour in 2 cups of water. Lay the ramekins on the rack and lock the lid onto the pot.

Cook for about 10 minutes. Reduce the pressure according to manufacturer's directions. Transfer the ramekins to a wire rack to cool completely. Serve and enjoy!

Traditional Rice Pudding

(Ready in about 15 minutes | Servings 6)

Ingredients

1 tablespoon butter

3/4 cup white rice

1 ½ cups milk

1/2 cup sugar

1/2 teaspoon ground cinnamon

1 tablespoon vanilla extract

A pinch of kosher salt

1/2 teaspoon ground cardamom

1 large egg plus 1 large egg yolk, at room temperature

1/4 cup heavy cream

Directions

Melt the butter in a pressure cooker set over medium heat. Add the rice and cook, stirring for 1 to 1 ½ minutes.

Stir in the milk, sugar, cinnamon, vanilla, salt, and cardamom. Cook for an additional 1 minute, stirring constantly.

Lock the lid onto the pot. Cook for 10 minutes under HIGH pressure. Reduce the pressure according to manufacturer's directions.

Unlock and open the cooker. In a separate bowl, beat the egg, egg yolk, and heavy cream. Add the egg mixture to the cooker. Whisk your pudding continuously for about 30 seconds. Turn off the cooker and serve warm.

Aromatic Rice Custard

(Ready in about 40 minutes | Servings 6)

Ingredients

2 ⅔ cups whole milk

2 large eggs plus 2 large egg yolks, at room temperature

2 cups basmati rice, cooked

1/3 cup sugar

1/3 cup golden raisins

1/4 cup dried cranberries

1½ tablespoons vanilla extract

A pinch of kosher salt

1/2 teaspoon anise seed

Directions

Treat the inside of a soufflé dish with non-stick cooking spray. Set a rack inside a pressure cooker; pour in 2 cups water.

In a bowl, combine the milk, eggs, and egg yolks until smooth. Stir in the rice, sugar, raisins, cranberries, vanilla extract, kosher salt, and anise seeds; pour the mixture into the prepared baking dish. Cover tightly with aluminum foil.

Make an aluminum foil sling and lower the dish onto the rack in the pressure cooker. Seal the cooker's lid. Set the pot over HIGH heat. Cook for 38 minutes.

Turn off the cooker and allow the pressure to come back to normal naturally. Then, open the cooker. Let it cool for 1 hour before serving.

Easiest Lemon Cheesecake Ever

(Ready in about 25 minutes | Servings 6)

Ingredients

1 pound cottage cheese

4 eggs

1/2 cup sugar

2 teaspoons finely grated lemon zest

2 tablespoons fresh lemon juice

1/2 teaspoon vanilla paste

1/4 cup all-purpose flour

Directions

Set the rack inside a pressure cooker; pour in 2 cups of water. Generously grease the inside of a springform baking pan.

Place the cheese, eggs, sugar, lemon zest, lemon juice, and vanilla paste in a food processor. Then, process the ingredients until smooth, stopping the machine to scrape down the inside of the bowl. Add the flour and pulse a few more times until uniform and smooth.

Pour the batter into the prepared baking pan and cover with foil. Make an aluminum foil sling and lower the baking pan onto the rack in the pot

Lock the lid onto the cooker. Cook for 15 minutes under HIGH pressure. Afterward, let the pressure come back to normal naturally.

Unlock and open the pot; serve warm.

Orange Chocolate Holiday Treat

(Ready in about 15 minutes | Servings 6)

Ingredients

6 ounces chocolate, chopped

1 cup half-and-half

1 cup heavy cream

4 egg yolks, whisked

1 tablespoon sugar

1 teaspoon fresh orange juice

1 tablespoon orange zest, finely grated

1/4 teaspoon vanilla extract

Directions

Put the chocolate into a large-sized mixing bowl. In a saucepan, heat the half-and-half and heavy cream over low heat.

Immediately pour the warm mixture over the chocolate in the bowl; whisk until the mixture has completely melted. Whisk in the egg yolks, sugar, orange juice, orange zest, vanilla extract.

Pour the mixture into six heat-safe ramekins; cover each ramekin with an aluminum foil.

Set the pressure cooker rack in a pressure cooker; pour in 2 cups of water. Set the ramekins on the rack and seal the lid onto the cooker.

Set the pot over HIGH heat. Cook for 10 minutes. Reduce the pressure according to manufacturer's directions. Serve garnished with gingersnaps and enjoy.

Old-Fashion Caramel Flan

(Ready in about 20 minutes + chilling time | Servings 4)

Ingredients

1/2 cup sugar

1/4 cup hot water

8 egg yolks

1 cup sugar

1/4 teaspoon anise seeds

1/4 teaspoon cinnamon powder

1/2 teaspoon lemon zest, grated

1 teaspoon vanilla paste

4 cups milk

Directions

First, make the caramel. Melt sugar in a saucepan over medium heat; stir continuously. Add hot water and keep stirring. Pour the caramel into a greased cookie tin.

Pour the water into the pressure cooker (2 inches). Lay the cookie tin in the pressure cooker. Pour the remaining ingredients into the cookie tin.

Close the lid; cook for 15 minutes under HIGH pressure. Serve chilled and enjoy.

Rhubarb and Prune Compote

(Ready in about 15 minutes | Servings 6)

Ingredients

1/2 cup water

1 pound rhubarb, cut into small pieces

1/2 pint prunes, pitted and chopped

1/4 teaspoon cinnamon powder

1/4 teaspoon freshly grated nutmeg

1/4 cup crystallized ginger, chopped

1 tablespoon maple syrup

Directions

Bring the water to a boil in a pressure cooker; then, add rhubarb and prunes.

Next, add the cinnamon, nutmeg, and ginger to your pressure cooker. Bring up to HIGH pressure; turn off heat and allow the cooker's pressure to come down naturally.

While the compote is still warm, stir in the maple syrup. Allow the compote to cool completely and serve with vanilla ice cream.

Dried Fruit Compote with Pecans and Ice Cream

(Ready in about 10 minutes | Servings 4)

Ingredients

6 cups water

1 cinnamon stick

1 vanilla bean, sliced lengthwise

1 teaspoon freshly grated nutmeg

1/2 cup prunes, halved

1 cup raisins

1 ½ cups dried cherries

1 cup pecans, toasted

Vanilla ice cream, for serving

Directions

Add the water to your cooker together with the cinnamon stick, vanilla bean, nutmeg, prunes, raisins, and dried cherries.

Next, cook the compote under HIGH pressure for 5 minutes. Quick release the pressure. Allow the compote to cool slightly.

Add pecans; serve over vanilla ice cream and enjoy!

Apples Stuffed with Figs and Almonds

(Ready in about 25 minutes | Servings 4)

Ingredients

4 apples, cored

1/2 cup raisins, chopped

4 dried figs, chopped

1/4 cup almonds, chopped

1/2 teaspoon ground cloves

1/2 teaspoon cinnamon powder

1/4 teaspoon grated nutmeg

Directions

Place the apples in an ovenproof dish. Then, make the filling. Mix the raisins, figs, almonds, cloves, cinnamon, and nutmeg. Then, stuff the apples with this mixture.

Next, pour 1 cup of water into a pressure cooking pot. Place a metal rack in the cooker. Cover the ovenproof dish with an aluminum foil and lower it into the pressure cooker.

Cook under HIGH pressure; maintain the pressure for about 20 minutes. Serve with the cream of choice.

White Chocolate Cheesecake with Strawberry Sauce

(Ready in about 35 minutes | Servings 10)

Ingredients

1 ¼ cups graham cracker crumbs

5 tablespoons butter, melted

1 pound cream cheese

7 tablespoons milk

2 large eggs plus 1 large egg yolk, at room temperature

4 ounces white chocolate, melted and cooled

1 tablespoon all-purpose flour

1/4 teaspoon cardamom

1/4 teaspoon anise seed

1 teaspoon vanilla extract

1½ cups fresh strawberries

1/2 cup seedless strawberry jam

2 teaspoons cornstarch

Directions

Set the rack inside a cooker; pour in 2 cups of water. In a mixing dish, combine the graham cracker crumbs with melted butter.

Treat the inside of a soufflé dish with non-stick cooking spray. Pour in the crumb mixture; press gently to form an even crust.

Drop the cream cheese and condensed milk in a food processor; process until smooth. With the machine running, add the eggs and egg yolk one at a time. Then, add the chocolate, flour, cardamom, anise seeds and vanilla extract; process until creamy. Pour the batter into the soufflé dish.

Make an aluminum foil sling and lower the dish onto the rack in the pressure cooker. Set the pot over HIGH heat; bring it to low pressure. Now, reduce the heat as much as possible while maintaining this pressure and cook for 35 minutes.

Allow to cool. Replace to a refrigerator for a couple of hours.

Meanwhile, place the strawberries in a fine-mesh sieve and use a rubber spatula to wipe them back and forth across the mesh to make a puree. Pour the puree into a saucepan along with the jam; heat over medium-low heat, stirring occasionally.

Combine the cornstarch with two teaspoons of water in a small mixing bowl; stir the mixture into the simmering strawberry mixture. Cook until the sauce has thickened, stirring often. Lastly, pour strawberry sauce onto the top of the cooled cheesecake. Serve well chilled.

Mom's Orange Cheesecake

(Ready in about 25 minutes | Servings 8)

Ingredients

2 pounds Cottage cheese

4 whole eggs plus egg yolk

1/2 cup sugar

Zest and juice of 1/2 orange

1 teaspoon orange juice

1/2 teaspoon anise seeds

1/2 teaspoon cardamom seeds

1/4 teaspoon vanilla extract

1 cup dates, soaked and chopped

Directions

Beat the Cottage cheese until creamy and smooth. Then, in another bowl, beat the eggs, the egg yolk, and sugar. Stir in the cheese.

Whisk in the remaining ingredients. Pour the batter into a well-greased heatproof dish. Cover with an aluminum foil.

Lay a trivet at the bottom of the pressure cooker. Set the pressure to HIGH and cook for 20 minutes. Serve dusted with powdered sugar and enjoy.

Ginger Maple Cheesecake

(Ready in about 35 minutes | Servings 8)

Ingredients

1 ¼ cups gingersnap crumbs

5 tablespoons butter, melted and cooled

1 pound Ricotta cheese

1/2 cup maple syrup

1 whole egg plus 2 egg yolks

2 tablespoons all-purpose flour

1/2 teaspoon anise seeds, ground

1 teaspoon vanilla extract

A pinch of salt

Directions

Place the rack in a pressure cooker; pour in 2 cups water.

Mix the gingersnap crumbs and melted butter in a bowl until moist. Grease the inside of a baking pan. Stir in the crumb mixture; press to form an even crust.

Then, in a food processor, blend the Ricotta cheese and maple syrup. With the machine running, add the whole egg and egg yolks, one at a time; blend until smooth.

Next, add the flour, anise seeds, vanilla extract, and a pinch of salt. Process until the mixture is creamy. Then, pour the batter into the prepared baking pan.

Make an aluminum foil sling so that use the sling to lower the baking pan onto the rack. Lock the lid onto the pot. Set the pot over HIGH heat and bring it to low pressure. Once the pressure has been reached keep the pot at that pressure. Cook for 35 minutes. Let cool slightly. Then, remove to your refrigerator and chill for a couple of hours. Enjoy!

Rice Pudding with Zante Currants

(Ready in about 15 minutes | Servings 8)

Ingredients

1 cup jasmine rice

1 pound carrots, shredded

1 ½ cups water

A pinch of salt

2 cups milk

1/2 cup sugar

1/2 teaspoon cinnamon powder

2 eggs

1/2 teaspoon vanilla paste

3/4 cup Zante currants

Directions

In a pressure cooking pot, combine rice, carrots, water, and salt. Cover and select HIGH pressure and 4 minutes cook time. Then, use a natural pressure release; open the cooker. Add the milk, sugar, and cinnamon powder; give it a good stir.

In a mixing bowl, whisk the eggs with vanilla paste. Pour the mixture into the pressure cooker. Then, cook uncovered, stirring continuously, until the mixture begins to boil. Turn off the cooker and stir in Zante currants.

Serve well chilled and dolloped with an ice cream.

Sunday Apricot Cheesecake

(Ready in about 35 minutes | Servings 8)

Ingredients

1 ¼ cups gingersnap crumbs

6 tablespoons butter, melted and cooled

1/2 cup dried apricots, soaked

1 pound Ricotta cheese

1/2 cup maple syrup

1 whole egg plus 2 egg yolks

2 tablespoons all-purpose flour

1 teaspoon vanilla paste

Directions

Set the rack in a pressure cooker; pour in 2 cups water.

Mix the crumbs and butter in a bowl until moist. Treat the inside of a baking dish with cooking spray. Stir in the crumb mixture; press to form an even crust.

Then, in a food processor, blend the apricots, Ricotta cheese, and maple syrup. With the machine running, add the whole egg and egg yolks, one at a time; blend until smooth

Next, add the flour and vanilla paste. Process until everything is well incorporated. Then, pour the batter into the greased baking dish.

Make an aluminum foil sling so that use the sling to lower the baking pan onto the rack. Lock the lid onto the pot. Set the pot over HIGH heat and bring it to low pressure. Once the pressure has been reached keep the pot at that pressure.

Cook for 35 minutes. Let cool slightly. Then, remove to your refrigerator and chill for a couple of hours. Afterward, serve well chilled.

Aromatic Stewed Fruits

(Ready in about 10 minutes | Servings 6)

Ingredients

1 ½ cups water

1/2 cup red wine

1/2 cup agave syrup

2 cinnamon sticks

1/2 teaspoon vanilla paste

1 tangerine, sliced

1/2 pound dried prunes

1/4 pound dried figs

1/4 pound raisins

Directions

In a pressure cooker, combine the water, red wine, agave syrup, cinnamon sticks, vanilla paste, and tangerine. Bring the mixture to a boil.

Add prunes, figs, and raisins. Cook for 4 minutes at HIGH pressure. Serve with vanilla ice cream.

Stewed Spiced Apples

(Ready in about 10 minutes | Servings 4)

Ingredients

2 cups moderately dry white wine

1/2 cup sugar

1/2 ground cinnamon

1/4 teaspoon grated nutmeg

8 whole cloves

4 Honeycrisp apples, peeled, cored and halved

Directions

Bring the white wine, sugar, cinnamon, nutmeg, and cloves to a boil in a pressure cooker over medium heat. Drop in the apples. Lock the cooker's lid onto the pot.

Set the pot over HIGH heat and bring it to high pressure. Cook for 4 minutes.

Use the quick-release method to bring the pressure back to normal. Now open the cooking pot. Transfer the apple halves to serving dish.

Bring the sauce to a boil. Cook, stirring periodically until you have a thick syrup, approximately 5 minutes. Lastly, pour the syrup over the apples and serve.

Poached Pears in Vanilla-Orange Sauce

(Ready in about 10 minutes | Servings 4)

Ingredients

2 cups dry red wine

2 cups sugar

1 tablespoon vanilla paste

1 vanilla bean

1 cinnamon stick

A few strips of orange peel

4 firm pears, peeled, cored, and halved

1/2 cup dried apricots, coarsely chopped

Directions

Combine the red wine, sugar, vanilla paste, vanilla bean, cinnamon stick, and orange peel in a pressure cooker.

Bring to a simmer over medium heat., stirring occasionally. Fold in the pears; stir to coat.

Lock the lid onto the cooking pot. Cook for 4 minutes under HIGH pressure. Use the quick-release method and open the pressure cooker. Serve well chilled.

Winter Dried Fruit Compote

(Ready in about 10 minutes | Servings 6)

Ingredients

2 cups unsweetened apple juice

1/2 cup sugar

1 cinnamon stick

1 vanilla bean

3 ounces dried banana

9 ounces dried apricots

1/2 cup dried cranberries

1/4 cup raisins

Directions

In a pressure cooker, combine the apple juice, sugar, cinnamon stick, and vanilla bean. Bring the mixture to a boil.

Add dried fruits and give it a good stir. Cook for 4 minutes at HIGH pressure. Serve with vanilla ice cream.

Healthy Apple and Fig Compote

(Ready in about 10 minutes | Servings 8)

Ingredients

2 ½ cups sweet white wine

1/4 cup agave syrup

2 cinnamon sticks

1 teaspoon vanilla paste

1/2 pound dried apples

1 pound dried figs

Directions

Add the wine, agave syrup, cinnamon stick, and vanilla paste in a pressure cooker; stir until the sugar dissolves. Stir in the dried apples and figs.

Lock the lid onto the pot. Set the pot over high heat and bring it to HIGH pressure (15 psi). Cook for 5 minutes. Serve warm.

Pumpkin Custard with Whipped Cream

(Ready in about 10 minutes | Servings 6)

Ingredients

1 ½ cups whole milk

4 whole eggs

3/4 cup pumpkin puree, canned

2/3 cup maple syrup

1/2 teaspoon freshly grated nutmeg

2 cups water

Whipped cream, for serving

Directions

Scald the milk in a pan. In a mixing bowl, whisk together the eggs, pumpkin puree, and maple syrup; mix until smooth.

Then, add the milk slowly in a thin stream. Sprinkle with the nutmeg. Pour into six individual custard cups. Then, cover with an aluminum foil.

Place a trivet and steamer basket in a pressure cooker. Add the water. Lay the custard cups in the basket.

Close and lock the cooker's lid. Set the burner heat to HIGH. Set a timer for 10 minutes. Open the cooker with the Natural Release method. Serve chilled with a dollop of whipped cream.

Mango Rice Pudding

(Ready in about 15 minutes | Servings 6)

Ingredients

2 cups half-and-half

2 cups milk

1 ½ cups white rice

3/4 cup sugar

Zest of 1 lemon, grated

1/4 cup dried mango, diced

1/2 teaspoon cinnamon powder

1/2 tablespoon vanilla essence

Directions

Coat the inside of a pressure cooker with nonstick cooking spray. Combine the half-and-half, milk, white rice, sugar, and lemon zest in the cooking pot.

Close and lock the lid. Set the burner heat to HIGH. When the cooker reaches the pressure, adjust the heat to maintain pressure. Set a timer to cook for 4 minutes at HIGH.

Remove the pot from the heat. Open the cooker using the Quick release method.

Stir in the dried mango, cinnamon powder, and vanilla essence. Serve well chilled.

Coconut Cranberry Rice Pudding

(Ready in about 15 minutes | Servings 6)

Ingredients

2 cups half-and-half

2 cups milk

1 ½ cups white rice

3/4 cup sugar

Zest of 1 lemon, grated

1/4 cup coconut flakes

1/4 cup dried cranberries, diced

1/2 tablespoon vanilla essence

Directions

Treat the inside of a pressure cooker with nonstick cooking spray. Combine the half-and-half, milk, white rice, sugar, lemon zest, and coconut in the cooking pot.

Close and lock the lid. Set the burner heat to HIGH. When the cooker reaches the pressure, adjust the heat to maintain pressure. Set a timer to cook for 4 minutes at HIGH.

Remove the pot from the heat. Open the cooker using the Quick release method.

Stir in the dried cranberries and vanilla essence. Serve well chilled.

Gingered Jasmine Rice Pudding

(Ready in about 10 minutes | Servings 4)

Ingredients

2 tablespoons butter, room temperature

3 cups milk

1 cup jasmine white rice

1/4 cup agave nectar

1/4 cup heavy cream

1 whole egg plus 1 egg yolk, beaten

1 teaspoon vanilla essence

2 tablespoons crystallized ginger, finely chopped

Whipped cream

Directions

Coat the bottom of a pressure cooker with the softened butter. Add the milk, jasmine rice, and agave nectar.

Close and lock the lid. Then, cook for 8 minutes under HIGH pressure.

Remove the cooking pot from the heat and open it with the Natural release method.

In a small bowl, beat the cream, egg, egg yolk, and vanilla essence. Spoon a small amount of the hot rice into the cream mixture. Add back to the pot. Cook, uncovered, over medium heat for 5 minutes.

Stir in the crystallized ginger. Serve chilled and garnished with whipped cream.

Coconut Jasmine Rice Pudding

(Ready in about 15 minutes | Servings 6)

Ingredients

Non-stick cooking spray

1 cup sweetened coconut, shredded

1 cup whole milk

1 ½ cups half-and-half

1 (14-ounce) can coconut milk, unsweetened

1 ½ cups jasmine rice

1/2 cup agave syrup

1 teaspoon vanilla essence

1/2 teaspoon coconut extract

Directions

Treat the inside of a pressure cooker with nonstick cooking spray. Combine the coconut, milk, half-and-half, coconut milk, and jasmine rice, in the cooking pot.

Close and lock the lid. Set the burner heat to HIGH. When the cooker reaches the pressure, adjust the heat to maintain pressure. Set a timer to cook for 4 minutes at HIGH.

Remove the pot from the heat. Open the cooker using the Quick-release method.

Stir in the agave syrup, vanilla essence, and coconut extract. Transfer to a refrigerator before serving time.

Classic Chocolate Custard

(Ready in about 10 minutes | Servings 4)

Ingredients

2 cups milk

2 whole eggs plus egg milk, at room temperature

1/3 cup sugar

1 tablespoon cocoa powder

1/2 teaspoon vanilla paste

1/4 teaspoon cinnamon powder

1/4 teaspoon grated nutmeg

1 cup water

Directions

Begin by scalding the milk in a small saucepan; let the milk slightly cool.

Add the eggs, egg yolk, sugar, cocoa powder, vanilla, cinnamon and nutmeg to a mixing bowl; add reserved milk and stir to combine well. Pour the mixture into four custard cups; cover the cups with an aluminum foil.

Add water to the cooker's base; set the trivet and steamer basket in the pressure cooker. Place prepared custard cups in the steamer basket.

Lock the lid in place and cook for 3 minutes under HIGH pressure. Allow the pressure to drop using the quick-release method.

Quinoa Pudding with Pecans

(Ready in about 10 minutes | Servings 6)

Ingredients

2 ¼ cups water

1 ½ cups quinoa

1/4 cup brown sugar

1/2 teaspoon vanilla extract

1/4 teaspoon coconut extract

1/2 teaspoon cinnamon powder

Chopped pecans, toasted

Directions

Add the water, quinoa, sugar, vanilla extract, coconut extract, and cinnamon powder to the pressure cooking pot.

Select HIGH pressure; cook for 5 minutes. Next, turn your cooker off; release the pressure according to manufacturer's directions.

Fluff the quinoa and serve sprinkled with chopped pecans. Enjoy!

Apple-Cranberry Dessert

(Ready in about 20 minutes | Servings 2)

Ingredients

1/4 cup sugar

1 cup dry bread crumbs

1/2 cup dried cranberries

1 teaspoon apple pie spice blend

2 tablespoons orange juice

1 teaspoon vanilla essence

3 apples, cored and sliced

1/4 cup butter, melted

2 cups water

Directions

Brush a baking dish with a non-stick cooking spray. Combine the sugar, bread crumbs, dried cranberries, apple pie spice, orange juice, and vanilla essence in a mixing bowl.

In the baking dish, alternate layers of apples and crumb mixture.

Pour melted butter over the layers; cover the baking dish with an aluminum foil.

Prepare your pressure cooker by adding the water to the cooker's base; place a metal rack at the bottom of the cooker. Place the baking dish on the rack.

Cook for 15 minutes under HIGH pressure. Allow to cool slightly before serving.

Pear and Apple Winter Delight

(Ready in about 20 minutes | Servings 2)

Ingredients

1 cup dry bread crumbs

1/4 cup brown sugar

1/2 cup sultanas

2 tablespoons apple juice

1 teaspoon fresh orange juice

1 teaspoon vanilla extract

1 teaspoon cinnamon powder

2 pears, cored and sliced

2 apples, cored and sliced

1/4 cup butter, melted

2 cups water

Directions

Treat a baking dish with a non-stick cooking spray (butter flavor works the best). Combine the bread crumbs, sugar, sultanas, apple juice, orange juice, vanilla extract and cinnamon powder in a mixing dish.

In the baking dish, alternate layers of apples and pears with crumb mixture.

Pour melted butter over the layers; cover the baking dish with an aluminum foil.

Next, add the water to the cooker's base; set a metal rack in the pressure cooker. Place the baking dish on the rack. Cook for 15 minutes under HIGH pressure. Serve and enjoy!

Aromatic Thanksgiving Pudding

(Ready in about 30 minutes | Servings 6)

Ingredients

3 cups whole milk

1/3 cup fine-ground cornmeal

1/4 teaspoon sea salt

1/4 teaspoon cardamom

1/2 teaspoon ground cinnamon

1/2 teaspoon ground ginger

1/3 cup molasses

2 tablespoons light brown sugar

2 tablespoons butter

2 cups water

Directions

In a pan, combine the milk and cornmeal using a whisk. Heat over medium-high heat, whisking constantly. Add the salt and spices. Bring to a boil over low heat, whisking continuously for about 15 minutes.

You can also use an immersion blender to smooth it out.

Then, add the molasses, brown sugar, and butter. Remove from the heat.

Place a trivet in a pressure cooker. Add the water. Coat a soufflé dish with butter-flavored cooking spray. Pour the cornmeal mixture into the soufflé dish. Cover the dish tightly with an aluminum foil.

Place the soufflé dish in the pressure cooker. Close and lock the lid. When the cooker reaches HIGH pressure, reduce the burner heat as low as you can and still maintain HIGH pressure. Set a timer to cook for 28 minutes.

Remove the pot from the heat. Open the cooker with the Natural Release method.

Eggnog Bread Pudding

(Ready in about 20 minutes | Servings 6)

Ingredients

4 tablespoons unsalted butter, melted

6 cups day-old Italian bread, torn into pieces

1/2 cup raisins

1/2 cup chopped walnuts

2 cups eggnog

4 large eggs, lightly beaten

1 teaspoon vanilla extract

1/4 teaspoon rum extract

1/4 cup firmly packed light brown sugar

1/4 teaspoon freshly grated nutmeg

2 cups water

Whipped cream, for serving

Directions

Coat a soufflé dish with butter-flavored cooking spray. In the dish, toss the melted butter, bread pieces, raisins, and walnuts together.

In another medium-sized bowl, whisk the eggnog, eggs, vanilla extract, rum extract, brown sugar, and nutmeg.

Pour the eggnog mixture over the bread mixture. Let soak for 10 minutes. Cover the soufflé dish with some foil.

Place a trivet in the pressure cooker. Pour in the water.

Close and lock the lid. When the cooker reaches HIGH pressure, reduce the burner heat as low as you can and still maintain HIGH pressure. Now cook for 20 minutes.

Remove the pot from the heat and open the cooker following the manufacturer's directions. Serve with whipped cream and enjoy.

Coconut Rice Custard with Figs

(Ready in about 20 minutes | Servings 2)

Ingredients

2 ⅔ cups milk

2 eggs plus 2 egg yolks, at room temperature

2 cups jasmine rice, cooked

1/3 cup sugar

1 cup figs, chopped

1 ½ tablespoons vanilla extract

1/4 teaspoon kosher salt

1/2 teaspoon coconut extract

1/2 teaspoon anise seed

Shredded coconut, for serving

Directions

Treat the inside of a baking dish with a butter-flavored non-stick cooking spray. Set a metal rack inside a pressure cooker; pour in 2 cups water.

In a bowl, combine the milk, eggs, and egg yolks until frothy. Stir in the remaining components; pour the mixture into the prepared baking dish. Cover tightly with aluminum foil.

Make an aluminum foil sling and lower the dish onto the rack in the pressure cooker. Seal the cooker's lid. Set the pot over HIGH heat. Cook for 38 minutes.

Turn off the cooker and allow the pressure to come back to normal naturally. Then, open the cooker. Let it cool for 1 hour. Serve and enjoy!

Spiced Caramel Custard

(Ready in about 35 minutes | Servings 4)

Ingredients

2 eggs plus 2 egg yolks

1/4 teaspoon cardamom

1 teaspoon vanilla extract

3 cups milk

1/2 cup sugar

1/2 cup water

1/4 teaspoon cinnamon, ground

Directions

Beat the eggs and egg yolks until frothy and smooth; stir in the cardamom and vanilla extract. Whisk in the milk, stirring constantly.

Dissolve sugar with water. Add cinnamon and pour the mixture into a lightly buttered soufflé dish.

Pour the custard over the prepared caramel. Cover with an aluminum foil. Prepare your pressure cooker by adding the water and the trivet. Place the dish on the trivet.

Seal the pressure cooker and cook for about 20 minutes without the pressure. To serve, turn the pudding upside down onto a plate.

Coconut Tapioca Pudding

(Ready in about 15 minutes | Servings 4)

Ingredients

1 ½ cups water

1/2 cup tapioca pearls

1/4 cup agave nectar

A pinch of salt

1 whole egg plus 2 egg yolks

1/2 cup milk

1 teaspoon cornstarch with 1 tablespoon water mixed in

1 teaspoon coconut extract

1/2 teaspoon vanilla extract

1/2 cup toasted coconut, for garnish

Directions

In a pressure cooker, place together the water and tapioca pearls; give it a good stir.

Now turn off pressure cooker; perform a natural pressure release for a few minutes. Stir in agave nectar and salt.

In a mixing bowl, whisk together the whole eggs, egg yolks, and milk. Pour the mixture into the cooker. Add the cornstarch mixture and cook, stirring often, until the content begins to boil. Turn off your pressure cooker. Stir in the coconut and vanilla extracts; stir until everything is combined well.

Divide the pudding among four individual bowls and scatter toasted coconut over the top. Serve chilled.

Carrot Cake with Pecans and Rum

(Ready in about 1 hour 10 minutes | Servings 8)

Ingredients

1/2 cup sugar

2 tablespoons molasses

2 eggs

1/2 cup all-purpose flour

1/2 teaspoon cardamom

1/2 teaspoon cinnamon powder

1 teaspoon baking powder

1/2 teaspoon baking soda

A pinch of salt

2/3 cup shortening

1/2 cup carrots, grated

1/2 cup pecans, chopped

1 cup dry bread crumbs

For the Rum Sauce:

1/2 cup sugar

4 tablespoons butter

1/4 cup heavy cream

2 tablespoons rum

Directions

In a medium-sized bowl or a measuring cup, whisk together the sugar, molasses, and the eggs.

Stir in the flour along with the spices, baking powder and baking soda; add a pinch of salt; mix to combine. Fold in shortening, carrots, pecans, and dry bread crumbs.

Transfer the batter to a baking pan lightly buttered with non-stick cooking spray. Cover with an aluminum foil; now poke a hole in the middle of the foil.

Pour 1 ½ cups of water into the base of the cooker; lay the trivet in the bottom. Now lower the baking pan in the pressure cooker.

Next, lock the cooker's lid in place. Select HIGH pressure and set the timer for 60 minutes. Now release the pressure using the cold water release method.

Next, make the Rum Sauce by adding sugar and butter in a medium saucepan over medium heat; cook for about 2 minutes. Add heavy cream and rum; let the sauce simmer till it has thickened slightly. Serve at room temperature.

Classic Tapioca Pudding

(Ready in about 15 minutes | Servings 4)

Ingredients

1 ½ cups water

1/2 cup tapioca

1/2 cup brown sugar

1/4 teaspoon kosher salt

1 whole egg plus 2 egg yolks

1/2 cup whole milk

1/2 teaspoon cinnamon powder

1/2 teaspoon vanilla extract

Directions

In a pressure cooker, combine water and tapioca. Cover and select HIGH pressure; cook for 6 minutes. Then, turn off pressure cooker and use Natural pressure release for several minutes. Stir in the brown sugar and kosher salt.

In a measuring cup, whisk the whole egg, egg yolks, and whole milk. Pour the whisked mixture through a fine mesh strainer into the pressure cooker. Cook until the content begins to boil. Turn off your cooker. Stir in cinnamon powder and vanilla extract.

Serve chilled and garnished with maraschino cherries.

Soft Pineapple and Cottage Cake

(Ready in about 35 minutes | Servings 8)

Ingredients

2 cups hot water

2 tablespoons sugar

2 cans (8-ounce) pineapple slices, well drained

4 tablespoons butter, melted

1 cup graham cracker crumbs

3/4 cup sugar

1 tablespoon molasses

1 ½ cups Cottage cheese, softened

1 teaspoon vanilla extract

3 whole eggs plus 2 egg yolks

Directions

Start by adding hot water to the bottom of a pressure cooker. Now place a steamer basket in the cooker.

Next, coat a heat-proof dish with non-stick cooking spray. Then, dust the bottom of the dish with a little white bleached flour. Place a wax paper at the bottom of the heat-proof dish.

Sprinkle the bottom of the dish with sugar; arrange the pineapple slices artistically over the bottom.

In a mixing bowl, combine the remaining components. Stir well until everything is mixed. Pour the mixture over the pineapple slices.

Next, turn the heat up to HIGH pressure. Cook for 20 minutes under HIGH pressure. Check for the doneness by inserting a toothpick or a wooden stick in the middle of the pineapple cake.

Lastly, turn pineapple cake out onto a serving platter. Serve chilled.

Rum Chestnut Spread

(Ready in about 20 minutes | Servings 16)

Ingredients

1 ½ pounds fresh chestnuts, peeled and halved

2 cups white sugar

1/4 teaspoon grated nutmeg

1/2 teaspoon cardamom, grated

1/4 teaspoon cinnamon powder

1/4 teaspoon vanilla extract

12 ounces water

1/8 cup rum liqueur

Directions

Drop all the above ingredients, except for rum liquor, in a pressure cooker.

Now unlock the cooker. Turn the heat up to HIGH; then, lower the heat, maintaining the pressure. Cook for 20 minutes.

Next, open the cooker naturally and gradually. Stir in the liquor; stir to combine well. Puree the mixture with an immersion blender. Serve over cakes.

Bread Pudding with Crème Fraîche

(Ready in about 20 minutes | Servings 6)

Ingredients

2 cups water

1/2 cup dried cherries

1/3 cup brandy

1 1/3 cups chocolate chips

1/2 cup sour cream

1 cup heavy cream

1/2 cup granulated sugar

3 large eggs, whisked

1/4 teaspoon ground cinnamon

1 teaspoon vanilla extract

4 cups day-old Challah egg bread chunks

1 cup Crème Fraîche

1 tablespoon powdered sugar

1/4 teaspoon vanilla extract

Directions

Prepare the pressure cooker by adding the water. Butter a soufflé dish. Place a trivet in the pressure cooker.

In a small bowl, combine the cherries and brandy. Let soak at least 20 minutes. In a separate bowl, melt the chocolate chips in the microwave.

In a large-sized mixing bowl, whisk the sour cream, heavy cream, sugar, eggs, cinnamon, and vanilla extract.

Whisk in the warm chocolate. Add the bread cubes and soaked cherries; let it stand for 15 to 20 minutes.

Pour the mixture into the prepared soufflé dish. Cover the dish with foil. Place the dish in the pressure cooker. Close and lock the cooker's lid.

Then, cook for 20 minutes under HIGH pressure. Open with the Natural release method.

In a small-sized bowl, whisk the crème fraîche, powdered sugar, and vanilla extract. Serve the bread pudding with a cream on top.

Easiest Chocolate Fondue Ever

(Ready in about 10 minutes | Servings 12)

Ingredients

2 cups lukewarm water

4 ounces dark chocolate

1/2 cup cream

1 teaspoon powdered sugar

1/2 teaspoon cinnamon powder

1/4 teaspoon grated nutmeg

1 teaspoon Amaretto liqueur

Directions

Prepare a pressure cooker by adding 2 cups of water into the bottom; place trivet in the bottom.

In a heat-proof mug, melt the dark chocolate. Add the remaining components. Put the container into the pressure cooker. Close and lock the cooker's lid.

Cook for 2 minutes under HIGH pressure. Open the pressure cooker according to manufacturer's instructions.

Lastly, pull out the container with tongs. Serve with fresh fruits.

Coconut Rice Pudding with Berries

(Ready in about 10 minutes | Servings 8)

Ingredients

1 cup rice

1 ½ cups water

1 tablespoon coconut oil, melted

A pinch of salt

1 (14-ounce) can coconut milk

1/2 cup white sugar

2 whole eggs

1/2 cup milk

1/2 teaspoon coconut extract

1/2 teaspoon vanilla extract

1 cup mixed berries

Directions

In a pressure cooker, combine rice, water, coconut oil, and salt. Lock the lid in place; set the cooker to HIGH; maintain the pressure for 3 minutes.

Then, turn off your cooker; use a natural pressure release method and open the cooker. Stir in the coconut milk and white sugar; stir to combine well.

In a mixing bowl, whisk the eggs, milk, coconut extract, and vanilla extract. Pour the mixture into the cooker. Then, cook, stirring continuously, until it starts to boil. Turn off the pressure cooker. Stir in mixed berries. To serve, divide among serving glasses and garnish with some extra berries.

Persimmon and Raisin Bread Pudding

(Ready in about 20 minutes | Servings 6)

Ingredients

2 cups lukewarm water

3 soft, ripe persimmons

1/2 cup milk

1 cup heavy cream

1/2 cup packed light brown sugar

3 large eggs, whisked

1/4 teaspoon ground cinnamon

1 teaspoon vanilla extract

6 cups day-old Challah egg bread chunks

1/2 cup raisins, soaked

1½ tablespoons cold unsalted butter

Directions

Prepare your cooker by adding the water. Treat a soufflé dish with cooking spray. Place a trivet in the pressure cooker.

In a mixing bowl, drop the persimmons, milk, heavy cream, brown sugar, eggs, cinnamon, and vanilla extract; whisk to combine.

Add the bread cubes and soaked raisins; let it stand approximately 20 minutes.

Pour the mixture into the buttered soufflé dish; cut in the butter. Cover the dish with foil and transfer it to the pressure cooker. Close and lock the cooker's lid.

Cook for 20 minutes under HIGH pressure. Open with the Natural release method.

Vanilla-Ginger Peach Compote

(Ready in about 10 minutes | Servings 6)

Ingredients

1/4 cup water

2 (15-ounce) cans sliced peaches, with syrup

1 tablespoon dry white wine

1/4 teaspoon ground cinnamon

1 vanilla bean

4 whole cloves

1 tablespoon candied ginger, minced

Honey, to taste

Directions

Add all the components to a pressure cooking pot. Stir to combine them well. Cover and seal the lid tightly. Now bring to LOW pressure; maintain pressure for 3 minutes.

Next, discard the vanilla bean. Return the pressure cooker to MEDIUM heat; simmer for 5 minutes, stirring often.

Garnish with a dollop of whipped cream and serve chilled.

Delicious Chocolate-Peanut Cheesecake

(Ready in about 35 minutes + chilling time | Servings 8)

Ingredients

1/4 cup turbinado sugar

1 (8-ounce) package cream cheese

1 ¼ cups peanut butter, softened

1/2 cup confectioners' sugar, sifted

1/4 cup light brown sugar

2 tablespoons cornstarch

3 whole eggs

1/4 cup sour cream

1 teaspoon vanilla extract

1/4 teaspoon hazelnut extract

8 ounces bittersweet chocolate, melted

2/3 cup toasted peanuts, chopped

4 ½ ounces chocolate wafers, crushed

1/4 cup butter, melted

1/4 teaspoon ground cloves

Directions

To prepare the batter: grease a cake pan; then, coat it with the sugar; wrap with an aluminum foil; set aside.

Using an electric mixer, beat the cream cheese and peanut butter. Stir in the confectioners' sugar, brown sugar, and cornstarch. Add the eggs, one at a time. Stir in the sour cream, vanilla and hazelnut extracts. Stir in the chocolate; mix until everything is well incorporated.

Pour the batter into the pan, spreading it evenly. Then, cover with a sheet of foil. Create the foil handle. Place the trivet in the bottom of the cooker. Now pour in 2 cups water. Then, lower the cake pan into the pressure cooker. Seal the pressure cooker's lid.

Then, cook for 22 minutes. Quick-release the pressure and let the cake cool on a wire rack. Refrigerate overnight.

To make the topping, combine the peanuts, chocolate wafers, butter, and cloves in a small-sized bowl. Spread the topping on top of the cake. Enjoy!

Tropical Pineapple Shortcakes

(Ready in about 10 minutes | Servings 8)

Ingredients

1 cup canned pineapple, cubed

1/4 cup water

1/2 cup apple juice

1/3 cup honey

1/2 teaspoon vanilla paste

1/2 teaspoon coconut extract

1 ½ tablespoons cornstarch mixed in 2 tablespoons water

Shortcakes

Directions

Drop pineapple, water, apple juice, honey, vanilla, and coconut extract in your pressure cooker. Cook for 2 minutes under HIGH pressure. Perform the Quick release method and open the cooker. Then, set the cooker to HIGH again. Add the cornstarch mixture; simmer for 2 minutes, till the mixture has thickened.

To serve, spoon the pineapple sauce over shortcakes.

A-Number-1 Banana Cake

(Ready in about 40 minutes | Servings 12)

Ingredients

1 ½ cups all-purpose flour

1/2 teaspoon baking soda

1 teaspoon baking powder

1 teaspoon vanilla essence

1 cup granulated sugar

A pinch of salt

A dash of cinnamon

2 medium-sized ripe bananas, mashed

1⁄2 cup butter, melted

1 cup soymilk

Directions

In a medium-sized bowl, combine together the flour, baking soda, baking powder, vanilla essence, sugar, and salt.

Add cinnamon and mashed bananas. Slowly stir in the butter and the soymilk. Gently stir until everything is well incorporated.

Pour the batter into a round pan. Lay the pan in the pressure cooker. Cover and cook the cake for 30 minutes over LOW heat.

Afterwards, carefully remove the cake from the pan. Serve at room temperature.

Orange Cornmeal Cake

(Ready in about 20 minutes | Servings 6)

Ingredients

2 cups milk

1⁄4 cup light brown sugar

1 teaspoon orange zest, grated

1⁄2 cup fine yellow cornmeal

2 large eggs

2 tablespoons butter, softened

2 tablespoons orange marmalade

1/2 teaspoon vanilla extract

1 cup water

Directions

To make the batter: Bring milk to a simmer over MEDIUM heat. Stir in the sugar and continue to simmer for about 2 minutes.

Whisk in the orange zest and yellow cornmeal. Simmer for 2 minutes longer, stirring continuously.

Remove from the heat. In a separate mixing bowl, whisk together the eggs, softened butter, orange marmalade, and vanilla extract. Stir the egg mixture into the cornmeal mixture.

Coat a heatproof glass dish with non-stick cooking spray. Add prepared cake batter.

Pour 1 cup of water into the pressure cooker; now place a rack in your cooker. Place the dish on the rack. Cook on LOW pressure for 12 minutes. Allow to sit for a few minutes before removing from the dish.

Old-Fashioned Chocolate Cake

(Ready in about 45 minutes | Servings 12)

Ingredients

1 ½ cups all-purpose flour

4 tablespoons cocoa powder

1/4 teaspoon grated nutmeg

1 teaspoon cinnamon

1 tablespoon maple syrup

1/2 teaspoon almond extract

A pinch of salt

1/2 teaspoon baking powder

1/2 teaspoon baking soda

2 eggs, beaten

4 tablespoons butter, melted

1 cup whole milk

2 cups hot water

Directions

In a mixing bowl, combine together the flour, cocoa powder, nutmeg, cinnamon, maple syrup, almond extract, salt, baking powder, and baking soda.

In another bowl, beat the eggs. Add to the dry flour mixture. Then, stir in the melted butter and the milk. Stir to combine well. Replace the cake mixture to a round cake pan.

Add the rack to the pressure cooker; pour in the water. Place the cake pan on the rack. Bring to HIGH pressure; then reduce to LOW and cook for 30 minutes. Let the cake sit for 10 minutes; carefully remove your cake from the pan. Cut into wedges and serve.

Coconut Rice Pudding with Raisins

(Ready in about 30 minutes | Servings 6)

Ingredients

1 ½ cups white rice, rinsed and drained

1 (14-ounce) can coconut milk

1 cup water

2 cups whole milk

½ cup granulated sugar

1/4 teaspoon cardamom

1/4 teaspoon nutmeg, freshly grated

1 teaspoons ground cinnamon

A pinch of salt

1 cup golden raisins

Directions

Add rice, coconut milk, water, milk, sugar, cardamom, nutmeg, cinnamon, and salt to your pressure cooker. Now cook over medium-high heat, bringing to a gentle boil.

Lock the lid into place; cook on LOW pressure for 15 minutes.

Afterwards, remove the lid according to manufacturer's directions. Stir in golden raisins. Allow the pudding to stand for about 15 minutes. Serve.

Vegan Chocolate Cake

(Ready in about 45 minutes | Servings 12)

Ingredients

1 ½ cups all-purpose flour

4 tablespoons cocoa powder

1 teaspoon cinnamon

1/2 teaspoon cardamom

1 teaspoon anise

1 tablespoon maple syrup

1/2 teaspoon vanilla extract

A pinch of salt

1 teaspoon baking powder

2 ripe bananas

4 tablespoons vegan margarine, melted

1 cup almond milk

2 cups hot water

Directions

In a bowl, combine together the flour, cocoa powder, cinnamon, cardamom, anise seed maple syrup, vanilla, salt, and baking powder. In a separate mixing bowl, whisk the bananas, together with vegan margarine, and almond milk.

Add banana mixture to the dry flour mixture; stir to combine well. Replace the batter to a round cake pan.

Place the rack in your pressure cooker; pour hot water into the bottom of your cooker. Place the pan on the rack. Now cook for 30 minutes on LOW. Allow your cake to rest at least 10 minutes. Serve.

Rice Pudding with Cranberries

(Ready in about 30 minutes | Servings 6)

Ingredients

1 ½ cups rice, rinsed and drained

2 cups almond milk

2 cups water

1/2 cup sugar

1/2 teaspoon allspice

1/4 teaspoon cardamom

1/4 teaspoon nutmeg, freshly grated

1/8 teaspoon sea salt

1 cup dried cranberries

Directions

Add rice, almond milk, water, sugar, allspice, cardamom, nutmeg, and sea salt to your pressure cooker. Set the cooker over medium-high heat; bring to a boil.

Cover with the lid and cook for 15 minutes on LOW pressure.

Remove the lid according to manufacturer's instructions. Stir in cranberries. Allow the pudding to sit approximately 15 minutes. Serve and enjoy.

Apple and Dried Cherry Treat

(Ready in about 10 minutes | Servings 10)

Ingredients

4 tart apples, peeled, cored and grated

4 sweet apples peeled, cored and grated

1 cup dried cherries

Grated rind and juice from 1 medium-sized orange

1/2 cup brown sugar

1/2 cup granulated sugar

1 tablespoon butter

1/2 teaspoon ground cloves

1/8 teaspoon salt

1/2 teaspoon cardamom

1/2 teaspoon cinnamon

Directions

Add the apples and dried cherries to your pressure cooker. Place the remaining ingredients over the fruits.

Next, lock the lid into place, and bring to LOW pressure; maintain pressure approximately 5 minutes. Afterwards, allow pressure to release naturally and remove the lid.

Stir well and serve at room temperature.

Walnut Butter Cheesecake

(Ready in about 35 minutes | Servings 10)

Ingredients

For the Crust:

1/2 cup graham cracker crumbs

1/4 cup walnuts, chopped

2 tablespoons margarine, melted

For the Filling:

1 pound Ricotta cheese, softened

2/3 cup nut butter

3/4 cup granulated sugar

3 eggs

1/4 teaspoon almond extract

3/4 teaspoon vanilla extract

Directions

Coat two metal cake pans with non-stick cooking spray. Make two crusts by mixing graham cracker crumbs, together with walnuts, and margarine.

Process the filling ingredients in your blender or a food processor. Spread the filling over the top of each crust.

Next, place a metal rack at the bottom of the pressure cooker. To create a water bath, pour 2 cups of water into the bottom of your cooker.

Place the cake pans on the metal rack in prepared cooker. Cover with an aluminum foil. Cook for 25 minutes on HIGH. Remove the lid according to manufacturer's instructions. Place in the refrigerator until chilled.

Mom's Cranberry Jubilee

(Ready in about 15 minutes | Servings 8)

Ingredients

16 ounces dried cranberries

1/2 cup fresh apple juice

1/4 cup water

1/4 cup white sugar

1/2 teaspoon lemon rind, grated

1/4 teaspoon vanilla extract

1/4 cup light brown sugar

1 tablespoon cornstarch mixed with 2 tablespoons of water

Directions

Place cranberries, apple juice, water, white sugar, grated lemon rind, and vanilla extract in your cooker; securely lock the cooker's lid and set for 7 to 8 minutes on LOW.

Perform a quick release to release the pressure. Mash the mixture in the cooker with a heavy spoon in order to create a chunky sauce.

Then, set cooker to HIGH and stir in brown sugar and cornstarch mixture. Let simmer for about 3 minutes, or until sauce has thickened.

Serve over vanilla ice cream if desired.

Favorite Rice Pudding

(Ready in about 10 minutes | Servings 6)

Ingredients

2 tablespoons butter

1 cup Arborio rice

2 cups water

1/2 teaspoon vanilla extract

1/4 teaspoon grated nutmeg

2 cups milk

1 cup sweetened coconut, shredded

1 cup raisins

1/3 cup sugar

Directions

In your cooker, warm the butter until melted. Pour in Arborio rice and sauté for 1 minute.

Add the water, vanilla extract, and grated nutmeg. Then, securely lock the cooker's lid; set for 6 minutes on HIGH.

Next, perform a quick release to release the pressure.

Stir in the rest of the ingredients. Serve in individual bowls. Enjoy!

Coconut and Date Rice Pudding

(Ready in about 10 minutes | Servings 6)

Ingredients

2 tablespoons butter

1 cup rice

2 cups water

1/2 teaspoon ground cinnamon

2 cups almond milk

1 cup coconut, shredded

1/2 cup fresh dates, pitted and chopped

1/3 cup sugar

Mini chocolate chips, for garnish

Directions

Warm the butter in your pressure cooker over medium-high heat. Add the rice and sauté for 1 minute.

Add the water and ground cinnamon. Cover the cooker and set for 6 minutes on HIGH.

Then, perform a quick release to release the pressure.

Add the remaining ingredients. Stir to combine; while the pudding is still hot, garnish with chocolate chips.

Spicy Blackberry Sauce

(Ready in about 15 minutes | Servings 8)

Ingredients

2 cups frozen blackberries

2/3 cup grape juice

1/2 cup water

1/8 teaspoon grated nutmeg

1/4 teaspoon cardamom

1/4 teaspoon ground cinnamon

1/2 cup sugar

1 teaspoon vanilla extract

1 tablespoon cornstarch, mixed with 2 tablespoons water

Directions

Throw blackberries, grape juice, water, nutmeg, cardamom, and cinnamon in your cooker. Cook for 7 minutes on LOW.

Use a quick-release to release the cooker's pressure.

Next, use a potato masher to mash the blackberries in the cooker until the mixture is nearly puréed.

Set the cooker to HIGH, and stir in sugar, vanilla, and cornstarch mixture. Then, simmer the mixture for 3 minutes more.

Serve over pancakes or waffles. Enjoy!

Easy Mango Shortcakes

(Ready in about 10 minutes | Servings 8)

Ingredients

3 mangos, peeled and cubed

1/4 cup water

1/2 cup pineapple juice

1/3 cup sugar

1/2 teaspoon vanilla essence

1 1/2 tablespoons cornstarch, mixed with 2 tablespoons water

Shortcakes

Directions

Place mangos, water, pineapple juice, sugar, and vanilla extract in your pressure cooker.

Cook for 2 minutes on HIGH. Perform a quick release to release the pressure.

Then, set the cooker to HIGH and stir in cornstarch mixture; allow to simmer for 2 minutes, or just until the mixture has thickened.

Spoon mango sauce over shortcakes. Serve dolloped with whipped cream if desired.

Rice Pudding with Dried Figs

(Ready in about 40 minutes | Servings 8)

Ingredients

1 cup rice

1 ½ cups water

A pinch of salt

2 cups whole milk, divided

1/2 cup sugar

A dash of cinnamon

2 eggs

1/2 teaspoon vanilla extract

3/4 cup dried figs, chopped

Directions

In your pressure cooking pot, combine rice, water, and salt. Place the lid on and select HIGH pressure and 3 minutes cook time. Remove from heat and allow pressure to release naturally.

Add 1 ½ cups of milk, sugar and cinnamon to the rice mixture in pressure cooking pot; stir to combine well.

In a small-sized bowl, whisk the eggs, remaining 1/2 cup of milk, and vanilla extract. Add to the cooker and cook until mixture begins to boil; make sure to stir frequently. Turn off your cooker.

Stir in dried figs. Served dolloped with whipped cream if desired. Enjoy!

Dried Fruit Compote

(Ready in about 10 minutes | Servings 6)

Ingredients

1 cup dried peaches, quartered

1 cup dried apricots, quartered

1/2 cup golden raisins

1/2 cup dried figs, halved

1 ½ cups orange juice

1 ground cinnamon

1/2 teaspoon vanilla extract

Sugar, to taste

Directions

Add the dried peaches and apricots to the pressure cooker along with the rest of the ingredients. Then, bring to HIGH pressure; maintain pressure for 3 minutes.

Carefully remove the cooker's lid.

Then, turn to MEDIUM heat and simmer for 4 to 5 minutes. Store in your refrigerator up to 1 week.

Winter Steamed Pears

(Ready in about 10 minutes | Servings 4)

Ingredients

4 pears, cored and halved

1 medium-sized lemon

1/2 teaspoon ground cinnamon

1/2 teaspoon grated nutmeg

1/2 cup water

Directions

Drizzle lemon juice over the pears. Sprinkle them with cinnamon and nutmeg.

Pour the water into the pressure cooker. Place a metal rack in the pressure cooker; lay a heatproof plate on the rack.

Lay the pears on the plate. Cook on HIGH pressure for 4 minutes. Turn off the heat; carefully remove the lid.

Serve at room temperature or chilled. Garnish with some whipped cream if desired.

Ginger Peaches in Syrup

(Ready in about 10 minutes | Servings 6)

Ingredients

2 (15-ounce) cans sliced peaches in syrup

1/4 cup water

1 tablespoon wine vinegar

1/8 teaspoon grated nutmeg

1 teaspoon ground cinnamon

4 whole cloves

1 tablespoon candied ginger, minced

A pinch of cayenne pepper

Sugar to taste (optional)

Directions

Add all the above ingredients to your pressure cooker. Stir to combine. Cover and bring to LOW pressure; maintain pressure for 3 minutes.

After that, discard the cloves. Return the pressure cooker to MEDIUM heat; simmer for 5 minutes, stirring frequently.

Garnish with a dollop of whipped cream or strawberry ice cream, if desired. Serve immediately or refrigerate before serving.

Coconut Rice Pudding with Pineapple

(Ready in about 10 minutes | Servings 8)

Ingredients

1 cup white rice

1 ½ cups water

1 tablespoon butter, melted

1/4 teaspoon salt

1 (14-ounce) can coconut milk

1/2 cup sugar

2 eggs

1/2 cup milk

1/2 teaspoon allspice

1/2 teaspoon almond extract

1/2 teaspoon vanilla extract

1 can pineapple chunks, well drained

Directions

In a pressure cooking pot, combine rice, water, butter, and salt. Lock the lid in place; cook on HIGH and maintain the pressure for 3 minutes.

Then, turn off your cooker and use a natural pressure release. Add coconut milk and sugar; stir to combine well.

In a small-sized bowl, whisk the eggs together with milk, allspice, almond extract, and vanilla extract. Pour into your cooker. Then, cook, stirring often, until it starts to boil. Turn off the cooker. Stir in pineapple chunks.

Rice pudding will thicken as it cools. Garnish with maraschino cherries and serve chilled.

Winter Apple Dessert

(Ready in about 15 minutes | Servings 6)

Ingredients

6 apples, cored

1 cup red wine

1/4 cup raisins

1/4 cup walnuts, chopped

1/2 cup sugar

1/4 teaspoon grated nutmeg

1/4 teaspoon cardamom

1 teaspoon cinnamon powder

Directions

Arrange the apples at the bottom of your pressure cooker. Pour in wine.

Then, sprinkle raisins, chopped walnuts, sugar, nutmeg, cardamom, and cinnamon powder. Close and lock the cooker's lid.

Cook for 10 minutes at HIGH pressure. Lastly, open the pressure cooker with the "natural release method".

Serve warm or at room temperature. Enjoy!

Hot Chocolate Fondue

(Ready in about 10 minutes | Servings 12)

Ingredients

2 cups water

4 ounces dark chocolate 85%

4 ounces cream

1 teaspoon sugar

1/2 teaspoon cinnamon powder

1/4 teaspoon grated nutmeg

1 teaspoon Amaretto liqueur

Directions

Prepare your cooker by adding 2 cups of lukewarm water into the bottom; place trivet and set aside.

In a heat-proof container, such as a mug, melt your dark chocolate. Add the rest of the above ingredients. Put this container into the pressure cooker. Close and lock the cooker's lid.

Cook for 1 to 2 minutes on HIGH pressure. Open the pressure cooker according to manufacturer's directions.

Then, pull out the container with tongs. Serve right now with fresh fruits. Enjoy!

Rum Chestnut Delight

(Ready in about 20 minutes | Servings 16)

Ingredients

1 ½ pounds fresh chestnuts, peeled and halved

2 cups white sugar

1/4 teaspoon cinnamon powder

1/4 teaspoon vanilla essence

11 ounces water

1/8 cup Rum Liquor

Directions

Simply throw all the above ingredients, except for Liquor, in your pressure cooker.

Then, lock the lid of the cooker. Turn the heat up to HIGH; when the pressure cooker reaches pressure, lower the heat. Cook for 20 minutes at HIGH.

Next, open the cooker naturally. Add Liquor and stir to combine. Puree the contents with an immersion blender until desired consistency is reached. Serve over cakes or the other sweets. Enjoy!

Upside-Down Apple and Cheese Cake

(Ready in about 30 minutes | Servings 8)

Ingredients

2 cups water

1/4 cup granulated white sugar

2 apples, cored and diced

1 tablespoon fresh lemon juice

1 egg

1 cup cream cheese

1/3 cup sugar

3 tablespoons butter, softened

1 teaspoon vanilla extract

1 cup all-purpose flour

1/4 teaspoon cinnamon powder

1/2 teaspoon anise seeds

2 teaspoons baking powder

1 teaspoon baking soda

Directions

Add the water to the base of your cooker; place a steamer basket in the cooker and set aside.

Coat with oil and dust with flour a shallow heat-proof dish. Then, place a disk of wax paper at the bottom of the dish.

Sprinkle the bottom of the bowl with sugar; arrange the apples artistically. Drizzle with lemon juice.

In a small-sized dish, whisk together the egg, cream cheese, sugar, butter, and vanilla. Then, add the flour, cinnamon powder, anise seeds, baking powder, and baking soda. Blend to combine well; pour the mixture over the apples.

Close and lock the lid. Turn the heat up to HIGH. Cook approximately 20 minutes at HIGH pressure. Test by inserting a wooden stick in the middle of your cake.

To serve: turn your cake out onto a serving platter. Serve.

Pineapple and Ricotta Cake

(Ready in about 35 minutes | Servings 8)

Ingredients

2 cups hot water

2 tablespoons granulated sugar

2 cans (8-ounce) pineapple slices, well drained

4 tablespoons coconut oil, melted

1 cup graham cracker crumbs

3/4 cup plus sugar

1 tablespoon honey

1 ½ cups ricotta cheese, softened

1 teaspoon vanilla extract

3 eggs

Directions

Begin by adding the water to the bottom of your pressure cooker. Now place a steamer basket in the cooker

Then, prepare a baking dish. Coat a shallow heat-proof dish with non-stick cooking spray. Then, dust the bottom of the dish with a little all-purpose flour. Place a disk of wax paper at the bottom of the dish. Sprinkle the bottom of the dish with granulated sugar; arrange the pineapple slices artistically over the bottom.

In a mixing bowl, combine the rest of the ingredients. Stir well until everything is incorporated. Pour the mixture over the pineapple in the heat-proof dish.

Cover and turn the heat up to HIGH pressure. Cook for 15 to 20 minutes at HIGH. Check for the doneness by inserting a toothpick in the middle of the pineapple cake.

Afterwards, turn pineapple cake out onto a serving platter. Serve and enjoy!

Chocolate Lava Cake

(Ready in about 10 minutes | Servings 10)

Ingredients

2 cups water

1/4 cup powder sugar

2 tablespoons flour

4 tablespoons butter, melted

1/2 cup chocolate chips

1 medium-sized egg

1/2 teaspoon almond extract

1/2 teaspoon vanilla extract

Directions

Butter the cake mold (e.g. oven or microwave safe container) on all sides.

Place a rack in your pressure cooker. Pour two cups of water into the bottom of the cooker. Measure powdered sugar and flour into a bowl; stir thoroughly using a wire whisk.

Microwave the butter and chocolate chips for about 30 seconds. Stir the egg, almond extract, and vanilla extract into chocolate mixture. Using a hand mixer, mix until well blended.

Add sugar-flour mixture. Now, continue to blend with the hand mixer.

Pour the batter into the cake mold (half full). Place your cake mold on the rack in the cooker. Cook on HIGH heat setting for 7 minutes. Remove your cake from the cooker. Invert it onto a serving plate. Serve.

Winter Tapioca Pudding

(Ready in about 15 minutes | Servings 4)

Ingredients

1/2 cup tapioca

1 ½ cups water

1/4 cup powdered sugar

1/4 cup brown sugar

1/8 teaspoon kosher salt

2 egg yolks

1/2 cup whole milk

1/2 teaspoon apple pie spice mix

1/2 teaspoon vanilla extract

Directions

In a pressure cooking pot, combine together tapioca and water. Now cover and select HIGH pressure and 6 minutes cook time. Then, turn off pressure cooker and use "natural pressure release" for several minutes. Stir in the sugars and kosher salt.

In a small-sized dish, whisk the egg yolks and whole milk. Pour the whisked mixture through a fine mesh strainer into the cooker. Cook until the content starts to boil. Turn off your cooker. Stir in apple pie spice and vanilla.

Transfer the pudding to a refrigerator in order to chill completely. Served garnished with maraschino cherries if desired.

Carrot Cake with Rum Sauce

(Ready in about 1 hour 10 minutes | Servings 8)

Ingredients

1/4 cup molasses

1/2 cup sugar

2 eggs

1/2 cup all-purpose flour

1/4 teaspoon nutmeg

1/2 teaspoon cardamom

1/2 teaspoon cinnamon powder

1/2 teaspoon baking powder

1/2 teaspoon baking soda

A pinch of salt

2/3 cup shortening

1/2 cup carrots, grated

1/2 cup walnuts, chopped

1 cup dry bread crumbs

For the Rum Sauce:

1/2 cup sugar

4 tablespoons butter

1/4 cup heavy cream

2 tablespoons rum

1/4 teaspoon ground allspice

Directions

In a mixing bowl, whisk together the molasses, sugar, and eggs. Stir in all-purpose flour along with the spices; add baking powder and soda; add a pinch of salt; stir until blended. Fold in shortening, carrots, walnuts, and dry bread crumbs.

Spoon prepared batter into a pan oiled with non-stick cooking spray. Cover with an aluminum foil; now poke a hole in the middle of that foil.

Pour 1 ½ cups of water into the pressure cooking pot; lay the trivet in the bottom. Now lower the pan into the pressure cooker.

Next, lock the cooker's lid in place. Select HIGH setting and set the timer for 60 minutes. Now release the pressure using the cold water release method.

Next, make the Rum Sauce by adding sugar and butter in a medium saucepan over medium heat; cook for about 2 minutes. Add heavy cream, rum, and allspice; let your sauce simmer until it thickens slightly. Serve right away and enjoy!

Vegan Coconut Tapioca Pudding

(Ready in about 15 minutes | Servings 4)

Ingredients

1 ½ cups water

1/2 cup tapioca pearls

1/2 cup powdered sugar

1/8 teaspoon kosher salt

2 egg yolks

2 cups coconut milk

1/2 teaspoon cinnamon powder

1/2 teaspoon vanilla extract

Coconut flakes, for garnish

Directions

In your cooker, combine together the water and tapioca pearls. Place the lid on and select 'HIGH" pressure and 6 minutes cook time.

Turn off the heat and release the pressure. Stir in powdered sugar and salt.

In a mixing bowl or a measuring cup, whisk the yolks with coconut milk. Pour the egg-milk mixture through a fine mesh strainer into the pressure cooking pot.

Next, cook the content until it begins to boil. Turn off your cooker; while the pudding is still hot, stir in cinnamon and vanilla.

Served garnished with coconut flakes. Enjoy!

Almond Tapioca Pudding

(Ready in about 15 minutes | Servings 4)

Ingredients

1/2 cup tapioca pearls

1 ½ cups water

1/3 cup agave syrup

1/8 teaspoon kosher salt

2 egg yolks

1/2 cup whole milk

1 teaspoon cornstarch with 1 tablespoon water mixed in

1 teaspoon almond extract

1/2 teaspoon slivered almonds, for garnish

Directions

In a cooker, place together tapioca pearls and water; stir to combine well. Lock the lid and cook for 6 minutes on HIGH setting.

Now turn off pressure cooker; perform a natural pressure release for a few minutes. Stir in agave syrup and salt.

In a measuring cup, whisk together the egg yolks and milk. Pour the mixture into the cooker. Add the cornstarch mixture and cook, uncovered, stirring frequently, until the content begins to boil. Turn off your cooker. Stir in almond extract; stir to combine well.

Divide among 4 individual bowls and scatter slivered almonds over the top. Serve chilled.

Easy Caramel Custard

(Ready in about 35 minutes | Servings 4)

Ingredients

2 eggs

2 egg yolks

1 teaspoon vanilla essence

3 cups milk

1/2 cup sugar

1/2 cup water

1/2 teaspoon cinnamon powder

Directions

Beat the eggs and egg yolks together; add vanilla essence. Whisk in the milk, stirring constantly.

Dissolve sugar with water until it is caramelized. Add cinnamon powder and pour the mixture into a dish.

Pour the custard over the caramel. Cover with an aluminum foil. Add the water to a pressure cooker. Add the trivet to the cooker. Place the dish in the cooker.

Seal the pressure cooker and cook for about 20 minutes without the pressure. Afterwards, turn the pudding upside down onto a plate and serve.

Lemon Apple Crunch

(Ready in about 20 minutes | Servings 2)

Ingredients

1 cup graham wafer crumbs

1/4 cup sugar

1/4 teaspoon freshly grated nutmeg

1/2 teaspoon cinnamon, ground

Rind and juice of 1 lemon

1 teaspoon vanilla essence

3 tart apples, sliced

1/4 cup butter, melted

2 cups water

Directions

Butter a baking dish. Combine graham wafer crumbs with sugar, nutmeg, cinnamon, juice and rind of lemon, as well as vanilla essence. Then, in the baking dish, alternate layers of apples and crumbs.

Pour melted butter over the layers; cover baking dish with an aluminum foil.

Pour the water into the cooker; then, place the trivet at the base. Place the baking dish in prepared pressure cooker.

Cover with the lid and bring to pressure; lower the heat and cook for 15 minutes. Allow pressure to drop naturally. Afterwards, loosen the foil. Serve in individual serving dishes.

Amazing Pumpkin Pie

(Ready in about 1 hour | Servings 6)

Ingredients

1 ½ cups pumpkin, sliced

1 cup sugar

1/8 teaspoon grated nutmeg

1/4 teaspoon ground cloves

1/2 teaspoons cinnamon

1/2 teaspoon ground ginger

1/4 teaspoon salt

1 ½ cups evaporated milk

1/2 cup milk

2 large-sized eggs

Directions

Place water, trivet, and steamer basket in your pressure cooker. To make the pumpkin puree: Place the pumpkin slices on the steamer basket. Cover and bring to pressure. Cook for about 4 minutes on HIGH pressure.

Then, perform a quick release method. Mash the pumpkin and transfer it to a large-sized bowl.

Preheat your oven to 425 degrees F. Add the remaining ingredients to the bowl; beat until the mixture is uniform and smooth.

Pour the batter into a lined pie pan. Bake for about 10 minutes. Now lower the heat to 300 degrees F, and bake for about 45 minutes. Serve at room temperature.

Apple and Cherry Delight

(Ready in about 20 minutes | Servings 2)

Ingredients

Non-stick cooking spray

1/4 cup granulated sugar

1 cup dry bread crumbs

1/2 cup dried cherries

1 teaspoon apple pie spice blend

2 tablespoons fresh orange juice

1 teaspoon vanilla essence

1/2 teaspoon almond extract

3 apples, sliced

1/4 cup butter, melted

2 cups water

Directions

Drizzle a baking dish with a non-stick cooking spray. Combine granulated sugar, bread crumbs, dried cherries, apple pie spice, orange juice, vanilla, and almond extract. In the baking dish, alternate layers of apples and crumb mixture.

Pour melted butter over the layers in the baking dish; cover the dish with an aluminum foil.

Prepare the pressure cooker by adding the water to the cooker's base; place a metal rack. Place the baking dish in the cooker.

Cook for 15 minutes under HIGH pressure. Serve.

Lemon Cottage Cake

(Ready in about 25 minutes | Servings 10)

Ingredients

2 cups water

3 tablespoons butter, at room temperature

1 cup graham wafer crumbs

12 ounces Cottage cheese, softened

1/2 cup sour cream

1/2 cup white sugar

2 whole eggs

1 tablespoon grated lemon zest

1/2 teaspoon vanilla extract

Directions

Prepare your cooker by adding two cups of water. Set a trivet in the cooker.

Next, combine the butter with crumbs. Press the mixture into a spring-form pan and set it aside.

Then, in a medium-sized bowl, combine the Cottage cheese, sour cream, and white sugar. Beat until smooth. Add the eggs, grated lemon zest, and vanilla extract. Pour the Cottage mixture over the crust in the pan.

Next, set the foil-wrapped pan onto the trivet in the cooker. Cook on HIGH pressure for 20 minutes.

Remove the pan from the cooker with the foil handle. Serve chilled and enjoy!

Orange Macchiato Cheesecake

(Ready in about 35 minutes | Servings 10)

Ingredients

2 tablespoons butter, softened

4 tablespoons cookie crumbs

16 ounces cream cheese

3/4 cup sugar

1/4 cup heavy cream

2 teaspoons orange zest, grated

1 teaspoon orange juice

2 tablespoons all-purpose flour

6 tablespoons sour cream

2 tablespoons brewed espresso coffee

2 egg yolks

2 eggs

2 cups water

Directions

Generously butter your cake mold. Sprinkle with cookie crumbs; set it aside.

Mix together the cream cheese, sugar, heavy cream, orange zest, orange juice, flour, sour cream, and espresso coffee; mix to combine well. Fold in the egg yolks and eggs; mix again.

Center the mold on a long piece of a foil. Take another piece of foil, and cover the top of your mold; seal the edges. Then, create a handle of the foil.

Lay a metal rack or a trivet in your cooker; pour in the water. Place the foil-covered mold on the trivet.

Lock the cooker's lid; cook for 30 minutes on HIGH.

Afterwards, using the prepared foil handle, remove the mold from the pressure cooker. Loosen the foil and transfer the cheesecake to the refrigerator; let it stand overnight. Serve chilled and enjoy!

Mint Chocolate Cheesecake

(Ready in about 35 minutes | Servings 10)

Ingredients

Non-stick cooking spray

5 tablespoons chocolate wafer crumbs

2 (8-ounce) packages cream cheese

1/2 cup semisweet chocolate chips

3/4 cup sugar

1/4 cup heavy cream

1 teaspoon lemon zest

2 tablespoons flour

6 tablespoons sour cream

2 egg yolks

2 eggs

1 teaspoon cinnamon powder

1/2 teaspoon mint extract

1 teaspoon vanilla extract

2 cups water

Directions

Spray a cake mold with non-stick cooking spray. Sprinkle with chocolate wafer crumbs; set it aside.

Next, combine together the cream cheese, chocolate chips, sugar, heavy cream, lemon zest, flour, and sour cream; whisk to combine. Fold in the egg yolks and eggs; add cinnamon, mint extract, and vanilla; mix again.

Center the mold on a long piece of a foil. Take another piece of foil and cover the top of your mold. Seal the edges and create a handle of the foil.

Place a metal rack in the base of your cooker; pour in 2 cups of water. Place the foil-covered mold on the metal rack.

Cover and cook on HIGH for about 30 minutes. Serve chilled and topped with cherry pie filling if desired.

Quinoa Pudding with Walnuts

(Ready in about 10 minutes | Servings 6)

Ingredients

2 ¼ cups water

1 ½ cups quinoa

1/4 cup agave nectar

1/2 teaspoon vanilla

1/4 teaspoon nutmeg, preferably freshly grated

1/2 teaspoon cinnamon powder

Chopped walnuts, toasted

Directions

Add the water, quinoa, agave nectar, vanilla, nutmeg, and cinnamon powder to the pressure cooking pot.

Select HIGH pressure and cook for 5 minutes. Next, turn your cooker off; use a Quick Pressure Release to release pressure.

Fluff the quinoa and serve warm with the toasted walnuts.

Old-Fashioned Cocoa Custard

(Ready in about 10 minutes | Servings 4)

Ingredients

2 cups milk

2 whole eggs

1/3 cup sugar

1 tablespoon cocoa powder

1/2 teaspoon vanilla essence

1 cup water

Directions

Start by scalding the milk; then, allow the milk to slightly cool.

Add the eggs, sugar, cocoa powder, milk, and vanilla to a mixing bowl; stir to combine well. Pour the mixture into 4 custard cups; cover cups with an aluminum foil.

Add water to your cooker's base; now put trivet and steamer basket into the cooker. Place prepared custard cups in the steamer basket.

Lock the lid in place; cook for 3 minutes on HIGH pressure. Let the pressure drop using the quick-release method. Serve chilled.

Summer Caramel Custard

(Ready in about 10 minutes | Servings 4)

Ingredients

2 cups milk

3 eggs yolks

1/3 cup caster sugar

1/2 teaspoon vanilla paste

1/4 teaspoon freshly grated nutmeg

A dash of cinnamon powder

1 cup water

Directions

Begin by scalding the milk and allow it to slightly cool.

In a mixing bowl, combine together the egg yolks, caster sugar, vanilla paste, nutmeg, and cinnamon; add reserved milk; whisk well to combine. Pour the mixture into 4 custard cups; cover cups with a foil.

Pour the water into the cooker. Then, lay a rack and steamer basket in the cooker. Lay prepared custard cups in the steamer basket.

Cover with the lid and cook for 3 minutes on HIGH. Let the pressure drop using the quick-release method. Transfer to a refrigerator to chill before serving.

Stewed Prunes and Dried Apricots

(Ready in about 10 minutes | Servings 6)

Ingredients

1 cup water

1 cup red wine

3/4 cup brown sugar

1 vanilla bean

3-4 cloves

1 cinnamon stick

2 lemon slices

1/2 pound prunes

1/2 pound dried apricots

Directions

In your cooker, mix together the water, red wine, brown sugar, vanilla bean, cloves, cinnamon stick, and lemon slices. Bring to a boil; let it simmer until brown sugar dissolves.

Add the prunes and apricots. Cook for 4 minutes on HIGH pressure. Serve warm or at room temperature. Enjoy!

Winter Stewed Fruits

(Ready in about 10 minutes | Servings 6)

Ingredients

1/2 cup red wine

1 ½ cups water

1/2 cup agave syrup

3-4 cloves

2 cinnamon sticks

1/2 teaspoon vanilla essence

1/2 orange, sliced

1/2 pound dried apples

1/4 pound dried prunes

1/4 pound dried figs

Directions

In your cooker, mix together the wine, water, agave syrup, cloves, cinnamon sticks, vanilla, and orange. Bring the mixture to a boil.

Add dried fruits. Cook for 4 minutes on HIGH. Serve with vanilla ice cream if desired.

Rice and Carrot Pudding

(Ready in about 15 minutes | Servings 8)

Ingredients

1 cup rice

1 pound carrots

1 ½ cups water

1/8 teaspoon salt

2 cups whole milk, divided

1/2 cup sugar

1/2 teaspoon cardamom seeds

2 eggs

1/2 teaspoon vanilla extract

3/4 cup Zante currants

Directions

In your pressure cooking pot, combine rice, carrots, water, and salt. Cover and select HIGH Pressure and 3 minutes cook time. Then, perform a natural pressure release for 10 minutes. Add the milk, sugar, and cardamom seeds; stir to combine well.

In a mixing bowl, whisk eggs with vanilla. Pour the mixture into the pressure cooking pot. Then, cook, stirring frequently, until your mixture begins to boil. Turn off your cooker. Stir in Zante currants.

Serve your pudding right now or well chilled. Serve dolloped with a cream.

Orange and Date Cheesecake

(Ready in about 25 minutes | Servings 8)

Ingredients

2 pounds cream cheese

4 medium-sized eggs

1/2 cup white sugar

Zest and juice of 1/2 orange

1/2 teaspoon cardamom seeds

1/4 teaspoon vanilla extract

1 cup dates, soaked and chopped

Directions

Beat cream cheese until smooth. Then, in a separate bowl, beat the eggs together with sugar. Add the cheese.

Whisk in the orange juice, orange zest, cardamom seeds, and vanilla extract; lastly, add the chopped dates. Pour the batter into a well-greased heatproof dish. Cover with a foil.

Lay a trivet at the bottom of the cooker, Set pressure to HIGH and cook for 20 minutes. Serve dusted with cocoa powder if desired.

Apples Stuffed with Dates and Walnuts

(Ready in about 25 minutes | Servings 4)

Ingredients

4 apples, cored

1/2 cup dates, chopped

1/4 cup walnuts, chopped

1/2 teaspoon ground cloves

1/2 teaspoon cinnamon powder

1/4 teaspoon grated nutmeg

Directions

Place the apples in an ovenproof dish. To make the filling: combine together the dates, walnuts, cloves, cinnamon, and nutmeg. Then, stuff the apples with date-walnut mixture.

Next, pour 1 cup of water into the cooker. Place a metal rack in your cooker. Cover the ovenproof dish with an aluminum foil; now lower this dish into the cooker.

Bring up to HIGH pressure; maintain the pressure for about 20 minutes. Serve with your favorite cream.

Fig-Cranberry Compote with Pecans

(Ready in about 10 minutes | Servings 4)

Ingredients

4 cups water

2 cinnamon sticks

3-4 cloves

12 dried figs, halved

2 cups dried cranberries

2 tablespoons crystallized ginger

1/2 teaspoon vanilla paste

1 cup pecans, toasted

Directions

Add the water to your cooker along with cinnamon, cloves, figs, cranberries, and crystallized ginger.

Cook under HIGH pressure for 5 minutes. Then, quick release the pressure. Add vanilla paste and stir to combine. Allow your compote to cool slightly.

Serve with toasted pecans, warm or room temperature. Enjoy!

Summer Compote with Almonds

(Ready in about 10 minutes | Servings 4)

Ingredients

6 cups water

1 vanilla bean, sliced lengthwise

2 cinnamon sticks

1/2 teaspoon freshly grated nutmeg

1/2 cup dried apricots, halved

1 cup dried strawberries

1 ½ cups dried cherries

1 cup almonds, toasted

Directions

Add the water to your cooker along with vanilla bean, cinnamon sticks, nutmeg, dried apricots, strawberries, and cherries.

Then, cook your compote for 5 minutes under HIGH pressure. Quick release the cooker's pressure. Allow the compote to cool slightly.

Add toasted almonds, and serve over ice cream while the compote is still warm. Treat your guests!

Rhubarb and Raspberry Compote

(Ready in about 15 minutes | Servings 6)

Ingredients

1/2 cup water

1 pound rhubarb, cut into small pieces

1/2 pint raspberries

1/4 teaspoon freshly grated nutmeg

1/4 teaspoon cinnamon powder

1/4 cup crystallized ginger, chopped

2 tablespoons honey

Directions

Bring water to a boil in your pressure cooker; then, add rhubarb pieces.

Next, throw raspberries, nutmeg, cinnamon, and crystallized ginger in your cooker. Bring up to HIGH pressure; turn off heat, and allow the cooker's pressure to come down gradually and naturally.

While the compote is still warm, stir in the honey. Allow the compote to cool completely. Keep refrigerated in jars for up to 10 days. Serve over vanilla ice cream, or topped with warm custard if desired. Enjoy!

Cranberry and Kumquat Relish with Walnuts

(Ready in about 10 minutes + chilling time| Servings 6)

Ingredients

1/2 cup water

36 ounces cranberries

2 ½ cups kumquats, rinsed and halved

1 cup crystallized ginger, chopped

1 teaspoon cloves

3 tablespoons agave syrup

1/2 teaspoon vanilla paste

1 cup toasted walnuts, chopped

Directions

Bring the water to a boil in your cooker. Add the cranberries, kumquats, crystallized ginger, and cloves.

Cover with the lid and bring to HIGH pressure. Let it cook for about 1 minute. Turn off the heat; let the pressure come down naturally for several minutes. Afterwards, release any remaining pressure.

Allow this relish to cool slightly, and add agave syrup and vanilla. Stir in the toasted walnuts just before serving. You can keep it in a fridge for up to 1 week.

Nana's Easy Caramel Flan

(Ready in about 20 minutes + chilling time | Servings 4)

Ingredients

1/2 cup sugar

1/4 cup hot water

8 egg yolks

1 cup sugar

1/4 teaspoon cardamom seeds

1/4 teaspoon cinnamon powder

1 teaspoon vanilla paste

4 cups milk

Directions

In a pan, melt sugar, stirring continuously. Add hot water; keep stirring. Pour the caramel mixture into a well-greased cookie tin.

Pour the water into the bottom of the pressure cook (2 inches). Place cookie tin in the cooker. Pour the remaining ingredients into your cookie tin.

Close the lid and cook for 15 minutes under HIGH pressure. Allow it to chill at list four hours. Serve.

Homemade Lemon Pudding

(Ready in about 15 minutes | Servings 4)

Ingredients

1/2 cup sugar

2 tablespoons all-purpose flour

A pinch of kosher salt

1 tablespoon butter, softened

3 tablespoons fresh lemon juice

Grated rind of 1 medium-sized organic lemon

2 egg yolks, beaten

1 teaspoon anise seeds

2/3 cup whole milk

2 egg whites, well beaten

2 cups water

Directions

In a bowl, combine together the sugar, flour, salt, and softened butter. Stir in fresh lemon juice and grated lemon rind; fold in the egg yolks, anise seeds, and milk; whisk to combine well.

Fold in well-beaten egg whites. Pour the mixture into individual custard cups. Cover each cup with a piece of an aluminum foil.

Pour the water into the base of your pressure cooker. Place a metal rack in the cooker; now lay cups on the rack. Close your cooker and cook for 10 minutes at lowest pressure setting. Serve dolloped with whipped cream if desired.

Sweet Chocolate Dream

(Ready in about 40 minutes | Servings 8)

Ingredients

2 ½ cups cream

2 cups milk

1/2 cup caster sugar

1/2 cinnamon powder

1/2 teaspoon vanilla paste

3 cups dark chocolate, chopped

6 egg yolks

4 cups water

Directions

In a pan, cook cream, milk, caster sugar, cinnamon powder, and vanilla over medium heat.

Turn off the heat and add dark chocolate; stir until the chocolate is melted. Whisk in the egg yolks.

Prepare the cooker by adding 4 cups of water. Pour the mixture into a porcelain dish; place the dish on a trivet in your pressure cooker.

Cook under HIGH pressure for about 30 minutes. Serve with fresh fruits.

Download a PDF file with photos of all the recipes from the link below: